38.99

136190

D0545056

Organization Design

As the purse strings tighten, company costs need to be cut without affecting performance or sales. A common solution to this problem is to restructure the organization of the company, i.e. adjust the lines and boxes on the organization chart with the aim of setting it up for high performance. This inevitably fails because an organization is a system: change one aspect and other facets will also change.

Organization Design: Engaging with Change looks at how to (re)design the organizational system in order to increase productivity, performance and value, providing the knowledge and methodology to design an agile organization capable of handling the kind of continuous organizational change that all businesses face. The book clarifies why and how organizations need to be in a state of readiness to design or redesign and emphasizes that people as well as business processes must be part of design considerations. Responding to developments across the world since the first edition, it covers, among other topics:

- technology changes that have had an impact upon organizations;
- increased demands for 'sustainability' and corporate social responsibility;
- the pressure on organizations to be smarter, more efficient and more effective.

Whilst the material on this subject targets a wide management audience, this book is specifically written for consultants, OD/HR practitioners and line managers working together to achieve the goal of organizational redesign for changing circumstances. Aided by a range of pedagogical features, it is a must-read for students or practitioners involved in the field of organizational design, development and change.

Naomi Stanford PhD is a consultant, teacher and author. Her work as a consultant is in organization design and development in all its manifestations. Before leaving the UK to live in the USA she worked for large multinational companies including Price Waterhouse, Xerox, British Airways, and Marks and Spencer. She is currently working in the USA consulting on organization design, development and change, in a range of sectors domestically and internationally. She has written four previous books on organizations. She teaches MBA students and supervises doctoral students. Her blog, www.naomistanford.com, showcases her interests.

Organization Design
Engaging with change

Second edition

Naomi Stanford

Routledge
Taylor & Francis Group

LONDON AND NEW YORK

ST HELENS
COLLEGE

658.406
STA~

136190

Nov 16

LIBRARY

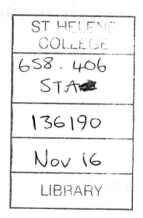

First published 2004
Second edition published 2014
by Routledge
2 Park Square, Milton Park, Abingdon, Oxon OX14 4RN

and by Routledge
711 Third Avenue, New York, NY 10017

Routledge is an imprint of the Taylor & Francis Group, an informa business

© 2014 Naomi Stanford

The right of Naomi Stanford to be identified as author of this work has been asserted by her in accordance with sections 77 and 78 of the Copyright, Designs and Patents Act 1988.

All rights reserved. No part of this book may be reprinted or reproduced or utilised in any form or by any electronic, mechanical, or other means, now known or hereafter invented, including photocopying and recording, or in any information storage or retrieval system, without permission in writing from the publishers.

Trademark notice: Product or corporate names may be trademarks or registered trademarks, and are used only for identification and explanation without intent to infringe.

British Library Cataloguing in Publication Data
A catalogue record for this book is available from the British Library

Library of Congress Cataloguing in Publication data
  Organization design : engaging with change / Naomi Stanford. – Second edition.
    pages cm
  Includes bibliographical references and index.
  1. Organizational change. 2. Business planning. 3. Personnel management. I. Title.
  HD58.8.S6958   2013
  658.4′02–dc23
  2013020814

ISBN: 978-0-415-63461-8 (hbk)
ISBN: 978-0-415-63462-5 (pbk)
ISBN: 978-0-203-09433-4 (ebk)

Typeset in Times New Roman
by Out of House Publishing

MIX
Paper from
responsible sources
FSC   FSC® C013056
www.fsc.org

Printed and bound in Great Britain by
TJ International Ltd, Padstow, Cornwall

Contents

Figures

Tables

Acknowledgements

Writing a book is a daunting task, and I've been helped along the way in the writing of this one by many, many people. Picking out those who deserve a special mention is hard too. I've been supported in multiple ways. I thank all of you who have asked questions, given feedback, provided stories and insights, and been curious about the writing process and about organization design.

I'd like to specially name some and acknowledge others:

- my family members have all been wonderfully understanding as I go off to write: Hannah Barugh, Rosa Barugh, Rosie Stanford, Michael Stanford, Roger Woolford, Patty Stratton;
- the clients and colleagues I work with have contributed in ways great and small: thank you Rich Larison, Kris Krail, Bill Nichols, Terry Huang and all of the participants in the various workshops and seminars;
- reviewers of the chapters who have made good comments and suggestions: Katie Aldridge has given sterling feedback;
- those individuals who have given me permission to use their work: Amy Kates, Chris Rodgers, Stuart Wigham, and Meg Wheatley among them;
- staff at Taylor & Francis: David Varley, Alex Krause, Rosemary Baron and others.

Additionally I would like to acknowledge the valiant, demanding, and unfortunately necessary work of Freedom from Torture (http://www.freedomfromtorture.org) to whom the proceeds of this book are donated.

Introduction

The first edition of this book was published as *Organization Design: The Collaborative Approach* in 2004. Since then there have been well-documented context changes that continue apace, all having a significant impact on the way organizations function. These changes include:

1 Accelerating swift and wide-ranging information and communication technology (ICT) changes that are having an impact on organizations. Since 2004 social media have burst upon the scene, cloud computing has become the norm and business intelligence software is getting increasingly sophisticated. All these have a huge impact on the traditional organization of enterprises.

2 Increasing requirements for 'sustainability' including carbon footprint savings, 'greening' the enterprise and so on. This again requires looking at the way work is done through a new lens.

3 Intensifying demands, brought about by fiscal and political conditions, to do more for less – smarter, more efficiently, more effectively. Just look at the impact the financial crisis of 2007–9 had on governments. Worldwide they were and continue to be faced with the challenge of offering better citizen services with vastly reduced budgets. No organization can keep pace with this type of demand without looking at its design.

4 Increasing involvement of architecture and design firms in the application of their world's design principles in the world of business operations and organization. This confluence of two disciplines is intriguing and perplexing, giving rise to questions such as: 'how does space become a strategic asset and not a cost to be borne?'; 'how relevant is space design to business performance?'; 'what can HR and facilities management learn from each other?'.

5 Building steam for a better work–life balance, coming particularly from people in their twenties and thirties in the USA and Europe. The introduction of flexible working, family-friendly policies, remote and virtual working all contribute to organizations having to take another look at the way they operate their people processes.

6   Emerging tensions around competition as companies seek to extend their range into new areas – both geographic and products/services. This gives rise to all manner of cultural and internal competition.

7   Changing global demographics that are leading to high youth unemployment and an increasing trend towards people over 65 staying in the workforce.

8   Heightening skills shortages in specific disciplines – engineering and computer sciences in the USA and Europe, for example.

9   Developing understanding of networks, 'organized complexity', neuroscience and biology, changing the way we think about organizations. This understanding is moving us away from thinking of them less as bounded systems, and more as complex, adaptive organisms.

10   Advancing product technologies that are changing the jobs landscape – many jobs previously done by humans are being done by robots or by other technologies. Self-checkout in supermarkets is an example, digital wallets are on the way and both are human job replacements.

These phenomenally fast-moving changes require three things from organizational leaders:

•   To think very differently about the way their organizations are structured: a growing number are thinking of their enterprises as networks with dependencies and interrelationships rather than fixed, hierarchical, bounded structures (see Figure 0.1).

•   To create a flexible, agile, adaptive, sustainable organization; one that continues to perform well and provide decent work (see Glossary).

•   To seek expert support in creating and maintaining this type of responsive organization and not feel they can go it alone. Design work is not for the layman, as findings from a survey carried out in 2012 found. It reported that about half of surveyed organizations viewed their organization design as only moderately successful, and none of them viewed themselves as very successful at organization design (University of Westminster, 2012).

This is where this book comes in. Its primary purpose is to:

•   provide the tools and techniques to enable HR/OD professionals to develop confidence and competence in organization design (and development).

Its secondary purposes are to:

•   give line managers an overview of the design process, their role in it and what support they can expect from their HR/OD colleagues;

•   suggest how HR/OD and the line manager can work most effectively together on design projects;

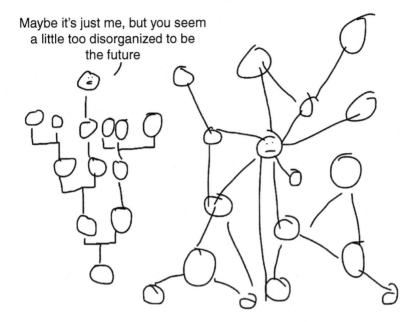

Maybe it's just me, but you seem a little too disorganized to be the future

Figure 0.1 The power of networks
Source: Lysy, 2013.

- provide insights into ways of handling the kind of ongoing change that all enterprises face and often find troublesome.

HR/OD professionals need the skills and technical expertise to guide, coach and support line managers through organization design and development. Capability in this respect is now a 'must-have'. A quotation from a European government line manager in 2012 illustrates this:

> In a context of increased pressure on resources within governmental institutions (10–15% of staff cuts over 5 years on average) the current mainstream message within these institutions is that staff need to 'do more with less'. We of course all understand that this is difficult to achieve and may lead employees to being in unbearable situations. Organizational design and development is therefore becoming central as we look for new ways of working, being together, learning to do better differently and finding the way to make the 'less that is actually more'.

Three things have occurred, since the first edition of this book, to help HR/OD staff develop their organization design and development competence:

1 The UK's Chartered Institute for Personnel and Development (CIPD) has added organization design to its HR Profession Map, requiring

demonstrated competence in this discipline from HR practitioners. The CIPD is now offering certification in organization design and several universities are including organization design as a module in their HR programmes.

2   The USA-based Organization Design Forum has opened chapters in both Europe and the Middle East and Africa. And other chapters are planned.

3   Software programs have been developed (and it is highly likely that more are in the works) that take a 'big data' (see Glossary) approach to organization design, drawing on an organization's multiple data sets to facilitate organization design visualization, scenario-planning and delivery.

This book has been extensively updated in the light of the context outlined above. It is grounded in a further eight years of my own experience of:

- consulting with organizations of all sectors, sizes and business models, on their design issues;
- leading public and tailored organization design programmes in Africa, China, the USA and Europe;
- writing and researching in the field.

During that period I have learned five things that help guide me in my work:

1   Unless you are clear on what the design is for (what it is supposed to do) you don't stand a chance of delivering something that works.

2   There is no one right way of doing organization design.

3   Even using a systematic approach, organization design is an evolving, iterative process which usually feels messy and complicated.

4   Faced with design options, take the one that makes most sense at the time.

5   The design you come up with is not one which will last for ever (or even for very long).

The book's approach is practical and pragmatic, systematic but flexible. It is more of a 'how to' guide than a textbook, so it is not academic or theoretical, although sometimes the theory or research is mentioned to clarify or illustrate. Each chapter is organized in the following sequence:

What you will learn: the purpose and outcomes of the chapter.
Input on the chapter topic: discussion and information, interspersed with 'OD shorts' that summarize the points made.
Tool: something that will help you in your organization design practice.
Summary: the key points covered in the chapter.

I hope that you will find the book helpful in developing your organization design thinking and practice, and that you find the whole field as fascinating as I have done over many years. I love the work that I do with clients in all its ups and downs, and I wish the same career fulfilment to you.

NOTE: Throughout the book the letters OD stand for Organization Design, and not Organization Development.

References

Lysy, C. (2013). 'The Power of Networks'. Retrieved 16 May 2013, from Freshspectrum: http://freshspectrum.com/the-power-of-networks.

SAS Institute Inc. (2012). *Big Data Meets Big Data Analytics*. Cary, NC: SAS.

University of Westminster. (2012). *Organisation Design Research*. London: Concentra.

1   What is organization design?

You can still be in a fog when surrounded by databases, information systems, knowledge sharing, learning environments, and people full of wisdom.

Jensen, 2000

What you will learn

This chapter introduces the concepts, models and methodology of organization design, providing the foundational knowledge needed to undertake a design project.

Preparing for organization design

An organization design (noun) is the output of an organization design process (verb). But there are several actions to take before starting the hands-on design process. These preparatory actions are to:

- develop insight about the relationship between organization design and organization structure;
- get an idea of the history of organization design in order to see how organizations have evolved;
- learn some of the basics of complex, adaptive, open systems theory that underpins the design process;
- choose a systems model to guide you through the design process;
- agree a definition of organization design;
- determine design principles;
- understand the five-phase design process – assess, design, plan to transition, transition and review – and the actions, deliverables and tools associated with each of the phases.

This list looks surprising to people who think that organization design is mainly about the structure of an organization – what they see represented on an organization chart. So this chapter opens with an explanation of the

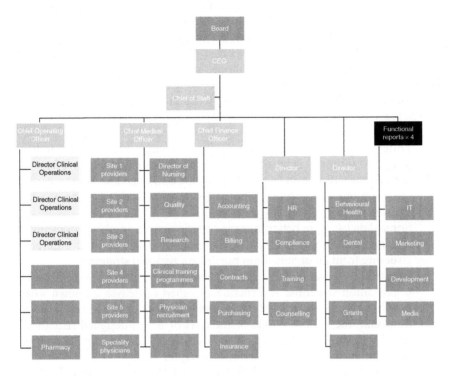

Figure 1.1 Example of healthcare provider organization chart

relationship between organization design and organization structure. Then each of the actions listed above is discussed and summarized.

The relationship between organization design and organization structure

Organization design is more often than not assumed to be the organization structure – that is, the series of boxes that are ordered in a hierarchy and are shown as an organization chart. One HR manager in a 300-person healthcare company was given a revised organization chart, similar to the one shown in Figure 1.1, by the new CEO and asked to realize it. The chart raised various questions, including: 'How will we know this is the right structure for our organization?' 'Is this how it should be structured?' 'Are ten direct reports to the CEO too many?'

Organizations race to 'restructure', i.e. change the organization chart, in response to some business issue, typically triggered by some external pressure (see Chapter 4) that is forcing a response. In this case the restructure was initiated by a combination of circumstances, including a new CEO, changes in the external healthcare market, requests from clients for a higher-quality level of service and loss of market share to competitors.

This CEO was not alone in taking this quick and common response to issues. It is all too easy to take the boxes on the chart and put them into a different configuration, usually without thinking through the consequences or the risks associated with doing so. But trying to solve a problem by attacking the organization chart is very unlikely to achieve the desired outcome, for seven reasons:

1   Different structures do different things. For example, in a hierarchical structure authority is based on level in the hierarchy, while in a flat, networked structure authority is based on knowledge and resources. The structure must be carefully chosen to position authority where it best delivers the business strategy.

2   Some structures are better in some situations than another. For example, an organization pursuing a global strategy is likely to need a different structure from an organization pursuing a regional strategy.

3   Business processes (which deliver the business strategy) should drive the organization structure. A structure designed to deliver a known workflow is more efficient and effective than one in which the workflow has to fit around the structure. One of the tests of a well-designed structure is whether it supports the flow of work efficiently and effectively and in a way that meets the client's needs (see Chapter 5).

4   A typical organization chart (see Figure 1.1) does not show the interdependencies, interactions, lateral co-ordinations and handover points that the people in the roles on the chart have. If the chart is restructured without reference to these crucial aspects then the workflow can be disrupted, with severe consequences. This sort of disruption can now be tracked by organizational and social network analysis (see Glossary).

5   Related to point 4, if a structure is developed without recognition of other stakeholders things can get difficult. It is not always easy to know what its boundaries are – should there be interfaces with strategic partners? What happens if there are several points of contact for the same stakeholder? How much of the work flows out of the organization – for example to compliance bodies?

6   In restructuring, people get confused with roles. In Figure 1.1 roles are shown. In most cases names are in the boxes and in certain cases a restructure is initiated because someone has left, someone needs a promotion or there is some issue that means, for example, that Pat cannot report to Jim. Restructuring around people is very risky. They may leave, move on, stop performing or become demotivated. Structuring around workflow is much less risky.

7   Fully employed members of staff work side by side with contractors, consultants and temporary workers. It is difficult to argue that this type of staff augmentation is not part of effective organizational functioning and

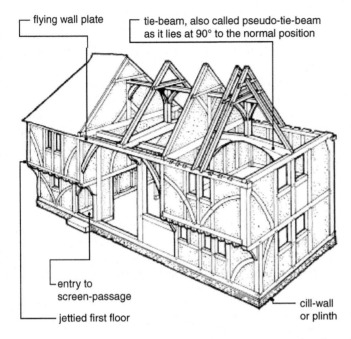

flying wall plate

tie-beam, also called pseudo-tie-beam
as it lies at 90° to the normal position

entry to
screen-passage

jettied first floor

cill-wall
or plinth

Figure 1.2 Exploded diagram of Wealden house, showing the timber-framed structure

Source: Curl, 2006, p. 839. By permission of Oxford University Press.

success (why pay for their services if not to have them contribute?), yet these people do not appear on a standard organization chart.

Well-designed structures are developed by, first, being clear about the business purpose; second, knowing what work needs to be done in order to achieve the purpose; and, third, developing an organization structure that optimizes the workflow both within the organization and to stakeholders outside it.

The organization chart (structure) is one part of the overall design. Think about a building: if the decision is made to 'restructure' it by repositioning a door or window, or taking out one of the tie-beams or a roof support, or bricking up one of the doorways then the design changes and there will be consequences – potentially damaging ones. In making structural alterations to buildings people tend to consult experts, or at least assess the risks of, say, cutting through a supporting beam, before they set to with the chainsaw. So it should be with restructuring.

Illustrating further, look at Figure 1.2 showing the timber-framed structure of a Wealden house. The overall design of the original house (its shape, interior layout, number of windows, etc.) came about by considering a set of questions, including:

1   What is the purpose of this building?
2   What are the constraints that it has to be constructed within? For example, time, cost, quality level.
3   What is the work or activity of the people who will be in the building?

Only when the three questions have been answered in some detail can some design options start to be developed, followed by the structure that supports the design. Organization designers ask these three questions, too, and each is discussed in more detail in the following chapters. For now it is sufficient to reinforce the point that the structure is only a part of the overall design and contributes to a coherent answer to a series of questions.

OD short

Like building design, organization design is not only about structure, i.e. what you see on the organization chart. But structure is one of the elements to consider in the design. The organization design process involves aligning the various elements of the organization, including the structure, to deliver a business purpose.

Quick history of organization design

One point to reinforce is that like houses, the design of organizations has got to change with the times or it becomes an anachronism that people can look at fondly or with curiosity as they might an original-state Wealden house (Figure 1.2). Look at the history of organization design, Table 1.1, and it is evident that the design of organizations also changes in line with changing internal and external operating contexts.

There is an extensive body of work on the various external forces that are having an impact on organizations, and as noted earlier some of these are covered in Chapter 4. Keeping up with these developments is almost a full-time job, yet it behoves any organization design consultant or HR manager to develop 'business savvy' by staying alert to the social, technological, environmental, economic, political, legal and ethical backdrops that are the main drivers of change in a company.

Look at the final column of Table 1.1, headed 'Adaptive open systems'. These types of organizations are designed to sustain the capacity to adapt to:

*   new jobs and new types of work in:
    *   routine work, i.e. repetitive, assembly-line type of work;
    *   in-person work, for example doctors, teachers, shop assistants;
    *   data manipulation of all types including problem-solving, information analysis, coding;

Table 1.1 A brief history of organization design

	1920–55	1955–65	1965–75	1975–85	1985–2000	2000s
Theoretical model	Mechanistic	Mechanistic with human relations	Open systems	Matrix and shared services	Entrepreneurial and self-managed work teams	Adaptive open systems
Attributes	Strict hierarchy of control, authority and rules. Tasks are highly defined and specialized. Few teams	Emphasis on the employee. Beginning of lateral career progression. Strict hierarchy of control	Combination of external focus and flexible structure. Transformation of inputs to outputs (output is the final product)	Dual hierarchy: vertical and horizontal. Flexible sharing of employees across product and organizational lines	Emphasis on teams. Sharing of tasks. Network of interaction. Learning environment encouraged	Flat hierarchy, flexible rules. Shared tasks, empowerment. Highly flexible and adaptable work environment. Customer-centric culture
Management power and control	Management knows best, tells employees what to do, low worker trust. Centralized decision-making, highly regimented	Preoccupation with the human side of the individual. Centralized decision-making. Limited employee empowerment	Project management. Break down of silos. Management controls information. Organization has to innovate	Project and product teams created across department lines. Management is the decision-maker. Moderate centralization	Employee empowerment. Strong horizontal collaboration and co-operation. Senior Management gives teams free range guided by the parameters and values they have set	Decentralized decision-making. Self-managed teams. Authority shared with employees, high trust, collaboration and partnership
Communication	Vertical: top-down, controlled	Concern for human and social needs. Vertical: top-down	Vertical and lateral. Mixed	Vertical mixed with horizontal. Specialized to project. Cumbersome including all parties	Information freely shared throughout the organization. Cross-fertilization of ideas. Teams and customers work together	Horizontal, vertical and networked communication. Open access to information and communication technologies at all levels

Table 1.1 (cont.)

	1920–55	1955–65	1965–75	1975–85	1985–2000	2000s
Pros	Efficient for one or a few products Allows economies of scale within specialized units In-depth, highly specialized skill development	Considered the employee as an individual, emphasis on motivation techniques	History of the organization considered important (causation) Multiple goals can be achieved by a lot of paths (diversification)	Opportunity for product and functional skill development Meets multiple customer demands Responsive to specific markets and products	Emphasizes team-building Encourages innovation Creates a sense of self-achievement Teams discuss conflicts and propose resolutions to problems	Highly creative and adaptive to the global market place Everyone has a broad view of organizational goals Employees empowered to share responsibility, make decisions and be accountable for outcomes
Cons	Slow response to environmental changes Inefficient Poor co-ordination across departments Innovation inhibited	Did not consider the effect it would have on production efficiency	Management focused on growth	Dual authority confusing for employee Requires great effort to balance vertical relationships Creates conflicting goals between vertical and horizontal lines of authority	Start-up may be time-consuming Shared decision making seen as time-consuming	Requires significant training of employees and managers

Source: Adapted from Beakey *et al.*, 2007.

- new work patterns in terms of work–life balance, self-employment and flexible working;
- high tension between young people trying to enter the workforce and those of pensionable age trying to stay in it.

Adaptability and agility are now essential organizational capabilities. Consider the fact that at the time of writing (2013) manufacturers are testing driverless cars with the prediction that they will be on public roads within five years. Now start to think through the implications driverless cars would have on any organization. The writer of an *Economist* article (Schumpeter, 2012) has done this, suggesting, among other things:

- Electronics and software firms will enjoy strong demand for in-car entertainment systems, since cars' occupants will no longer need to keep their eyes on the road.
- Bus companies might run convoys of self-piloting coaches down the motorways, providing competition for intercity railways.
- Cabbies, lorry drivers and all others whose job is to steer a vehicle will have to find other work.
- Driverless cars will be programmed to obey the law, which means no traffic cops or parking wardens.
- Driverless cars will not need driver insurance – so goodbye to motor insurers and brokers.
- Autonomous vehicles will mean fewer accidents and so much less work for emergency rooms and orthopedic wards.
- Roads will need fewer signs, signals, guard rails and other features designed for the human driver; their makers will lose business, too.

Clearly, a driverless car scenario is only one among many that would have an impact on the jobs, work patterns and social tensions mentioned above. Some of the other scenarios are touched on in the Introduction to this book. There are many, many more – look out for them and be ready as they start to emerge. Notice, too, that the driverless car scenario would have an impact not just on work associated with vehicles and travel but in many other spheres. So a scenario that might seem peripheral to an organization might, in fact, have a profound effect on it.

OD short

The history of organization design shows how designs have changed over the years in response to the context changes. Although details of the future of work cannot be predicted, clearly it will be different from what it is like now. Organizations which keep a very close eye on external trends, themes and emerging technologies will be better placed to see where and how they need to adapt to stay in business.

Basics of complex adaptive systems theory

Organizations and buildings are similar in that they comprise a number of aligned elements. For example, in a building the electrical system drives the solar blinds that are designed to fit the lighting conditions. But unlike an organization, once a building is built, for the most part it is 'done'.

Organizations, however, are basically purposeful social systems operating in a constant state of flux – people join and leave, compliance requirements change, a strong competitor erupts on to the scene. So, in organization design work it helps to think of the enterprise as an adaptive open system that is not self-contained, is interconnected with other entities in a complex dynamic relationship and is dependent upon its external environment for survival. Look back at the history of organization design (Table 1.1), and consider how thinking about designs has moved from the mechanistic to this adaptive, open-system form.

Open systems consist of 'the patterned activities of a number of individuals. Moreover, these patterned activities are complementary or interdependent with respect to some common output or outcome; they are repeated, relatively enduring, and bounded in space and time' (Katz and Kahn, 1978). Such systems are defined by nine characteristics:

1   They take in energy of some type. In organizations, money is one proxy for energy both as an input and as an outcome. For the most part a proportion of the money gained in sales is reinvested as an input to the organization – money is used to buy resources, e.g. raw materials, to pay wages and to continue the activity pattern. But organizations also take in other proxies for energy in the form of ideas, newcomers bringing new skills and so on.

2   They transform the energy into new products, services, processes and/or by-products.

3   They export something into the external environment – products, services, processes and/or by-products.

4   They perform patterns of activity in a cyclical way so that the output furnishes some part of the input, but it is the events or activities that form the cycle, while the social system is often dynamic. (Think of the production of the annual report that occurs as a repeated activity although the social systems and personnel producing it change over time.)

5   They move to acquire negative entropy. That is, they take in more energy than they expend in order to improve their chances of survival. Organizations do this by reinvesting, undertaking research and development, distributing shares and so on. Even so, each year many organizations are unable to maintain negative entropy and go out of business.

6   They interpret, decode and respond to signals and information about their environment and their own functioning in relation to the environment. Organizations have to continuously learn which signals and information

to respond to and which they can dismiss as 'noise' if they are to stand a chance of maintaining the negative entropy required for survival.

7 They maintain a reasonable constancy in energy exchange which results in a quasi-'steady state', although it is not motionless or a true equilibrium. Organization design work is aimed at aligning the various organizational elements to maintain that 'dynamic homeostasis'.

8 They move in the direction of differentiation/specialization and elaboration, that is they get more complex and nuanced as they evolve. In organization design work the more differentiated/specialized the systems of the organization are, the more integrative and linking mechanisms are needed.

9 They move towards a final state from differing initial conditions and by a variety of paths. (In systems theory this is known as equifinality.)

An in-depth knowledge of systems theory, complexity theory or chaos theory is not needed to do organization design work, but it is important to know that traditional organization structures based in mechanistic views of the world are no longer viable. There are many providers of good introductions to systems thinking: the UK's Open University, for example, offers a Postgraduate Certificate in Systems Thinking in Practice. A useful book on the topic is *Systems Thinking for Curious Managers: With 40 New Management f-Laws*, by Russell L. Ackoff, with Herbert J. Addison and Andrew Carey (Triarchy Press, 2010).

OD short

Organizations are now designed less from the perspective of a mechanistic view of the world, and more from the view that the world is complex and chaotic. Having a basic understanding of systems theory is a necessary attribute for organization designers.

A systems model for the design process

It is unusual for organization designers to talk to clients in the academic, theoretical or conceptual terms that underpin their organization design practice. Rather they talk about applying 'systems models' that graphically represent, in shorthand form, the various organizational elements that collectively comprise the system, including the IT infrastructures, the business processes, the skills of the workforce, the workforce profile, the policies and procedures and the operating context: all the interacting stuff that delivers the required organizational outcome – product, service, shareholder value or whatever.

A 'systems model' acts to guide the organization designers in their work and there are many models. Four in common use are the Burke–Litwin model, Galbraith's five-star model, McKinsey's 7S model and Nadler and Tushman's

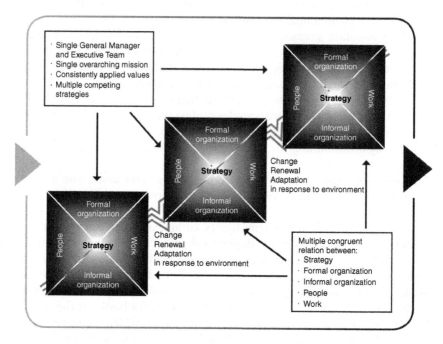

Figure 1.3 Organizational systems model
Source: Adapted from Nadler and Tushman, 1999.

model. The one used in this book is an adaptation of Nadler and Tushman's model. It is shown in Figure 1.3. This one was chosen because it:

- specifies that organizations have an informal component;
- highlights the independent but interconnected business units or divisions;
- recognizes the need for change, renewal and adaptation;
- indicates the concept of a unifying business mission and values;
- signals the inputs and outputs (the arrow heads on the left and right).

Many of the other models lack one or more of these elements.

Expanding on the points listed above, the model (Figure 1.3) shows three business units (or divisions or departments) connected – top left – to a single General Manager/CEO with a single vision. Each unit comprises four major elements which have sub-elements, although these are not shown in the graphic but some are given in Table 1.2. Across the three business units – bottom right – are multiple 'congruent relations' between them. These might be a common management information system or performance management process. But beyond these are elements that are specific to each business unit.

Table 1.2 Systems model element detail

Organizational element	Including
People	The characteristics of individuals in the organization including their skills, capabilities, aptitudes, talents, demographic profile, length of service and time in role.
Work	Workflow, IT infrastructure, functional systems, interdependencies, handover points, how work actually gets done. That is, the basic tasks to be done by the organization and its parts including the job roles and content, job design, number of positions, what work is done at what level.
Formal organization – things that can be documented and described easily to someone else. The explicit, objective parts of the organization. The sort of information you get on an induction programme.	Strategy, hierarchies, structures, layers and spans, organization chart, business processes, standard operating procedures, rules, policies, stated values, space/interior layout, floor plan. That is the totality of the systems and methods that are formally created to get individuals to perform tasks.
Informal organization – things that are not easily described, the shifting coalitions, the nuances, the implicit things.	Culture, relationships, lived values, behaviours, politics, communication, language, myths and stories, management style. That is, the implicit or emerging arrangements including variations to the norm, processes, and relationships, commonly described as the culture or 'the way we do things round here'. The informal organization also includes the 'shadow side' the way people 'decide' how to think and behave, the in-groups and out-groups, social routines, rites and rituals which reinforce the culture.

Thus each unit has a certain level of autonomy within an overarching strategy and some common platforms. And each takes in different 'energy units' from its environment but contributes them both to their own functioning and to the overall organization. Each division has different outputs or outcomes which again contribute to the total output.

The CEO of Sud Group (not the real name) found this graphical representation of an organization very helpful as he struggled to work out with his executive team how the organization should be designed both to be what he called 'One Sud' and to allow business units the autonomy and freedom to act. He wanted to arrive at a One Sud design that enabled 'freedom within a framework' as he put it. Here's how he described his challenge:

> We're a conglomerate – we have three large divisions Food, Agriculture and Bottling, and several smaller divisions. They're very different in customer base, workforce skills requirements, business strategies and so on. But we

want everyone to feel that they belong to One Sud – that lives the same values, that is focused on the same overarching vision and strategy, that has career paths across the divisions, that is run efficiently without duplication of function and that offers employees the same value proposition.

That's been hard to achieve, but our organization design is getting there. We used the graphic to clarify where the synergies lay, what we could run across the organization – like the financial and HR systems, compliance oversight and the supply chain. And what we needed to offer within divisions – like a sub-strategy clearly aligned to the One Sud strategy, technical and specialist training, some sales and marketing activity (within an agreed framework), decisions over numbers and roles of people (again within an agreed framework).

I wouldn't say that the divisions compete for customers but they certainly compete for share of organizational resources, and investment. They've been used to doing their own thing so the One Sud approach has not pleased some senior people. We've had to exit some who were not willing to commit to the One Sud strategy. Now it's clear that we are one brand with sub-brands, that the same values are evident and lived in all divisions, and that we are all working in the same direction. It's very exciting, and we're profiting by learning from each other, making efficiency gains as we constantly review the organization's functioning and increasing customer and supplier satisfaction as we get simpler to deal with.

Just looking at the organization chart would not have given us the full picture of what we needed to do to improve efficiency, effectiveness and customer/employee experience. Seeing a representation of the organization provided a useful hanger for challenging discussions.

For this CEO the systems model provided an easy-to-understand guide to the requirement to align organizational elements in order to achieve a design that delivered the business purpose and strategy. And as the book proceeds it becomes clearer how a systems model guides the design process. As mentioned, there are several to choose from, and some organizations develop their own. The tool at the end of this chapter helps identify a systems model that will work in a specific organization.

OD short

Finding an appropriate systems model and using it to guide organization design work keeps the idea of designing within a complex adaptive system in the front of your mind.

Definition of organization design

Dennis Crowley, CEO, Foursquare, believes that his product needs to be radically different every few months because he faces so much competition.

Believing this he wants to oversee 'a company under constant reinvention'. (Foursquare is a free app that helps people and their friends make the most of where they are.) As he said, 'Reorganizing a company is generally considered a bad thing. We're trying to see it differently. It has to be built into the culture, this idea that we haven't got it right yet – product or organization design' (Safian, 2012).

This perspective leads towards one of the definitions of organization design, that it is:

> Arranging how to do the work necessary to effectively and efficiently achieve a business purpose and strategy whilst delivering high-quality customer and employee experience.
>
> Arranging involves *aligning* the organization with the strategy, creating *coherent* designs, while building *trust* among key stakeholders.

Go back to the systems model, Figure 1.3, and it is evident that alignment of the work, the people, the informal organization and the formal organization is critical to organizational balance. This alignment should maintain the appropriate integrity of each business unit whilst enabling synergies between them to be exploited. Simultaneously it has to ensure that each business unit contributes to the 'greater good' of the whole organization (coherence). This must be done whilst maintaining (a) operational performance and customer satisfaction and (b) the goodwill, motivation and productivity of the workforce (trust).

There are many other definitions of organization design and it is worth finding a few of these and comparing them. Some will fit an organization's language, culture and business better than others. The value of having a definition of organization design is that it becomes easier to explain what organization design is and why it is about more than the structure/organization chart.

OD short

There are many definitions of organization design. Use the one given here or find one that is appropriate to your organization to serve as one of the guides that inform the way you deliver organization design work.

Design principles

Along with the definition of organization design go the principles that guide the way design work is conducted. The principles must reflect the values of the organization. For example, if the values are centred on collaboration and teamwork then credibility and goodwill will be lost if an organization redesign that will take immediate effect is summarily announced.

Develop design principles, and if appropriate embody them in an organizational policy, that specify the basis on which the work will be done.

**Policy Principles
of Engagement & Involvement**

PEOPLE SOLUTIONS

- Stakeholders are involved at the earliest opportunity (good practice would be during the Assess phase)

- Projects are managed on the basis of transparancy and openness

- Every effort made to involve all employees from the earliest opportunity (good practice would be during the Assess phase)

- The end users are involved to determine what their views and opinions are at the earliest opportunity (good practice would be during the Assess phase)

- The local trades unions are included and invited to contribute to Organization Design Projects at the earliest opportunity (good practice would be at the start of the Assess phase)

Figure 1.4 Policy principles of engagement and involvement

Birmingham City Council has both an organization design policy and a set of principles aimed at ensuring that organization design work involves and engages employees. Figure 1.4 shows these principles.

It is not necessary to develop design principles from scratch. Architect and designer Dieter Rams formulated a set of ten to apply to his work in building and product design. They are readily adapted to organization design as follows:

Good [organization] design:

- Is innovative – technological development is always offering new opportunities for innovative design. Innovative design always develops in tandem with innovative technology, and is not an end in itself.
- Makes an organization effective (Rams uses the word 'useful') – an organization is designed to be effective. It has to satisfy certain criteria, not only functional, but also psychological and aesthetic. Good organization design emphasizes effectiveness whilst aiming to eliminate anything that could possibly detract from it.

- Is aesthetic – the aesthetic quality (experience) of the organization is integral to its effectiveness because organizations and workplaces have an effect on people and their well-being. Only well-executed designs can feel motivational.
- Makes an organization understandable – it clarifies the organization's structure and functionality. Better still, it can make the organization clearly express its purpose in a way that stakeholders grasp. At best, it is self-explanatory.
- Is unobtrusive – organizations fulfilling a purpose are like tools. They are neither decorative objects nor works of art. Their design should therefore be both neutral and restrained, to leave room for the employee's self-expression.
- Is honest – it does not make an organization more innovative, powerful or valuable than it really is. It does not attempt to manipulate the employee or customer with promises that cannot be kept.
- Is sustainable – it avoids being fashionable and therefore never appears antiquated. Unlike fashionable design, it lasts many years – even in today's throwaway society.
- Is thorough down to the last detail – nothing must be arbitrary or left to chance. Care and accuracy in the design process show respect towards the employee and the customer.
- Is environmentally friendly – design makes an important contribution to the preservation of the environment. It conserves resources and minimizes physical and visual pollution throughout the enterprise.
- Is as little design as possible – less, but better – because it concentrates on the essential aspects, and the processes and systems are not burdened with non-essentials. Back to purity, back to simplicity.

Adapted from Vitsoe, n.d.

From the Birmingham City Council and the Dieter Rams examples note how having a set of principles helps approach organization design work in a particular way – principles act in a similar way to a code of ethics or behaviour as the design process proceeds. As with OD definitions, there are many sets of design principles and it is worth researching them to help in the development of an organization-specific set. The decision to develop a specific set working with other organizational members (as Birmingham City Council did) helps reflection and learning about *how* to approach design work before getting to the *what* of doing it. Principles make for consistency of approach, a basis for choices and a platform for evaluation.

OD short

Adopting and sticking to some design principles helps: (a) maintain a consistency of approach across organization design projects; (b) establish a basis for your design decisions; (c) contribute to objective evaluation of the design.

The five-phase design process

The HR manager of an Asia Pacific bank came with exactly the sort of thing an organization designer is typically asked to tackle. Read his story below and notice that using the acronym SPIN – situation, problem, implications, needs/ outcomes – provides a framework for organizing the case.

Here's the **situation**:

1   We are very slow to respond effectively to market conditions, which are changing all the time. Our customers and clients are not very happy with the experience they get from us.
2   We have about five managerial levels from manager to executive director. We are adding a sixth level this year with the role of assistant to the governor.
3   Our structure is rather similar to that of the military in that it is vertically organized, although not rigidly so.
4   We don't have any formal business architecture across the organization so things are not very aligned; for example, we introduced a grading system about four or five years ago but have not been very successful in this.
5   Department heads are always saying there is insufficient high-level talent but managers are not willing to manage or exit non-performing employees.
6   Our employee turnover is very low as people are comfortable here and there are not many other places to go to. But this means that career progression is slow and there are a lot of employees stuck in the middle ranks.
7   Our core business lacks good career management tools and pathways and we struggle with performance measurement.

We get a number of **problems** arising from this situation:

1   We have difficulty controlling the growth of the organization structure. Currently, department heads tend to create a new structure to accommodate someone who needs a job promotion.
2   We are not able to judge whether a function should be decentralized or centralized in one unit. That is, we are not sure whether, how and what we should centralize or decentralize.
3   It is very hard for us to calculate the volume of work in order to determine the number of workers needed – particularly knowledge workers, when we are not sure of performance measures for them.

4   Thus we cannot really determine the design, mix and content of jobs – how many functional jobs/individual contributions, how many managers and the relative positions and number of each in the hierarchy.

The **implications** seem to me to be that this situation and the problems arising are about more than structure and we are trying to put across the principle that structures follow strategy and business process, but this is proving uphill work.

What we **need** is a methodology and the tools to apply to make sure our organization design intervention results in cost-effective continuous performance improvement, with ongoing customer and employee satisfaction. Specifically I'd like to be able to give the organizational leaders confidence that the designs we suggest are scalable, flexible and appropriately responsive to the various external environmental changes.

Listening to this sort of thing, OD practitioners often feel the strong urge to leap in and do one of the following:

*   Tell the HR or line manager what the solution is.
*   Accept the new organization chart that his line manager has just given to him (note that this did not happen in this case, but it often does!).
*   Panic, because it all sounds too complicated and beyond his/her level of expertise.

Acting on this impulse is a big mistake. It is far better to develop the confidence to follow a systematic path leading to some design options that achieve the desired outcomes. Remember, organization design is about effectively arranging work (the definition), that an organization is an open system, that a systems model provides a proxy for the elements that need alignment to get the appropriate workflow and that agreed principles will guide the way the work is done.

So, the final piece of preparatory work before beginning an organization design project is getting clear about this systematic path that leads to the design of an aligned, adaptable, high performing, healthy, agile organization.

An organization design or redesign happens over five distinct phases, each with associated activities, tools and deliverables. Figure 1.5 shows these.

The phases look linear, continuous and sequential but in practice they are not. The organization design process is more like being on a playing field where there are principles, givens and guidelines to the game but the players are running around, acting, interacting, ducking and weaving in multi-dimensions: time, place and emotion.

Also the phases look very similar to those of any other type of organizational intervention, for example consulting, training design, organization development and change management. The differences lie in what happens in each of them – the activities within the phases – that make it more distinctively organization design than, say, change management.

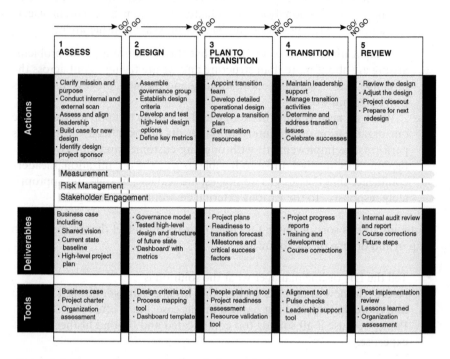

	1 ASSESS	2 DESIGN	3 PLAN TO TRANSITION	4 TRANSITION	5 REVIEW
Actions	· Clarify mission and purpose · Conduct internal and external scan · Assess and align leadership · Build case for new design · Identify design project sponsor	· Assemble governance group · Establish design criteria · Develop and test high-level design options · Define key metrics	· Appoint transition team · Develop detailed operational design · Develop a transition plan · Get transition resources	· Maintain leadership support · Manage transition activities · Determine and address transition issues · Celebrate successes	· Review the design · Adjust the design · Project closeout · Prepare for next redesign
	Measurement				
	Risk Management				
	Stakeholder Engagement				
Deliverables	Business case including · Shared vision · Current state baseline · High-level project plan	· Governance model · Tested high-level design and structure of future state · 'Dashboard' with metrics	· Project plans · Readiness to transition forecast · Milestones and critical success factors	· Project progress reports · Training and development · Course corrections	· Internal audit review and report · Course corrections · Future steps
Tools	· Business case · Project charter · Organization assessment	· Design criteria tool · Process mapping tool · Dashboard template	· People planning tool · Project readiness assessment · Resource validation tool	· Alignment tool · Pulse checks · Leadership support tool	· Post implementation review · Lessons learned · Organization assessment

Figure 1.5 Phases of an organization design project

Look back to the systems model shown in Figure 1.3: in organization design work the focus is on the formal organization, but the other elements are in clear sight and organization development and change management cannot be divorced from the design process. The relationship amongst these is discussed in Chapter 3.

In subsequent chapters, each of the five phases of the methodology is discussed in detail. Remember not to go into the work of designing before having the basics of a systems model, an OD definition and design principles.

OD short

An organization design project is organized in five phases with associated activities, deliverables and tools. The phases look linear and sequential but in practice they are iterative and invariably somewhat 'messy'.

Tool

Table 1.3 places five commonly used systems models in order from simplest to most complex and notes some strengths and limitations of each. Take a look at the table and the associated figures. Add in any other systems models – almost

Table 1.3 Systems models of organization design in common use

Originator	Model	Elements of model	Strengths	Limitations
McKinsey: 7S model (developed by Pascale and Athos, 1981 and then refined by Peters and Waterman, 1982)	See Figure 1.6	Systems Strategy Structure Style Shared values Staff Skills	Description of important organizational elements Recognition of the interaction between these	No external environment (input)-throughput-output element No feedback loops No performance variables
Galbraith: star model	See Figure 1.7	Strategy Structure People Rewards Process	Description of important organizational elements Recognition of the interaction between these	Does not 'call out' some key elements including inputs–outputs culture
Weisbord's six-box model	See Figure 1.8	Leadership (co-ordinates other five elements) Purpose Structure Rewards Helpful mechanisms Relationships	Includes some diagnostic questions in each box Requires the purpose to be stated	Focus on some elements may lead to overlooking others
Nadler and Tushman: congruence model	See Figure 1.9	Informal organization, formal organization, work, people (with inputs and outputs)	Easy to follow Allows for discussion of what comprises 'informal' and 'formal' organization Boxes must be congruent with one another	Few named elements may lead to wheel-spinning or overlooking of crucial aspects
Burke–Litwin	See Figure 1.10	Mission/strategy Structure Task requirements Leadership Management practices Work unit climate Motivation Organization culture Individual needs and values (plus feedback loops)	Includes feedback loops 'Calls out' more qualitative aspects, e.g. motivation	Very detailed Difficult to grasp at a quick glance

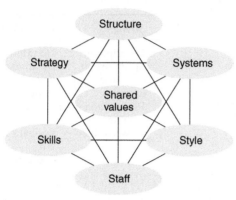

Figure 1.6 McKinsey's 7S model

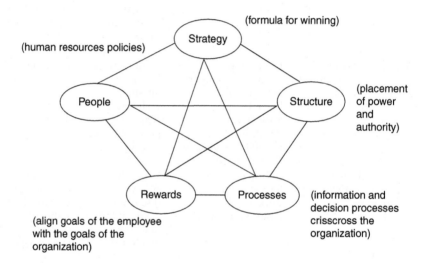

Figure 1.7 Galbraith's star model

all the big consultancies have their variation on these – and complete Table 3.1 for any added in.

Be aware that there is no one right choice of model for an organization design in the same way that there is no right choice of car for a family – there are tradeoffs and compromises in choosing. But to help select one that is best fit for an organization ask the following questions:

1   Does the model 'parcel' the organizational elements in a way that stakeholders will recognize; i.e. are there enough, are they ones that are important in the organization?

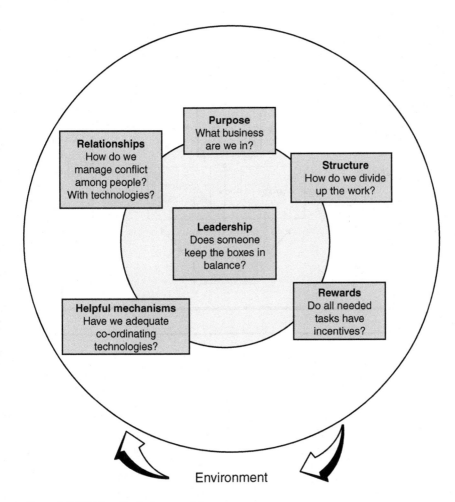

Figure 1.8 Weisbord's six-box model

2   How will stakeholders react to the presented model (is it jargon-free, simple to understand and communicate)?
3   Is it a model that will find favour across the organization or will it compete with other organization design models?
4   Does the model harbour implicit assumptions that might help or hinder design work? For example, does it include/exclude factors such as local culture (both national and organizational) and human factors (such as personalities), or does it suggest ways that elements may relate to one another?
5   How adaptable is the model for the specific context and circumstances in which it will be used? Does it enable any new perspectives or innovative

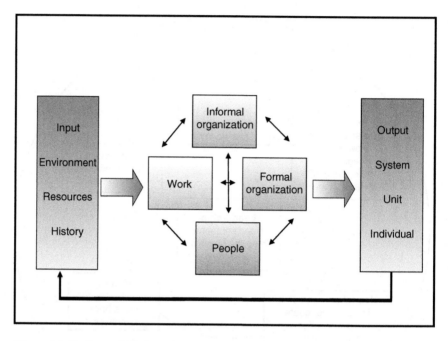

Figure 1.9 Nadler and Tushman's congruence model

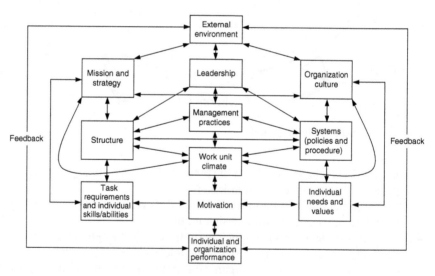

Figure 1.10 The Burke–Litwin model

thinking? Is it scalable to small work-unit design and whole-organization design?

6　Does the model work with other models in use in the organization (for example, change management or project management models)?

7　Are the costs to adopt the model acceptable (for example, training, communication and obtaining 'buy-in')?

8　Does the model allow for new and unconventional organization design that will help drive the business strategy?

9　Does the model have a sponsor/champion who will help communicate it appropriately?

10　Does the model allow for transformational design as well as transactional design? ('Transformational' means a design developed in response to environmental forces, either internal or external to the organization – for example, creation or closure of a business unit or a merger – that affect the mission, strategy and culture. 'Transactional' means changes related to the business or work unit structures, systems, processes, etc. that might be needed to carry out the mission and strategy but do not change them.)

Do not be purist about the models: any one of them can be adapted for a specific organization. But do make sure that:

- there is only one systems model in use across the organization;
- all internal and external organization design consultants work with the chosen organizational model and not their model.

Using multiple systems models in one organization creates difficulties around language, alignment, consistency of approach and so on.

Summary

This chapter has set the scene for practitioner organization design confidence-building. It has discussed the relationship between organization design and structure, given an outline of the history of organization design, presented the essentials of systems theory and pointed out the direction to learn more on this. It has provided a systems model to reflect on together with an activity to help choose one appropriate for a specific organization. It has considered one definition among many of organization design and again suggested that an organizationally tailored or developed one is a good option. It has talked about the value of adopting organization design principles and given an overview of the five phases of the design process.

References

ACASA. (2011). 'Ackoff Collaboratory: Types of Systems'. Retrieved 17 December 2011, from http://www.acasa.upenn.edu/4sys.htm.

Beakey, D., Wells, K. and Rubin, J. (2007). 'Organizational Design and Implementation', *Graziado Business Review*, **10**(4), at http://gbr.pepperdine.edu/2010/08/organizational-design-and-implementation.

Curl, J. S. (2006). *A Dictionary of Architecture and Landscape Architecture*. Oxford: Oxford University Press.

Jensen, W. (2000). *Simplicity: The New Competitive Advantage in a World of More, Better, Faster*. Cambridge, MA: Basic Books.

Katz, D. and Kahn, R. (1978). *Social Psychology of Organizations*. New York: John Wiley and Sons, Inc.

Nadler, D. A. and Tushman, M. (1999). 'The Organization of the Future: Strategic Imperatives and Core Competencies for the 21st Century', *Organizational Dynamics*, 1 July, 45–60.

Pascale, R. T. and Athos, A. G. (1981). *The Art of Japanese Management*. New York: Simon & Schuster.

Peters, T. J. and Waterman, R. H., Jr. (1982). *In Search of Excellence: Lessons from America's Best-Run Companies*. New York: Harper & Row.

Safian, R. (2012). 'Secrets of the Flux Leader', *Fast Company*, November, 96–106.

Schumpeter. (2012). 'The Driverless Road Ahead', *The Economist*, 20 October. Retrieved 21 October 2012, from *The Economist*: http://www.economist.com/news/business/21564821-carmakers-are-starting-take-autonomous-vehicles-seriously-other-businesses-should-too.

Stanford, N. (2012). *Organizational Health*. London: Kogan Page.

Vitsoe. (n.d.). 'Dieter Rams: Ten Principles for Good Design'. Retrieved 16 May 2013, from Vitsoe: https://www.vitsoe.com/us/about/good-design.

Worren, N. (2012). *Organisation Design: Redefining Complex Systems*. London: Pearson.

2 Organization design
Positioning, roles and skills

We are drowning in information, while starving for wisdom. The world henceforth will be run by synthesizers, people able to put together the right information at the right time, think critically about it, and make important choices wisely.

Edward O. Wilson

What you will learn

This chapter raises awareness about the 'ownership' of the design capability and the process-consulting relationship between client and consultant. It considers the skills needed to be an effective consultant, including the ability to build trust, to influence well and to demonstrate business savvy.

Who 'owns' organization design?

The previous chapter defined organization design. From the discussion it is evident that organization design is a lot more than adjusting the organization chart, i.e. the blocks and lines that show a formal reporting relationship between the jobholders.

As indicated in Chapter 1, when people are trying to decide the 'best' structure for their organization they often forget that work has to flow through it and that different structures have different attributes. For example, that adaptability is poor in a traditional hierarchy but good in a network. Instead, structure decisions are often made based on personalities, politics and expediency. This is a mistake on two counts. First, it fails to explicitly recognize that structure choices affect organizational capabilities, and, second, that getting work done efficiently in order to meet organizational goals is, or should be, the purpose of the organizing frameworks and structures.

The possibilities that technology now offers for charting the way work actually gets done in organizations and the advent of new business models raises some questions about who 'owns' the design of the organization and where the 'owner' should reside in the organization.

Identifying who owns the design is not always clear-cut. Consider the business model of LiveOps, established in 2000. It deploys cloud computing to virtualize its business services. It is a cloud-based call-centre service that manages a network of more than 20,000 independent at-home agents. Companies use the service on a pay-as-you-go model, either as a fully outsourced call centre or to augment their own. The technology enables an on-demand, scalable service to subscribers. The relationship of the stakeholders – LiveOps, the independent agents and the companies buying the services of the agents via Live Ops – is not easily depicted in a standard chart. Nevertheless the three parties together form an organization that delivers a service to a customer. In this instance who 'owns' the whole system design of LiveOps? Is it the CEO or leadership team, or the self-employed agents, or the purchasers of the services, who, by nature of their requirements, have an implicit voice in the design of the organization, or others who are not so obvious: regulators, or possibly unions or even more possibilities beyond these? Notice that so far none of the possible owners mentioned includes HR – a function which often sees itself as the guardian of organization design.

Listening to LiveOps founder and CEO Marty Beard speak it is obvious that the design of the organization is something he constantly thinks about. He is making continuous decisions of whether, in his words, to 'pivot or persevere' (LiveOps, 2012). As it says on the LiveOps website: 'He is responsible for all strategic and operational aspects of the company.' He is using his sophisticated technology to keep a constant eye on operations, and specifically the at-home agents. As he says: 'I have this real-time flow [of information] so that every day I can see what they're working on, what they're impacted by, what challenges they face. That's just input for me to figure out what products do I need to make, what changes do I need to make, what patterns am I seeing, where do I need to change my focus to provide better service?'

The LiveOps SVP of human resources, Norma Jean Lane, 'manages the planning, direction and implementation of all human resources programs and policies and participates in the overall executive management of the company. Her team serves all LiveOps employees in the areas of human resource services, compensation, benefits, organizational development, training, EEO compliance, recruiting, staffing, and all other aspects of human capital management.'

In this example you see a current trend: the overall 'design' is 'owned' by the business people, as a part of a business strategy, and its 'development' is 'owned' by the HR team. These are not independent, but integrated pathways. There is a business strategy that can only be delivered with the support of a corresponding HR strategy. Here is what one HR manager said on the topic:

> Our business leaders are currently designing a Target Operating Model and a five-year plan which will look at business development in emerging and existing markets. Therefore I see my [HR manager] role as instrumental in being able to plan the 'future-state' including assess skills requirements, analyzing labour markets, and developing a future plan talent

The HR Profession Map

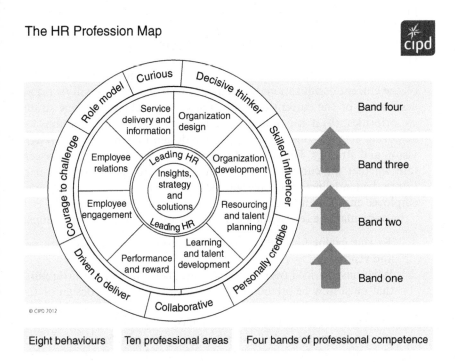

Eight behaviours   Ten professional areas   Four bands of professional competence

Figure 2.1 CIPD HR Profession Map

acquisition planning/internal mobility or other interventions for resource such as outsourcing and other flexible workforce solutions. I also aim to look at centres of competence for key skills in e-commerce and this could be on an international basis as my company has international span/ growth plans. Thus my role is strategic in terms of the business strategy as I have to integrate the HR strategy with it.

Although 'organization design' is often seen as vested in HR, and certainly required as an HR competence – it figures on the CIPD's HR Profession Map (Figure 2.1) – a new design is typically initiated and driven by the business. HR, with its focus primarily on the workforce, is only one of the parties that enable new organization design success. Other support service areas, among them IT, finance, facilities and communications, are also typically tagged as enablers of new design success, and often work alongside the business and HR in planning and implementing a (re)design piece of work.

Take a look at this extract from a request for proposal (RFP) from a tele-coms company.

Over recent years, Telco has undergone significant change, much of which is the result of influences of the external environment. This change has taken many forms: merger activity, entry into new markets, new channels, a new CEO, an emerging strategy, etc. During this period of change the overarching structures, roles, policies and processes, etc. have remained largely unchanged.

The CEO and his leadership team are now commissioning a review of the current organizational design. The outcome of this will be (a) an assessment of the current design's capability to achieve the new strategic priorities; (b) if it is found to be not capable, recommendations for achieving a more coherent and effective design that will deliver Telco's vision and strategy. The aim of this piece of work therefore is to ascertain whether the current organization design is robust enough to meet future demands including emerging strategy, external market pressures, employee engagement, etc.

In particular, the review should aim to answer the following questions:

1   To what extent does Telco's current form support our stated purposes and vision?
2   What has changed over recent years (either internally or externally) that must now be attended to in terms of the overall design of the organization?
3   What are the recommendations in determining next steps in achieving greater coherence and alignment (dependent upon findings)?
4   How can organizational agility be maintained in the light of ongoing organization-development activity?

This RFP was initiated by the business leaders. In consulting terms the key business owner of the project is the 'client'. Now think about who might respond to the RFP. If it were external consultants, what field of expertise would they demonstrate to qualify them: HR, business strategy, operations, organization development, change management, business analytics or finance? If it were an internal request, who would it flow to? It is not obvious that respondents would (or should) come from HR. In this RFP the only qualifier is that respondents should provide evidence of 'experience in this field and references of work previously carried out that are similar in nature to the proposal'. Whoever it is, the person(s) providing the expertise are the 'consultants'. Throughout the remainder of the book the terms 'client' and 'consultant' will be used to describe this key relationship in organization design work.

OD short

Organization design is 'owned' by a formal business leader (the client) and its implementation is facilitated and enabled by an expert practitioner (the consultant).

Where does organization design delivery expertise sit?

A recurring organizational question is about where the 'point people' with internal expertise to do the detailed technical work required to design and then keep an organization well designed should be situated in an organization. Are they best placed as part of an HR function, part of a strategy department, as an independent unit reporting to a COO or CEO or somewhere else? (The assumption is that technical organization design requires specific expertise.)

This is not an easy question to answer, as different organizations have different views on the added value of conscious organization design activity and this perspective seems to colour where it is 'put'. Furthermore, and unfortunately, many organizations are not clear on what OD is, why they need it, how it should be practised and the ROI (return on investment) they are expecting to get from it.

Those in a position to decide where OD should sit should aim to agree that OD:

(a) is integral to delivering the business strategy;
(b) is needed for developing the capability of the whole system;
(c) demands expertise in the integration of IT systems, work process improvement and business analytics;
(d) should be practised by engaging and involving internal and external stakeholders through humanistic values (see Glossary) using soft approaches;
(e) can be evaluated and measured to ascertain ROI (using hard approaches).

The decision can then be made on where it should be based. Decisions on this are founded on the size, market maturity, industry sector and local or global nature of the organization, but for a large organization the OD function is ideally an independent, objective multi-expert unit reporting into the strategy department or a COO.

However, the reality is that it is difficult to find an organization that has an independent, objective unit of this type. The predominant view seems to be that organization design technical skills are rightfully part of an HR function's services to clients and thus sit in HR. Where, within that function, is another matter. Fred Nickols is the author of a short, useful discussion paper on this.

Viewing organization design as a sub-set of organization development, he suggests that, generally speaking, internal organization development practitioners are found in one of three areas within HR: Learning and Development; as a stand-alone Organization Development unit; and as an Organizational Effectiveness (OE) unit. In the first two cases, the consultant is typically practising 'soft' elements of OD, i.e. biased towards organization development work, while OE units are typically practising 'hard' OD, i.e. biased towards organization design work (Nickols, 2004).

In his view, soft approaches include coaching, motivating, mentoring, conflict management, group facilitation and team-building, i.e. they are situated more towards what is thought of as the 'development end' of organization effectiveness. Hard approaches are things like business process re-engineering, total quality management, ISO 9000, six sigma and lean, i.e. what is thought of as the 'design' end of organization effectiveness. This design end requires certain technical skills – for example in determining what structures might fit which situations. Nickols does not specifically reference organization design, rather he sees it as the 'hard' end of organization development, noting that:

> External Organization Development practitioners fall into two groups as well: those practicing 'soft' Organization Development and those practicing 'hard' Organization Development.
>
> It's my guess that whether internal or external, those practicing 'hard' organization development find more favor with senior executives and other managers focused on measurably improving performance, whether of people, processes or the bottom line. Moreover, I'd also guess that external organization development consultants practicing 'hard' organization development are probably the better paid.
>
> It's been my observation that internal organization development practitioners using 'soft' approaches typically find themselves in supporting roles of limited influence and, in some cases, they have been there primarily for show, so an executive can say, 'Yeah, we have an organization development unit.' External consultants using 'soft' approaches are still in vogue and on occasion work in the rarefied atmosphere of the executive suite but these are few and far between. (Nickols, 2004)

An individual organization design practitioner may favour the 'hard' over the 'soft' approach or vice versa, but invariably most organization design work involves a blend of both sets of skills and experience. So which HR service area is the 'owner' and developer of these? Where does it sit in the HR organization?

Table 2.1 lists the job titles of the majority of attendees at a two-day CIPD organization design course run six times during 2012. These titles give some indication of the various HR service areas that lay claim to organization design.

The range of job titles gives the impression that organization design skills touch a number of traditionally more or less discrete HR areas of expertise. Thus it may not make sense to argue that organization design should be in a particular HR service line. A more pragmatic approach is to expect the OD technical skills to be present in whatever HR service line or other business function is appropriate for a specific organization and/or distributed across HR and other organizational functions with integration mechanisms that can call on the required competences as needed.

Table 2.1 Job titles of organization design programme participants

Title	Number	Percentage
Analyst	4	3
Change manager	4	3
HR business partner	12	8.5
HR consultant	4	3
HR director	8	6
HR manager, head of HR	35	25.5
HR officers	5	4
HR projects and programmes	7	5
HR strategy	6	4.5
Independent consultant (from an HR background)	5	4
Learning and development manager	7	5
Organization development manager	19	14
Organization effectiveness manager	1	1
Other job titles (including communications, HSE, HRIS, reward, recruitment, job architecture, talent manager, global marketing capability)	20	14.5
Total attendees	137	100

OD short

Organization design expertise covers a variety of 'hard' and 'soft' technical skills and knowledge. In most organizations the expertise sits somewhere in the HR function. As long as the expertise is organizationally present the specific location matters less than having the consulting skills capability required to deploy the expertise effectively.

Technical skills for organization design

Those currently in operational HR but moving towards organization design take on a very different role from that of a conventional HR practitioner. Organization design work (indeed any change management work) requires them to move well beyond the traditional boundaries of managing transactions to mobilizing a number of strategies to improve human performance and organizational effectiveness.

Examining the reasons why people register on an OD programme shows that HR people are aware that they will need new or different skills. The following three reasons given for enrolling on an organization design course are typical:

> My organization has grown significantly over the last few years and I want to think more effectively about its design, at global, national and

functional levels. Having done a lot of work around job design, I also wanted to think about how this relates to organization design. (Head of Organization Development)

As a result of acquisitions in the last two years I've had the opportunity to step away from my HR day role and get more involved with the merging companies. This has been fantastic in working with other processes, values and a different customer base. Whilst I understand the business rationale, I'd like to understand more about the strategy and process behind the scenes that helps to form design decisions and choices. (Learning and Development Manager)

I have a knowledge and awareness of organization design built through operational implementation. I would like to learn about best practice and also have a robust methodology that I can use as a framework. (HR Business Partner)

What follows here is an overview of the technical skills required. Note that these are discussed in more detail in subsequent chapters.

The discussion so far has focused on the business leader as initiator of an organization design project, with the OD consultant sitting somewhere in the HR function, or perhaps somewhere else in an organization, providing the operational skills and expertise to help business leaders design or redesign their organizations for optimum and sustainable performance. A certain skill-set and toolkit are needed to be able to deliver this support.

As mentioned, the UK's CIPD, in its HR Profession Map, gives a set of competencies for organization design. Its overall statement asserts that a competent OD practitioner: 'Ensures that the organization is appropriately designed to deliver organization objectives in the short and long term and that structural change is effectively managed.' It then lists, at each of four bands: 'Activities: what you need to do' and 'Knowledge: what you need to know'. Table 2.2 shows the content for band 3.

The CIPD Organization Design Map is a useful guide. But be aware that it has some limitations, as most competence frameworks do. Aiming to band specific aspects does not allow for the complexity and nuances of projects. The long 'laundry list' of stuff makes it rather difficult to know what is critical and what is nice to have as a practitioner. Some skills can be bought in from outside or found in other parts of the organization, and it might be a better option to look at this possibility. For example, the aspect of job evaluation methodology knowledge that calls for 'the limitations and advantages of leading-edge job-levelling and evaluation tools and how to use them' could well be delegated to someone with job design and evaluation expertise. An alternative is to challenge the whole concept of job levelling as organizations become flatter and more organic.

Participants in the organization design courses mentioned earlier are clear on what they want to know. Answers to the request 'Please list three topics you want addressed by this training' reflect predominantly technical content,

Table 2.2 CIPD HR profession map. Organization design, band 3: activities and knowledge

---

Organization design
Ensures that the organization is appropriately designed to deliver organization objectives in the short- and long-term and that structural change is effectively managed.

Activities: what you need to do

Set the context for design	Facilitate discussion with senior managers to identify situation or problems the need resolving in respect to the design of the organization.
	Work with senior managers to complete tools and frameworks which will help define the case for change.
	Develop a business case for redesigning the organization, including milestones and goals, benefits and timescales for delivery, investment required and critical success factors and key risks and mitigations.
	Ensure that senior managers clearly understand the likely impact/investment that will be required to make change happen.
Assess current organization design	Conduct benchmarking of other organizations.
	Use an appropriate model to systematically assess the impact of current design at the highest level on factors such as behavior, attitudes, culture, systems and communication flows.
	Complete 'as is' description of the organization and how it operates today.
	Translate the strategic requirements for the new design into a set of design criteria that will guide and inform the subsequent redesign work.
	Assess the impact of the new design by comparing the strategic requirements for change with the 'as is' organization.
Design organizational model	Propose design solution that better aligns structure, process, reward, metrics and talent. Assess opportunities to outsource activity to reduce cost or increase quality of work.
	Test the feasibility of design solutions and the extent to which they meet the design criteria.
Identify key organization processes	Lead the definition of end-to-end processes and how they will operate to ensure co-ordination of activities across departments.
	Identify required roles to deliver end-to-end process and create top-level organization charts
Define measures and governance	Identify measures that focus on shifting the emphasis inputs, processes and outputs, to measuring outcomes: impacts, benefits or consequences for the organization.
	Ensure boundaries and controls are in place to maintain the integrity of the new structure.
Implement and evaluate design	Plan implementation, identifying who will be the drivers of the proposed changes to design and how progress will be tracked.
	Identify benefits realization, what lessons have been learned and what further improvements need to be made to the structural design.

Table 2.2 (cont.)

Knowledge: what you need to do	
Situational organization design	How a business case is developed and the tools and frameworks that support this.
Organization design tools	How to work within an organization design framework that ensures integration of processes, governance, people and technology.
Design blockers and challengers	The organization culture that they are operating in and the approaches that will best encourage buy-in and engagement to design implementation
Job evaluation methodology	The limitations and advantages of leading-edge job-levelling and evaluation tools and how to use them

the 'hard' aspects of organization design: tools and techniques, models and methodologies, structure and culture alignment, planning and implementation. Handling the politics and influencing business leaders, the 'soft' aspects, get runner-up mentions.

The exercise at the end of this chapter is an Organization Design Skills Self-Assessment. Amy Kates, the originator, notes that 'Our clients really find this self-assessment helpful. We often use it before a training program to create a group profile. Not too long ago we looked at about 1,000 responses over the past few years from HR/OD staff at all kinds of companies around the world. The pattern was quite consistent and predictable – training course participants are much stronger on the talent and consulting skills than on the assessment and design skills.'

Take the self-assessment and decide in what respects you would like to develop your own expertise and in what respects you can involve colleagues or external support in filling the gaps in a specific piece of work. You will learn more on the technical skills in later chapters. The rest of this chapter concentrates on the relationship between client (business leader) and consultant (you). Having a trusting relationship makes for a well-orchestrated organization design project.

OD short

Organization design competences are outlined in the UK's CIPD HR Profession Map. For the most part the competences relate to technical skills, with some behavioural and role description aspects. Organization design technical skills training is the most sought-after by HR practitioners, who tend to have had some exposure to organization design work but wish to build their technical expertise.

Process consulting, client consultant roles and activities

Somewhat surprisingly none of the respondents registering on the programmes referred to above (Table 2.1) mentioned development of organization design consulting skills as one of their reasons for joining. There were some oblique mentions: for example, one person wanted to know how to 'build the case for Organization Design with business leaders and what skills of coercion and influence need be brought to bear to do this'. Another was interested in learning 'how to make bold change happen'. Although the process of designing in sequential phases, as discussed in Chapter 1, is the ideal approach, in the reality of day-to-day and business-as-usual (BAU), organization design work is stressful, messy and complex. Therefore it requires:

- a trusted, partnering client–consultant relationship;
- individual capability to manage competing roles;
- clear differentiation between the HR consultant and the line manager's role in the organization design work.

And this is best conducted using process consulting techniques.

Edgar Schein (Schein, 1990) defines process consulting, which he says is basically a 'helping model', by contrasting it with two other forms of helping models 'that seem to me substantively quite different': providing expert information and playing doctor. These are explained below.

Providing expert information

This, Schein suggests, is giving information that is directly relevant to a client's problem. So if the client says, 'The performance appraisal system doesn't work to raise productivity in my department. What is a better system for my group?', the consultant gives the answer. This makes an assumption that the consultant has the right skills, knowledge and expertise to do this and the client does not. The client believes that the consultant is an expert with the 'right' answers. Take a car analogy. The client takes his car to the garage and says, 'The brake-pads are worn and need replacement, please fix them.' The mechanic has the expertise to do this but the car-owner does not – he only has the skills to see that something is wrong with the brakes. The issue here is that the client may not know that brakes can fail for reasons other than worn brake-pads. Similarly the client may not know that his group's productivity levels may have nothing to do with the appraisal system, but in this case the consultant is not being hired to find this out but simply to give an expert answer to a specific question.

Playing doctor

When a client asks a consultant to come and assess a situation, find out what is wrong and suggest a cure, the consultant is in the role of 'playing doctor'. Schein suggests that playing the doctor role is somewhat of an ego trip for consultants and that the efficacy of the role is based on a number of assumptions that may or may not be accurate. Again using the car analogy, the client may take the car to the mechanic and say, 'This car is taking a long time to slow down, please find out what the problem is and suggest a way of fixing it.' The mechanic might come back with several suggestions – too little brake-fluid or air and water in the brake-fluid or the brake-pads are worn. The client expects the mechanic to diagnose which of these it is (or if it is something else) and suggest a remedy.

Process consulting

Schein discusses this in terms of helping people who know something is awry but are not sure what or why. Once they have been helped to work out what is wrong they are usually in a position to fix whatever it is themselves (i.e. they don't need an expert). This means that the consultant has to suspend judgment on what the issue is, and/or how to fix it, and with the client develop an inquiry process where together they find out what is going on and what to do about it.

Schein sees this as a robust way of involving the client, ensuring that he/she takes responsibility for the issues and feels a sense of ownership of the outcome and commitment to it. Again in the car scenario, the client might start noticing that coming up to a traffic-light the car isn't slowing down very quickly. In this case the client and the consultant would determine together how to tackle this issue – they might decide to look at the car's manual, or take a course on car maintenance or examine the levels of brake-fluid to rule out one of the possible causes. In this process consulting mode, the consultant is helping the client learn how to address problems himself and develop skills to apply in future situations.

As Schein points out, in practice consultants are usually moving from one of these three helping models to another as the intervention proceeds. A practical and readable book on process consulting is Peter Block's *Flawless Consulting* (Pfeiffer, 2011). It is a gold-mine of tips, tools and sound advice.

One of the tensions inherent in the organizational client–consultant partnering process is that in addition to the roles both players have in the OD project are the roles that they have elsewhere in the organization. These can cause conflicts or dilemmas. One line manager spoke eloquently on this:

> Now there are a whole heap of strategic projects coming at us like a tidal wave and on top of that we're doing a restructure. We still have

Table 2.3 Role of line manager (client) in organization design work

Strategic management	→ Tactical management	→ Operational management
Giving direction: why do we want to do this?	Planning oriented: how do we achieve the goals	Driving actions: what, when, where, who
Thinking long term, beyond the immediate problem	Thinking 3–6 months ahead	Thinking days or a few weeks ahead
Challenging the organization	Coming up with solutions	Listing jobs to be done, quick fixes
Redefining the problem to be tackled	Organizing, planning, co-ordinating	Spotting opportunities for immediate action
Giving an innovative perspective	Planning within an appropriate and flexible framework	Mitigating risks

At whichever point on the continuum, defining the task, planning, briefing staff, controlling, evaluating, motivating, organizing and setting a positive example.

to concentrate on getting the day job done. This has to be a priority. Individuals are being asked to manage a colossal amount of change. It's like a wall of change. How are we going to scale it? Is it going to grind the organization to a halt? Who is prepared to speak for prioritization – against what measures? People can't cope with the day-to-day work combined with the tidal wave of change and the redesign simultaneously. There are cracks appearing – for example turnover is starting to creep up. Where shall I put my energy?

An HR consultant talked about the dilemmas he faced:

My advice is to employ an outside facilitator to run the discovery phase workshop but that will cost money that we have not got in the current budget. So I will have to do it and I am not seen as truly objective. And really, I'm not. I know that the redesign is likely to result in lay-offs and unwanted redeployments and all of us in HR are already suffering from the fall-out and flack of previous reduction in force programmes.

For both client and consultant, successful multiple-role working requires the ability to balance the various demands of each role without becoming stressed and demoralized. This can be helped if client and consultant are clear what each other's role is in a redesign and how the skills and expertise of each can complement the other's.

In most cases the line manager (client) will take one or more of the management roles along the continuum summarised in Table 2.3 and the HR consultant will adopt one or more of the roles shown along the continuum Table 2.4.

Table 2.4 Role of HR consultant in organization design work

Facilitator role →	→	→	→	→	→		Expert role
Objective observer and commentator	Process counsellor	Fact finder	Alternative identifier and linker	Joint problem solver	Trainer educator	Informational expert	Advocate

Table 2.5 Continuum of process consultant style

Non-directive style →	→	→	→	→	→		Directive style
Questions to encourage reflection	Observes problem solving process and gives feedback	Gathers data and stimulates thinking	Identifies alternatives for the client and helps assess consequences	Proposes alternatives and participates in decisions	Develops, trains, educates the line manager/ client	Determines policy or practice	Represents the line manager/ client; puts the case on his/her behalf

Table 2.6 Continuum of line manager (client) style

Directive style →	→	→	→	→	→		Non-directive style
Decides to restructure based on context change	Informs workforce and selects and directs consultant	Controls pace and resources of project	Manages upwards, downwards, laterally the consequences of design decisions	Invites participation in project design and implementation	Delegates much of design decision to staff within framework	Forms collaborative teams to work on redesign life cycle	Empowers staff to self-organize their workflow and structure within framework

Additionally, the client and the consultant will be flexing their operational style depending on the situation and the project phase. Typically, the consultant will be operating as a process consultant (see Glossary), judging when and how to operate at a specific point on the continuum outlined in Table 2.5. While the client will be moving more or less on the opposite continuum, shown in Table 2.6.

Each one of the five phases requires the client and the consultant to be working together but on different aspects of the project, as Table 2.7 shows.

This difference in consultant/client activities dictates the role that each plays. As a rule of thumb, each phase requires a slightly different role emphasis from the client and consultant, outlined in Table 2.8.

Knowing the roles and activities of client and consultant and the general orientation of process consulting as a 'helping' approach is not enough. Both

Table 2.7 Client and consultant activity by phase

Design phase	Client activity	Consultant activity
Assess	Deciding that a new design or redesign is necessary to achieve business outcomes (including assessing the drivers for this) Evaluating the chosen route (OD or not) in order to feel confident about the way forward Ensuring key leaders and stakeholders are aligned on the way forward	Coaching the manager in making a sound decision Providing information and support to the manager to help him/her make the right choices Probing and challenging to ensure the manager is on solid ground in his/her decision
Design	Initiating the design process Keeping the day-to-day business running Balancing the trade-off between time, cost and quality, in choosing a design option to implement	Drafting the high-level scoping document and project charter Following up with sponsors and stakeholders Guiding and suggesting on potential project team leaders and members
Plan to transition	Guiding the governance of the project Allocating resources to project (time, staff, skills, budget, etc.) Communicating with peers and other stakeholders on progress	Working with the project manager to manage the assignment Supporting creation of the project structure and plan Identifying issues and opportunities for improvement
Transition	Leading the transition process Motivating people to work with the changes and projecting confidence and optimism Adjusting plan appropriately	Surveying responses to change and relaying to manager Recommending actions as needed to maintain progress Supporting and guiding people into new state
Review and evaluate	Commissioning a post-implementation review after project closure Taking action to address issues and concerns to ensure benefits of change are delivered Transferring to peers knowledge, skills and learning gained in the OD process	Ensuring post-implementation review is thorough and reliable Guiding and supporting manager to understanding, communicating and acting on the findings Following through on the agreed actions

Table 2.8 Client and consultant roles by phase

Phase	Client role	Consultant role
Assess	Strategic management	Fact finder Objective Process counsellor
Design	Strategic management moving towards tactical management	Fact finder
Plan to transition	Tactical management moving towards operational management	Alternative identifier Joint problem solver
Transition	Operational management	Trainer educator Informational expert
Review and evaluate	Strategic management	Advocate Facilitator Objective Process counsellor

client and consultant have to hold the basic assumptions on which process consulting is predicated:

- The consultant and the client act as equals. The client provides the knowledge of the organization's nature, business and issues; the consultant provides the knowledge of the techniques, ways of thinking and practices that can solve the problem.
- The client owns the problem and determines the solution. The consultant helps the client to see the issues and find what needs to be done. By not imposing a point of view, the process consultant ensures that a real solution, not an attractive, trendy or unstable fix, is obtained.
- The consultant operates from a position that two-way learning and collaborative problem solving will skill the client to continue to deal with the situation.
- The sharing of problem and opportunity identification and action planning/implementation leads to shared vision. The expert consultant may have a toolkit of best practice methods, but the process consultant will ensure that the tools which are employed will best fit the organization's needs and interests. (21st Century Process Consultation, 2001)

These assumptions can clash with some of the realities of organizational life – that trust is often at a premium, and consultants – particularly if they come from HR – are often hierarchically junior to the client and have no real power base from which to approach the relationship as an equal. The consultant in this position has to build trust and trade on influence and credibility to make the relationship successful. The following section considers these attributes.

OD short

Process consulting is particularly suited to organization design work as it is based on the assumptions that the client knows the answers and the consultant is helping surface these. Consultants who combine subject expertise with process helpfulness are best suited to organization design work. Part of the 'helping' approach is being clear about the roles and activities of client and consultant at each stage of the project.

Trust, influence and credibility

Trust between consultant and client is the critical underpinning for the relationship to have any chance of resulting in successful project outcomes. Solomon and Flores (Solomon and Flores, 2003) say that 'Trust is dynamic. It is part of the vitality … of relationships. It involves personal responsibility, commitment and change and is characterized by sincerity, authenticity, integrity, virtue, and honor (matters of *ethics*).' From this perspective trust could be viewed as part of the portfolio of 'humanistic values' (see Glossary) that inform organizational development work. Almost certainly the opposite of trust – what Solomon and Flores describe as 'cordial hypocrisy' – is not going to result in a motivated and energetic workforce or a well-designed organization.

One way to build trust is to apply an appropriate trust-based model. In 'Trust in Business: The Core Concepts' (Green, 2007), Charles Green lays out the Trust Creation Process: a process model of trust creation through personal interaction, mainly conversations. This is appropriate for developing the client–consultant relationship, not least because its principles are equally applicable to other stakeholders in design work. It works by:

1 Engaging the stakeholders in an open discussion about issues that are key to them.
2 Listening to what is important and real to the stakeholders; earning the right to offer solutions.
3 Framing the true root issue, without the language of blame, via caveats, problem statements and hypotheses; taking personal risks to explore sensitive issues – articulating a point of view; creating by giving away.
4 Encouraging them to envision an alternate reality, including win-win specific descriptions of outcomes and results, including emotional and political states; clarifying benefits – making clear what's at stake; being tangible about future states.
5 Inviting them to commit to actionable next steps that imply significant commitment and movement on the part of each party.

As Green points out, 'The order in which these sentences occur in a conversation has as much impact as the sentences themselves. That is, you could do a wonderful job on framing the issue or on the commitment to action – but if you do them before you do listening, then the trust process breaks down, or freezes.'

Although trust has to be two-way, it is usually the organization design consultant, in the first instance, who has to work to build it. This means using influencing skills and demonstrating high levels of business credibility. Read more on trust in a book, *The Trusted Advisor*, by David Maister (Free Press, 2000).

Influencing is the ability to get what one wants without threat of punishment or promise of reward, and the ability to influence results largely from the respect and esteem in which a person is held by others. Influence occurs when people perform actions because they have been convinced they are the right actions to take, not because someone with power told them to do them (Cialdini, 2006). Internal organization design consultants can feel disadvantaged if they are working with someone higher than them in the organizational hierarchy. But influencing is a core consultant skill.

Read this extract from an advertisement placed by a large multinational company for an OD consultant; it is evident that a challenging and questioning ability is described in terms of influencing skills:

> This is largely a role of influence, balance between strategy and tactics is critical. This will be a person who leads from behind. It is critical that he/ she has a customer-focused perspective and orientation to the process. To make the point again, this person must be exceptionally strong in a role of influence and flawless in their approach related to managing people and expectations.

Being able to influence without authority is at the heart of an OD practitioner's ability to challenge and question effectively – often a tricky thing to do in difficult situations where, for example, there is no opportunity for a second chance, or there is a lot of resistance from another person or group.

The first step in learning how to influence effectively is to find out what your current influencing capability is. There are many influencing skills surveys available and it is worth finding out more about these, as a good diagnosis can help you find out where to focus your efforts to develop your influencing skills. One assessment tool suggests that there are five core skills required for effectively influencing others (PI Worldwide, 2010):

1   Openness, which asks how well you set agendas, build trust, handle concerns and manage the other person's expectations.
2   Investigation, which assesses your ability to diagnose the situation, ask good questions to uncover needs, listen attentively and help people take another look at their decisions.

3   Presence, which examines the way you can help people consider the potential consequences of their choices and decisions and how they might benefit from exploring a range of options.
4   Confirmation, which explores how well you do at handling concerns and gaining agreement even if there are a number of different ideas in the room.
5   Rapport-building, which considers your ability to build long-term relationships that are mutually beneficial.

Further on in the job specification mentioned above comes the requirement for a 'business-oriented' approach:

> While this person will be expected to have deep technical skills in organizational design, their holistic business acumen and practical results-orientation will be critical for their internal credibility. This position's success will be measured by the job holder's business orientation and the continuing demand for their involvement by operational line executives throughout the company.

The ability to talk the same business language as line managers, and to realize that they have time, budget and cost constraints as they try to drive performance, is an essential part of OD consultants proving that they are truly business-aware.

What they need to do this is 'business savvy'. This is explained by Ed Griffin in an engaging podcast (Griffin and Roebuck, 2012) from the CIPD as being

> about a deep and comprehensive understanding of the organization. I think fundamentally it's about understanding what makes your organization viable. So that's about understanding where does the funding or the finances come into the organization. It's knowing who are the people who bring that in and who are the people who support those who bring in the money. So what's the relationship between what your people do and the value that achieves the purpose of the organization? I think there's also something about understanding how your organization really works in terms of its processes, its procedures and its systems, and then there's a piece which is about the human dynamics. So it's about understanding what you might call organizational politics, who's really influential and who's not, who are the noise-makers but not necessarily the powerbrokers.
>
> And then there's a massive external piece. So actually business savvy is about understanding what's going on outside your organization, what's the context within which your organization sits. It's about understanding your customers, it's understanding the competition, it's understanding how products and services are developing in your field. It's about being

able to get in the mind. I think somebody said once if you're not serving a customer you'd better be serving someone who is. So it's that proximity to the people who are the beneficiaries of your organization and its work.

Without 'business savvy', organization design consultants (largely seen as part of HR) will not get their desired 'seat at the table' – a place on the management/executive team of the business.

OD short

Organization design consultants need to be highly skilled in building trust, influencing and demonstrating business savvy in order to work effectively with their line-manager clients, who are often in a hierarchically superior role.

Tool

Organization design competencies: self-assessment

Assess to what degree you have the following competencies, using the scale below. Refer to Table 2.9, and enter the appropriate rating into the cell in the right-hand column for each competency. This tool can also be used to establish a baseline for an HR or OD group and to determine where training, coaching and development investments are best made.

Ratings

1   I have no experience with this area.
2   I have had limited exposure or experience in this area.
3   I have some experience in this area; I can effectively engage internal or external experts to either do the work or show me how.
4   I have experience in this area; I can apply basic skills to solve routine challenges and knowledgeably consult with internal or external experts to solve more complex problems.
5   I have significant experience in this area; I can independently apply advanced skills.
6   I am considered an expert in this area; I am qualified to teach it to others.

Summary

This chapter first explored the organizational 'ownership' of organization design, noting that although it is often positioned in an HR function it is more appropriately deployed as a strategic lever and should be owned by a strategy function. The discussion moved on to consider the respective roles of client

Table 2.9 Organization design self-assessment

	Rating

Diagnostics

A. **Assessment**: Can use a variety of methods to gather and analyse data within the organization specifically related to organization design issues; know the appropriate questions to ask to assess the business and distinguish underlying causes from observed symptoms. ....

B. **Diagnostics**: Able to draw accurate conclusions from the data and determine appropriate organization design interventions to address business challenges; can identify the systemic and interrelated nature of issues. ....

Structure and process content areas

C. **Design criteria**: Translate the strategic goals of the business into capabilities that the organization must have; can guide a group through developing design criteria and use them effectively in the decision-making process. ....

D. **Structure design**: Propose structural options that support the organization's strategy by segmenting the work and grouping resources and outlining reporting relationships, levels of authority, and hierarchy for management and decision-making; able to evaluate and articulate the benefits and drawbacks of different options. ....

E. **Lateral organization design**: Identify the integrating mechanisms and horizontal and vertical processes that will move information and work through the 'white space' (e.g., networks, teams, matrixed structures, decision-making, etc.); guide a group through designing high-level activities, hand-offs and key decision points. ....

F. **Role design**: Define the new roles for individuals/groups in the reshaped organization and the success factors that are unique to the role; guide individuals in the new roles through role-clarification exercises. ....

G. **Job design**: Define job specifications (position and candidate requirements); create staffing models and career progression lattices that are aligned with related structures, processes, jobs and talent. ....

H. **Management structures**: Design management roles, executive teams, and governance structures that support the strategy, have an appropriate span of control, and aid in good decision-making for the organization. ....

I. **Process mapping**: Map core processes, group the work appropriately, develop several grouping options from which to determine the structure. ....

Related content areas

J. **Organizational measurement frameworks**: Identify both leading (process) and output (result) measures that gauge performance at the organizational, group, and team level; determine the key, underlying drivers of performance that need to be monitored to ensure that organization executes on its strategy. ....

K. **Individual performance management systems**: Modify or design performance management processes for guiding and assessing the work of individuals; able to identify the most important behaviors that will support organizational performance. ....

Table 2.9 (cont.)

	Rating
L. Reward and recognition systems: Design reward and recognition frameworks that align and incent individual and team actions with the goals of the overall organization design.	....
M. Talent assessment: Assess individuals against new role and job requirements; articulate fit, potential, risks and development needs to decision-makers.	....
Enabling consulting skills	
N. Contract with clients: Clearly define project objectives, phases and the resources, involvement and support needed; identify sponsors and key decision-makers and build commitment to the project outcomes and process at each phase.	....
O. Work collaboratively (with internal peers, clients, and consultants): Identify the appropriate expert and implementation resources and engage them in the work; keep roles clear and everyone aligned; create a sense of partnership.	....
P. Facilitate decision-making: Identify and articulate the key decisions that need to be made at each step of the organization design process; guide decision-makers through generating and evaluating options.	....
Q. Project management: Define project plan milestones, success criteria, risks, and contingencies; develops plans that are appropriately comprehensive but realistic for the context; monitor progress and follow-up to meet deadlines and outcomes.	....
R. Change management: Identify effective strategies to transition the organization from the current to the 'new' state; anticipate risks and create plans to address them; build both the project (task) and 'engagement' (communication, feedback, commitment) plans.	....

Source: Kates Kesler Organization Consulting.

and consultant, and the use of process consulting in the design work. Finally the skills required by an organization design consultant were described. The three key skills needed are building trust, influencing and demonstrating business 'savvy'.

References

21st Century Process Consultation. (2001). Retrieved 2 December 2012, from Manage2001: http://www.manage2001.com/pc.htm.

Cialdini, R. (2006). *Influence: The Psychology of Persuasion.* New York: HarperBusiness.

Green, C. H. (2007). 'Trust in Business: The Core Concepts', 29 April. Retrieved 2 December 2012, from Trusted Advisor: http://trustedadvisor.com/articles/trust-in-business-the-core-concepts.

Griffin, E. and Roebuck, C. (2012). 'Business Savvy HR – Podcast 63', 6 February. Retrieved 6 December 2012, from CIPD: http://www.cipd.co.uk/podcasts/_articles/hr-business-savvy.htm?view=transcript.

LiveOps. (2012). 'All About LiveOps'. Retrieved 22 November 2012, from LiveOps: http://www.liveops.com/company.

Nickols, F. (2004). 'What Kind of OD Practitioner Are You?'. Retrieved 22 November 2012, from Distance Consulting: http://www.nickols.us/ODTypology.pdf.

PI Worldwide. (2010). 'PI Worldwide'. Retrieved 6 December 2012, from Influence Skills Assessment Tool™ (ISAT): http://www.piworldwide.com/Solutions/Leadership-Development/Influence-Skills-Assessment-Tool.aspx.

Schein, E. (1990). 'A General Philosophy of Helping: Process Consultation', *MIT Sloan Management Review*, 15 April, 57–64.

Solomon, R. and Flores, F. (2003). *Building Trust, in Business, Politics, Relationships and Life*. Oxford: Oxford University Press.

3 Organization design, organization development and change management

The future is not some place we are going, but one we are creating. The paths are not to be found, but made. And the activity of making them changes both the maker and their destination.

John Schaar

What you will learn

This chapter opens by discussing the triggers of organization design work from both reactive and proactive stances. It moves on to look at the connections between organization design, organization development and change management.

Triggers of organization design

Think about what triggers a redesign. Triggers can be classified as one of two types – external and internal. A simple acronym, STEEPLE (but also seen as SLEPT, EPISTLE, PESTLE, PEST), helps categorize the triggers, as the examples in Table 3.1 show.

In either case, internal or external, the triggers can be:

- Immediate ones that an organization has to react to, leading to reactive design.
- Known medium-term events that it is worth taking a further look at in case design work is needed, leading to proactive design.
- Future 'what if' things (for example, the driverless car mentioned in Chapter 1), leading to designs that build capacity to meet the future.

In most cases organization members are able to identify immediate triggers and known events: Table 3.1 has examples of this type of trigger – but they have a harder time with foreseeing potential or future triggers that if acted on early enough could give a clear market advantage.

Table 3.1 STEEPLE in use

	Examples of internal triggers	*Examples of external triggers*
Social/demographic	Employees lobbying for flexible working hours	Retirement from the workforce being increasingly delayed
Technological	People starting to bring their own devices to work (BYOD, see Glossary)	Availability and security of cloud computing accelerating
Environmental	Refurbishing of office becomes due	Competitors seizing market share
Economic	Desire to contain/reduce costs of real estate resulting in move to mobile and remote working	Financial accounting compliance requirements changing
Political	New CEO or other leader deciding to shake things up	Change of ruling government party changes business climate
Legal	Harassment case highlighting deficiencies	New laws coming into force on trading conditions
Ethical	People are inflating their travel and expenses for personal gain	Lobbying groups surface issues resulting in reputational damage
Other stuff	*NOTE: People doing this exercise often come up with factors that do not fit into any of the above categories, for example 'governance'. Having a catch-all alleviates the desire to fit something into a specific box.*	

The short-term design tendency is attributable to several factors, including: the requirement to hit short-term earnings targets, lack of management or leadership time to reflect and discuss the future, constant 'firefighting', being rewarded only for immediate results and/or not caring about the future of the organization because current decision-makers will not be part of it. However, short-termism comes at the expense of creating long-term value and the risk of sacrificing an organization's future (Silverthorne, 2012).

It is important, therefore, for organization designers to understand that only by taking a longer view can they design sustainable organizations. Ron Ashkenas, consultant and author, offers three points for developing designs that have a longer-term horizon (5–15 years, rather than quarterly).

1   First, make sure that you have a dynamic, constantly refreshed strategic 'vision' for what your organization (or unit) will look like and achieve 3–5 years from now. I'm not talking about a strategic plan, but rather a compelling picture of market/product, financial, operational, and organizational shifts over the next few years. [Keep this rolling].

2   Second, make sure that your various projects and initiatives have a direct line of sight to your strategic vision. Challenge every potential investment of time and effort by asking whether it will help you get closer to your vision, or whether it will be a building block to help you get there. Doing this will force you to continually re-balance your portfolio of projects, weeding out those that probably won't move you in the right direction.

3   Finally, be prepared to take some flack. There may be weeks, months, or quarters where the results are not on the rise, or don't match your (or analyst) expectations. Long-term value, however, is not created in straight lines. As long as you're moving iteratively towards the strategic vision on a reasonable timeline, you're probably doing the right things. (Ashkenas, 2012)

In adopting these three points it is important to communicate to stakeholders the reasons for taking a longer-term approach and to back up the communication with narrative and quantitative information that 'provides a holistic picture of the business describing the economic, environmental, and social performance of the corporation as well as the governance structure that leads the organization. By embedding environmental, social, and governance (ESG) data into financial reports, a company achieves an effective communication of its overall long-term performance' (Silverthorne, 2012).

Organizations that know they are weak at horizon scanning, future thinking and forecasting can look for help in various quarters. The World Future Society and the Institute for the Future are two organizations that are worth keeping in touch with in terms of predicted external futures. On 21 December 2012, for example, Thomas Frey posted on the World Future Society website four macro trends that he thinks will have a dramatic effect on the future (Frey, 2012). As he points out 'since no one has a totally clear vision of what lies ahead, we are all left with degrees of accuracy. Anyone with a higher degree of accuracy, even by only a few percentage points, can offer a significant competitive advantage.' His four trends are:

1   The shift to natural gas vehicles.
2   The great insourcing movement – the pendulum swings back again.
3   Multidimensional literacy – the evolution of consumable information.
4   The legalized marijuana movement – nudging the snowflake that started the avalanche.

The end of one year and the beginning of the next are good times to look out for predictions of one type or another – many business bloggers, business journals, professional associations and management consultancies publish theirs.

The Organizational Design Community makes explicit the relationship between potential futures and organization design, saying that 'Big Data is predicted to become a key basis of competition, underpinning new waves of productivity growth, innovation, performance and consumer surplus. Big Data also holds great potential for the public sector in terms of operational efficiency improvements and new services. *To grasp these opportunities the design of the organizational architecture has to support and drive the value creation of Big Data'* (Organizational Design Community, 2012, author italics).

Think about these types of annual predictions. If any one of them came to pass, and the insourcing one is gaining ground in many organizations, there would be profound effects on an organization's design: being prepared to meet these possibilities may offer greater competitive advantage than either reacting to them once they are evident or looking for clues and symptoms that suggest a more proactive response is required.

To help decide whether a prediction requires follow-up action, the Institute for the Future 'has pioneered tools and methods for building foresight ever since its founding days'. It has developed a toolkit that includes:

- signals;
- scenarios;
- forecasts and perspectives;
- maps;
- artifacts from the future;
- immersive videos;
- collaborative forecasting games (Institute for the Future, 2012).

Using these types of techniques helps develop the organizational outlook and skills required for designing for a positive, sustainable organizational future.

Design triggers: two examples

Someone (usually a new leader) deciding to juggle the boxes and lines in an organization chart without thinking through why he/she thinks it is necessary and what the ramifications might be is neither designing nor redesigning. Thoughtful organization design is better triggered, as previously discussed, by a combination of a number of internal and external events which can be ones that require immediate reaction; that are known to be coming in the medium term; or that are longer-term preparations for a less-known possible future. Two examples illustrate this.

Example 1

In mid-2012, a US community healthcare organization asked the question 'How do we grow bigger and better with ...':

1   The new leadership personnel, including the CEO. (This is an internal social and current trigger.)

2   Our moving from five buildings to one building (This is an internal environmental and current trigger.)
3   Healthcare reform (This is an external legal and known trigger.)
4   Change in reimbursement of medical costs. (This is an external economic and known trigger.)

At the time it had just bought a new headquarters building and was planning to move five departments scattered around the town into the new building. In their case, the number of triggers, listed above, converged to a point where a total redesign made perfect sense and they initiated a whole-organization design which encompassed not only the five departments in the single town, but also the five satellite centres in adjoining counties. This involved whole-organization changes in working practices, policies, procedures, processes, the departmental structures, IT systems and so on. It also involved making decisions about a new relationship between the head office and the satellite centres.

Notice though that the first two triggers on the list are ones the organization was reacting to, and the second two suggest known events where pro-activity is required. None of the four triggers looks at possible futures. If this healthcare organization were reflecting on what healthcare might be like in the future they might be referencing, for example, IBM's supercomputer, Watson. At the end of 2012 Watson was being taught how to help in medical diagnosis with the possibility that:

> Someday, Watson might be able to provide reliable clinical decision support to physicians in their daily work. If this scenario became a reality it could be a paradigm change in how we practice medicine. It could be a powerful, easy-to-use bedside decision support tool with deep understanding that helps make sure that our lists are complete and that there's concordance between the physician's thinking and the decision support thinking. (Terry, 2012)

Or the healthcare organization might be asking questions like:

•   What if new technologies enable us to experience the future effects of present-day behaviour choices?
•   What if patient self-tracking goes mainstream and shapes research and treatment practices?
•   What's the future of doctors when sensors in your electronics diagnose disease? (Institute for the Future, 2012)
•   What if organs could be grown using 3D printing techniques? (Thompson, 2012)

These types of future thinking queries pave the way for designing for organizational resilience and agility – that is, the ability to meet whatever future comes into play. Designing for resilience and agility means building in methods of:

Anticipating. This means developing a view of possible or likely changes – not trying to predict actual changes. Anticipating includes a rigorous review of customer needs and industry forces, and an evaluation of likely scenarios of industry consolidation, product development, pricing and customer needs.

Sensing. This involves continual reviews of market conditions, looking for trends and especially anomalies in customer behavior, competitor moves, supply chain shifts, supply/demand changes, and macro- and microeconomic developments. It requires strong analytics capabilities.

Responding. The key is to respond to market shifts faster than competitors do. This includes rapid decision-making, testing responses on a pilot basis and then scaling for a broader response. It frequently includes preset 'plays,' where management teams have agreed ahead of time how they will respond to certain situations – for instance, to a price drop by a competitor or the merger of two rivals.

Adapting. Once initial market changes have been identified, organizations often find that they need to rework some of their business processes. Some may tailor their organizational structures to better handle ongoing changes in their markets. (Shill *et al.*, 2012)

Example 2

John Chambers, CEO Cisco, a network company, is well known for restructuring the organization and said as much in his communication to employees in 2011 that heralded another big shake-up.

> Over the years as your leader here at Cisco, I've also learned many things. I've learned to read market transitions by listening deeply to our customers and partners. And I've learned to adjust when and where it's needed, quickly and transparently.

The previous restructure had taken place in 2007/2008 and comprised:

> [A] network of councils and boards empowered to launch new businesses, plus an evolving set of Web 2.0 gizmos – not to mention a new financial incentive system – encouraging executives to work together like never before ... leaders of business units formerly competing for power and resources now share responsibility for one another's success. What used to be 'me' is now 'we.' (McGirt, 2008)

But by many measures (particularly financial), this design was ultimately deemed a failure. Four years later Chambers noted in 2011:

Today we face a simple truth: we have disappointed our investors and we have confused our employees. Bottom line, we have lost some of the credibility that is foundational to Cisco's success – and we must earn it back. Our market is in transition, and our company is in transition. And the time is right to define this transition for ourselves and our industry. I understand this. It's time for focus.

The 2011 restructure had several triggers:

- Disappointing investors. (This is an external economic and current trigger.)
- Confusing employees. (This is an internal social and current trigger.)
- Losing market credibility: some questioned Chambers's ability to retain his role of CEO. (This is an external social and known trigger.)
- Transition in the market. (This is an external economic predicted trigger.)
- Transition in the company. (This is an internal social known trigger.)

The last two are to do with transition towards the future. In this case 'transition in the market' is specified as a trigger of redesign, and Cisco employs Dave Evans, chief futurist, internet business solutions group, to keep close watch on what the future environment will be like in order to support Cisco in its development of products and services. One of his predictions is that the Internet will evolve to connect more and more things, becoming – in a marketing tag-line – 'The Internet of Everything' (IoE). In a Point of View paper on this topic Evans puts the question 'How will the Internet evolve to continue changing and improving the world?' He states that: 'The purpose of this paper is to address this important question in order to provide industries, individuals, and countries with the information they need to begin planning and making strategic decisions for the coming decade.' He then asks several thought-provoking questions for organizational leaders:

- How do I set priorities to match the opportunities that will exist in the connected world of IoE?
- Given the impact the Internet already has had on my business, what happens when new categories of things are connected at exponential rates?
- What are the potential benefits and risks of IoE for my business or government organization?
- How should organizations be structured around information and processes?
- How will governance, control, and responsibility change in an IoE world? (Evans, 2012)

All of these are useful types of questions for organizations to ask as they consider designing to meet the unfolding future, and John Chambers has made use of them in thinking about his own organization's design, demonstrating skills in both reacting to triggers for redesign and designing for the future. As one analyst remarked, 'Chambers hasn't met a market transition he couldn't either see coming or fix in retrospect with quick action or an acquisition' (Higginbotham, 2012).

These two examples of the healthcare organization and Cisco illustrate another key point for organization designers: that the design is always in motion. One blogger put it like this:

> Any organizational structure should be temporary. Organizations have no separate existence; they function as tools of the business. When businesses change their priorities (like Nokia is doing right now) then organizations must be changed, sometimes even discarded. That is why it is so wrong to encourage employees to identify with the organization – they need to identify with the business. If you are a Bedouin, it's the difference between the tent and the tribe. As for building an organization I think [Henry] Mintzberg got it right when he suggested that two things must be settled – the division of labor and coordination after that. But again, any division, any organization is always temporary. (Corkindale, 2011)

OD short

There are numbers of triggers of organization design work. Triggers can be internal or external; immediately obvious requiring reactive design; medium-term calling for proactive design; or lie in the potential future, suggesting futuring design. In practice, organizations are grappling with all these three types of triggers simultaneously – although less often with those associated with future thinking, where potentially more benefit lies.

Organization design and organization development

Look back at the organization design definition (Chapter 1) and now at three of the many definitions of organization development. Organization design definitions generally do not mention behaviours or organizational health, while the organization development definitions are all about these.

> Organization development is a system-wide application of behavioral science knowledge to the planned development and reinforcement of organizational strategies, structures, and processes for improving an organization's effectiveness. (Cummings and Worley, 1997)
>
> Organization development is an effort (1) planned, (2) organization-wide, and (3) managed from the top, to (4) increase organizational effectiveness and health, through (5) planned interventions in the organization's 'processes', using behavioural science knowledge. (Beckhard, 1969)

> Organization development is the activities engaged in by stakeholders in order to build and maintain the health of an organization as a total system. It is characterized by a focus on behavioral processes and humanistic values. It seeks to develop problem solving ability and explore opportunities for growth. (Finney and Jefkins, 2009)

This doesn't mean that design and development work is neatly boxed into different packages. In most cases it is not possible to do design work without doing development work: the two are integral. It is, however, possible to do development work without design work – for example coaching a team to manage conflict effectively. Additionally, development work can highlight the need for design work, as the comment from this financial services retail branch manager illustrates:

> We are training our staff to give good customer service but that is almost an empty gesture: the front-end sales process desperately needs an overhaul if we are to achieve our strategic objectives. How staff make it into a wonderful experience staggers me but they do. It's a mismatch of forms, paper, re-asked questions, things stapled together. We cannot carry on with this. Nothing is properly integrated. Anything that needs to be changed is a nightmare. Skills training is simply not enough.

A practical way to think of the difference between design and development is to imagine that the design is the tacit, explicable part of the organization – the sort of thing that can be written down and explained to people; for example, the organization chart, rules, policies, standard operating procedures, the code of ethics, training and development opportunities, the career paths and so on.

The development aspect of the organization is the implicit part, which is more complex and nuanced – the culture, the behaviours, the leadership style, the motivation and engagement of staff. A telecoms organization explained the difference between the two as follows:

> The Programme Steering Committee recognizes the synergies between the Organization Development project and the Organization Design project in developing a customer centric organization.
>
> These two projects are closely linked and have a complementary focus on alignment, but distinct perspectives on the overall design:
>
> • Organization design is the 'hard knitting'. Its work is to agree and articulate the tangible components of the design, to inform the transformation journey and drive alignment with strategy throughout the business (customers, brands, channels, products and services, roles and responsibilities, structures, functions, processes, systems and management information, etc.).

- Organization development is the 'soft knitting'. Its work is to articulate and embed the competencies, skills and behaviours which need to wrap around the tangible dimensions of the organization design to create capability and sustain/improve performance (culture, working practices, decision-making, leadership, reward and recognition, performance management and communication, etc.).

Another way of thinking about design in relation to development is to take a car analogy. Organization design is deciding, first, the purpose of the car that you are about to design, for example is it to cross the desert? Is it to win a Formula 1 race? Is it to transport two adults and three children to a party? The next step is designing and delivering a car that is fit for that purpose.

Organization development is about keeping that vehicle in the condition necessary to achieve the purpose, for example using the right fuel, having it serviced regularly, teaching the driver how to drive it to maximize its performance and so on.

Clearly this is not a perfect analogy, as an organization is in a constant state of flux, unlike the vehicle, but it does serve an illustrative purpose. Another analogy is that of the human body. The underpinning 'design' of the human body is a given – skeleton, cardio-vascular system, etc. But keeping the human body fit and healthy is the development aspect: nutrition, exercise, learning, managing stress, for example. This analogy works reasonably well as the human body is adaptive to its environment, but, unlike an organization, the underpinning design of the human body is not necessarily affected in the adaptation process (apart from ageing).

As discussed in Chapter 2, the notion that design is the tacit (hard) part of the organization and the development is the implicit (soft) part is reflected in the CIPD's HR Profession Map description of what a competent organization development consultant does. He/she:

> Ensures that the organization culture, values and environment support and enhance organization performance and adaptability. Provides insight and leadership on development and execution of any capability, cultural and change activities.

Contrast this with their description of what an organization design consultant does. He/she:

> Ensures that the organization is appropriately designed to deliver organization objectives in the short and long term and that structural change is effectively managed.

To do their work effectively organization development consultants, like organization design consultants, require a good understanding of the organization as whole system, including:

- the business model and strategy;
- the systems;
- the structures;
- the processes;
- how organizational performance is managed;
- the methods of leadership and management of the organization.

Below, an organization development consultant talks about a typical day in her life. Notice where there are, or might be, connections between design and development, and think about the impact of the various development activities referenced on the whole organizational system.

It's difficult for me to talk about a 'typical' day, as the hallmark of my role is its variety. It's easier for me to describe a work day in my life. So here goes.

I began the day with a self-reflection writing exercise. [See Bryan and Cameron, 1998.] I've been doing that for a while now because it's helpful in my work and I've been reading a lot recently about the reflective leader. I'm wondering if development of reflective capability would be a good organization development project for me to initiate with our executives.

I then went to the new office building to see how the people who had moved there over the weekend were doing, and chatted to them about how they'd found the move. It was good to hear that everything had run smoothly and they'd had excellent service from the IT department in getting everyone up and running the moment they reached their desks. My role in this move project is to prepare staff for the move in all sorts of ways including:

- the skills development in working with new processes and new IT systems;
- the behavioural and management changes required to work in an open-plan rather than an individual office environment;
- the emotional responses and anxieties people may have as they give up known routines, or as their immediate social community is changed. People who've worked together for years are now in different locations.

My organization design colleagues are working on the more structural elements of the move, for example alignment of the business processes with the IT infrastructure, and the new terms and conditions and reward structures and policies associated with mobile working. They're also grappling with the merger of two departments and what that entails – the move was one of the triggers for this decision.

Yes, we have to be clear who is taking the lead on what as there are some grey areas but we keep communication lines open and things are working well right now.

Once at the new building I participated in a meeting about the move. The meetings had very different feels, one informal with just three of us face to face, and one much more formal with several people in the room including the architects and interior designers and several more participants dialing in from other locations. Later in the day, I had another couple of meetings, one using a video conference line and one a teleconference line.

These different meetings styles made me think about whether some meeting forums were better than others. Is it 'better', i.e. more productive, to have face-to-face or dial-in meetings. What is the value of the face-to-face-ness? This is a substantive question as we are ramping up teleworking (mobile working). I'm wondering if there are any criteria that can be applied to help people decide this. In what circumstances does 'presence' in a physical sense add value to a meeting? Back at home, a quick interrogation of an online university library that I have access to showed me that there's a significant amount of research on the topic of team effectiveness comparing virtual with face-to-face interactions.

My challenge is to convert the various academic findings into practical and relevant recommendations for managers who are wrestling with building a sense of community accountability and productivity among their work teams, who are increasingly working off the office site.

Leaving that aside I started to prepare a one-day workshop on the topic of teleworking. Getting the balance of behaviors, skills and technologies for confident teleworkers was the order of the day. The program is being developed for intact work teams, not for individual teleworking, though that forms a part of the section on organizing yourself for teleworking.

Beyond the meetings and phone calls I answered in the order of 60 emails on a range of topics including an office community garden, conference room-booking protocols, meeting scheduling and leadership development programs.

So another typical day passes.

Reading this 'day in the life' it is easy to see that organization design and organization development have different focuses but are interdependent in any design project. But as mentioned earlier, organization development can be independent of organization design work. In this case, for example, the consultant could develop the reflective capability of leaders (the soft 'knitting') without doing any of the hard 'knitting' of organization design. But design work cannot be undertaken independently of development work.

OD short

Organization design work cannot be effective in the absence of organization development activity. However, organization development work can be undertaken in the absence of design activity. Design work focuses on the 'hard', tacit elements of an organization, while development work focuses on the people, their behaviours, their culture and their performance capability.

Change management

People often ask whether 'change management' is part of organization design work and if so how. The answer is clearly that change management is integral to any design project. Obviously, both organization design and organization development involve change. There is no way of, say, integrating a company acquisition into the acquiring company without something changing. So how can it best be 'managed'?

The prevailing view is that it is not managed well. A journal article on the topic recorded that the bulk of change literature 'regularly quotes failure rates of between 60% and 90%' (Burnes, 2011).

In a study of critical human capital issues three of the top six issues were to do with change (coping with change, managing change and embracing change in the culture). This same study reported that:

> While the importance of managing change-related issues is on the rise, the ability to improve in this most vital capability remains highly elusive. In fact the research reveals that only 35% of high-performance organizations in this study – those in the top quartile of performers in year-over-year growth in revenue, profit, market share and customer satisfaction – indicate they are highly effective at doing so. And among low-performance organizations – those in the bottom quartile – the story is even worse, with only 13% perceiving their ability to manage and cope with change as highly effective. (Martin, 2013)

One reason for this could be that traditional change management approaches, developed when organizations were more stable and information and communication technologies less all-pervasive and sophisticated, have outlived their value. A second reason could be that many of these myriad off-the-shelf, well-known change management methodologies (take a look at Google Images to see a number of the models available) have adherents and practitioners who imply that there is one best way to manage change.

Given the number of 'one best way' approaches to change, this is somewhat confusing (Burnes, 2011) to stakeholders in an organization design project: it raises the question of what approach to take and why. A different way is to deploy an approach that is flexible and situational, that recognizes the changing context in which the organization design work is taking place.

Further, it makes sense to say that as organizations are increasingly being researched and designed from a perspective of systems, complexity and chaos theory, so there must be a corresponding shift in the way change management is being approached. As one commentator noted:

For many years, the training field has viewed organizational change as a process that is both linear and sequential. Instead, change has revealed itself to be non-linear and chaotic. It's time to find a new model – one that incorporates insights from neuroscience research and takes into account 21st century workplace dynamics and realities. (McFarland, 2012)

This means thinking about organizational change differently:

*   Not as a 'thing' to be managed in 'project' way, but as a continuously present process.
*   Not that people resist change but that they are innately equipped to handle change.
*   Not as an orderly process to manage via a methodology but as an emerging process to manage via flexibility and pragmatism.

In their personal lives, people often welcome change (getting married, moving house or trying out a new restaurant, for example) and *can* handle change as a continuous and emerging process. We all demonstrate this capability constantly. A small event – missing a train, for example – triggers a series of actions in response to that change. People deal with this sort of thing on a continuous basis.

Think back over the technology changes you have handled perfectly well in the last five years – there was unlikely to be a 'change management' manager supporting your transition from one technological gadget to the next.

What makes the organizational landscape different from the personal landscape is the much reduced capacity for individual agency. Often people feel (and are) pushed and manipulated into new situations. What employees find particularly difficult is a planned, disruptive organizational change. (Paradoxically in an unplanned disruptive crisis they often work well and handle things beautifully.)

One, or a combination, of four types of disruptive change is typically associated with organization design project work:

1   Structural change: where the formal 'shape' of the organization is being changed, as in an acquisition or a move from a functional organization to a matrix organization.
2   Cost cutting: introducing desk-sharing, mobile working, home-working as a practice to reduce the cost of real estate space is a common current example.
3   Process change: which involves doing the work differently as in digitizing records or changing the technology (and the number of people or their skills) for doing the work.
4   Cultural change: where leaders want to generate a new culture perhaps of 'customer service' or 'innovation' to meet a business need.

The challenge is to create a situation where people feel they have agency and control in organizational change. Here is one government leader's experience:

> I realized I'd made a mistake in just announcing something. Essentially, I'd imagined that in making people aware of what we were trying to do in introducing hoteling [see Glossary] then they would do it. I'd forgotten that the leadership team had been working on the project for a good while and were familiar with what the strategy was and what we wanted to achieve. During this period we'd gradually recognized the changes that would be required and were ready to make them.
>
> I decided to do four things to help salvage the situation and engage the employees:
>
> (a) Set up what I called a 'Show and Say' period of two weeks. We planned out a whole series of events, activities, webinars, and forums which were targeted at raising awareness – basically making the business case about what we were trying to do and why we were trying to do it. During this period we invited comment, responses, and questions from employees about the organization development strategy. These were all debated in online forums, at management meetings, and in my blog to staff.
>
> (b) Help employees really feel what it would be like working in a hoteling environment. We set up one of the office floors as hotel space and invited work-groups to come and try it out for a day. We more or less insisted that everyone experimented with this or at least talked to someone who had. We got a lot of good feedback with this and realized that we needed to do things like provide useful tip sheets, where to go for help, and 'how to' information, like 'How to change the height of your desk', etc. When I think about it, it's the sort of information you find in a standard hotel room – that explains how to order room service, amenities in the neighborhood, and so on.
>
> (c) Highlight the gains they would get from this – which were linked to the business processes, and technology we were introducing at the same time to support the hoteling principles. We wanted to make sure that people, process, space, and technology were all aligned in service of the organization development strategy. We made this a two-way process – it wasn't just management saying 'Look what you gain from this', it was employees putting forward points on what they felt the gains would, and could, be. I was surprised and pleased to find that employees put forward some gains that we hadn't thought of like they would be learning to use some new technologies that would be useful in streamlining their work – putting all documents online was one of these.
>
> (d) Recognize and reward people who volunteered to start hoteling. We had to be careful with this one so we had a phased process. Each

week for eight weeks we told a story both of an individual employee's experience of hoteling and a group's. They weren't all glowing praise either; we learned to improve the process substantially in that time period.

This leader realized that if he forced the hoteling issue he could end up with a demotivated workforce and drops in productivity. So he decided to take a step back and invest the time in doing things differently. It paid off for him, and it would pay off in most organization development and design situations.

Any organizational design strategy must be partnered with a pragmatic change-management approach that will gain employees' support. Other things that can help are:

* Using the forces of social influence to generate enthusiasm for the change. This is described at a popular level in Malcolm Gladwell's book *The Tipping Point* (Little, Brown, 2000) or can be seen in action when things 'go viral'.
* Ensuring that the business processes, technology and office space are also changed/aligned appropriately.
* Being willing to change course as you see resistances or people experimenting in ways that others could benefit from.

OD short

Any organization design work requires change management. Traditional change management approaches have had their day, and are giving way to different ways of thinking about change. People are well equipped to handle change if they have power and agency in the situation. The aim of organization-design-related change management is to gain high awareness of the business goal and high support for it.

Tool

This set of ten principles is a useful discussion document for provoking thinking in how to set up and manage a piece of work associated with organizational change. Use the principles to help frame a non-mechanistic approach to change management that involves and engages people rather than 'gets them to do something'.

Margaret Wheatley's 'Ten Principles for Creating Healthy Organizational and Community Change'

Margaret J. Wheatley (commonly Meg Wheatley) is a writer and management consultant who studies organizational behaviour. Her approach includes systems thinking, theories of change, chaos theory, leadership and the learning organization: particularly its capacity to self-organize. She describes her work as opposing 'highly controlled mechanistic systems that only create robotic behaviors' (Wikipedia, 2012).

Principle 1: people support what they create

The only way to create ownership is to involve people in creating the project. This does not mean that everyone has to be involved in every aspect of the project but it does mean that everyone has to feel they have touched it or had a voice in it. People don't always do what you tell them to do. They do what they feel engaged with. Involve them in aspects of the creation of the work.

Questions: Are we engaging all those people who have a stake in the issue/ project?
Whatever the problem or opportunity have we involved all the people who care?

Principle 2: people act responsibly when they care

You do not get accountability by bringing in more measures, punishments or fear. You get it by creating care. We create care by caring. Caring whether this person, this work, this client gets well served by our organization. A fundamental act of leadership is identifying the things that matter to people. If people don't care about something, it does not matter how engaged you hope they will be, they will not be.

Question: Are we working on an issue or opportunity that people truly care about?

Principle 3: conversation is the way human beings have always thought

We have always talked together to think well together. Problem-solving techniques have demoted conversation. We have tended to think that conversation is too casual, that it doesn't go anywhere, that it is nonlinear and messy. So we go back to the flipcharts. We go back to the project planning techniques. But is important to remember that it is only through conversation that people discover what they care about. They discover shared meaning and they discover each other. It is also important to notice where the conversations happen. Do they happen inside meetings or do they happen in the parking lots, bathrooms, in the hallways or on email late at night?

Questions: How often are we confident enough to use conversation as a legitimate problem-solving, thinking together process rather than using these very technical processes which not only bore us, they disengage us and they separate us from one another?

Can we legitimize conversations so that we strengthen our relationships as well as develop much better thinking?

Principle 4: to change the conversation, change who is in it

Sometimes you are in a conversation that is not going anywhere. Every time you talk about the topic it is the same conversation going round and round. The only thing that changes is that people stop coming to the meetings to talk about the issue because it has got so demoralizing or boring.

If you want to change the conversation that is going nowhere simply change who is in that conversation. Invite in new people, people who have different perspectives. This is where diversity comes into play. It is a very simple technique and it works wonderfully.

Question: Who can join the conversation, who has a different perspective, who will help take it out of the loop it has got stuck in and open the way to new thinking?

Principle 5: expect leaders to come from anywhere

This principle introduces the element of curiosity and surprise. Leadership can emerge from anywhere – from people we never thought of. What causes someone to step forward as a leader is their interest – their caring for the issue. A leader is anyone who is willing to help because they have made a connection between something that needs to be fixed or changed and their own heart. They step forward.

In our organizations where we are all sitting in our little boxes and we are told what to do, we can soon forget that leadership is not a function of title and role leadership is a function of caring enough to want to step forward to help with an issue.

Questions: Is our organization willing to let leaders emerge from anywhere?
Do people in our organization feel they have the agency and permission to take the lead in making things better?

Principle 6: we focus on what works and it releases our creative energy

When we focus on what is wrong people get depressed and disengage. Marvin Weisbord, who developed Future Search [see Glossary], said he used to go into organizations and ask what was wrong and how could it be fixed it. That is a question we all ask; we do it in order to seem responsible and open and we want to know what is wrong so we can fix it. But when you are in the meetings asking those questions you realize they are very depressing.

The right question is: 'What is possible here and who cares?' When we ask that question what we are actually releasing or inspiring is human creativity, that can-do attitude.

This is a hard principle to enact as we are brought up to be analytical, to complain, to worry, and we think we need to focus on what is wrong. But once we focus on what is right, what is possible and what we can do, although it seems fanciful, all the things that are wrong actually get fixed. We do not energize ourselves by focusing on the negative questions.

Questions: What are the questions that will energize us?
What is going well that we can focus on?

Principle 7: the wisdom resides within us

This is why principle 6 works: the wisdom is within us to solve our problems. When people are in regular reflective practice together and are in good, trusting relationships with their colleagues what becomes available to them is their own wisdom. It is not imported from outside. We have to slow down and reflect together and we will find that we are wise and smart and compassionate. If we can't find the solution we will go and look for it.

Questions: Where we look for our solutions – do we benchmark – do we look for best practice – do we always routinely leap outside our organization to find the solution?
Or do we gather together with the assumption that the wisdom is within us – do we spend enough time thinking together to discover whether we do have a solution?

Principle 8: everything is a failure in the middle

Anything we are doing we can expect to feel disappointing, not be working well, or get stalled somewhere along the line. This is the way life works. Things are going really well and then they are not going so well but they will be working well again because life works in cycles. It is when things are not going well, when things are falling apart that we actually have the opportunity to learn a lot and to reorganize in ways that will succeed.

If it was all just success, success, success, first of all it wouldn't be life and secondly we really wouldn't be learning. And it's in those moments of darkness when things do truly fall apart that we can get together, be together, and think together and come up with solutions that will really work. Now the question is, what do we do?

Questions: What does your organization do when things are falling apart?
Does it quickly look for scapegoats, someone to blame? Do managers change the team leader, and does the Board fire the boss? Do they re-organize (that's guaranteed)?

Principle 9: humans can handle anything as long as we're together

This is why relationships are the centre of my work. I have seen so many communities that are suffering from desperate problems such as health and illiteracy, poverty or recouping from major natural disasters and I have found that it is the quality of our human relationships, and being in it together, that actually gets us through. In modern organizations relationships have been denigrated, we call them touchy-feely, etc. This is not only a misnomer; it paralyses us and prevents us from being effective responders in the age of uncertainty. So we need to take relationships much more seriously than we have up till now.

Questions: Are we paying attention to our relationships?
Are we supporting each other?
How often do we gossip, judge or scapegoat?

Principle 10: generosity, forgiveness and love

How we have to be together is in a spirit of compassion, generosity, forgiveness. That when things go wrong people aren't going to gossip and spread rumours, they are going to help you learn from your failure, learn from your mistakes and move on in ever more trusting relationships. We each have to be accountable for any negative things we say about each other on the workplace. We need to get off of blame. And exercise our great human capacity to be in good, trusting relationships, to be generous, forgiving and to be kind to one another. Otherwise we're not going to get through.

Question: What would it really feel like to know that your colleagues were all really there for you?
Source: Wheatley, 2007.

Summary

This chapter has examined three time-framed triggers of change: current triggers that require an immediate reaction; forthcoming triggers that are known and which can be responded to proactively; future triggers that are predictions rather than certainties, which require adaptive designs capable of effectively meeting what happens.

As any design work involves change, thinking about 'change management' as a separate 'thing' is not sensible. Rather, adopting principles that involve employees in the change to the new design, where they have power and agency in helping to decide what happens, is a more effective change-management approach than those traditionally advocated.

Similarly, organization development work is part and parcel of organization design work – the 'soft' development side of the project works in complementarity to the 'hard' design side. Design work cannot be done without development work, but development work can be done without design work.

References

Ashkenas, R. (2012). 'Thinking Long-Term in a Short-Term Economy', 7 August. Retrieved 28 December 2012, from HBR Blog Network: http://blogs.hbr.org/ashkenas/2012/08/thinking-long-term-in-a-short-.html.

Beckhard, R. (1969). *Organization Development: Strategies and Models.* London: Addison-Wesley.

Bryan, M. and Cameron, J. (1998). *The Artist's Way at Work: Riding the Dragon.* New York: William Morrow Paperbacks.

Burnes, B. (2011). 'Introduction: Why Does Change Fail, and What Can We Do about It?', *Journal of Change Management*, **4**, 445–50.

Cisco. (2011). 'Cisco Restructures Consumer Business', 12 April. Retrieved 8 December 2012, from Cisco, the Network: http://newsroom.cisco.com/press-release-content?type=webcontent&articleId=775104.

Corkindale, G. (2011). 'The Importance of Organizational Design and Structure', 11 February. Retrieved 26 December 2012, from HBR Blog Network: http://blogs.hbr.org/corkindale/2011/02/the_importance_of_organization.html.

Cummings, T. G. and Worley, C. G. (1997). *Organizational Development and Change*, 6th edn. Cincinnati: North Western.

Evans, D. (2012). 'Cisco'. Retrieved 26 December 2012, from The Internet of Everything: https://www.cisco.com/web/about/ac79/docs/innov/IoE.pdf.

Finney, L. and Jefkins, C. (2009). *Best Practice in OD Evaluation.* Roffey Park Institute.

Frey, T. (2012). 'Four Unexpected Macro Trends for 2013 and Beyond', 21 December. Retrieved 23 December 2012, from World Future Society: http://www.wfs.org/blogs/thomas-frey/four-unexpected-macro-trends-for-2013-and-beyond.

Higginbotham, S. (2012). 'John Chambers on the Future of Cisco', 12 February. Retrieved 26 December 2012, from Gigaom: http://gigaom.com/2012/02/24/john-chambers-on-the-future-of-cisco.

Institute for the Future. (2012). 'Institute for the Future'. Retrieved 23 December 2012, from Foresight Toolkit: http://www.iftf.org/what-we-do/foresight-toolkit.

McFarland, W. (2012). 'This is Your Brain on Organizational Change', 16 October. Retrieved 3 January 2013, from HBR Blog Network: http://blogs.hbr.org/cs/2012/10/this_is_your_brain_on_organizational_change.html.

McGirt, E. (2008). 'How Cisco's CEO John Chambers Is Turning the Tech Giant Socialist', 1 December. Retrieved 26 December 2012, from Fast Company: http://www.fastcompany.com/1093654/how-ciscos-ceo-john-chambers-turning-tech-giant-socialist.

Martin, K. (2013). 'Managing Change is More Difficult Than Ever, Top Executives Say', 3 January. Retrieved 4 January 2013, from IC4P: http://www.i4cp.com/trendwatchers/2013/01/03/managing-change-is-more-difficult-than-ever-top-executives-say.

Organizational Design Community. (2012). *Organizational Design Community Newsletter*, December. Retrieved from http://orgdesigncomm.com.

Shill, W., Engel, J., Mann, D. and Schatteman, O. (2012). 'Corporate Agility: Six Ways to Make Volatility Your Friend', October. Retrieved 23 December 2012, from Accenture: http://www.accenture.com/us-en/outlook/Pages/outlook-journal-2012-corporate-agility-six-ways-to-make-volatility-your-friend.aspx.

Silverthorne, S. (2012). 'The High Risks of Short-Term Management', 11 April. Retrieved 25 December 2012, from HBS Working Knowledge: http://hbswk.hbs.edu/item/6965.html.

Terry, K. (2012). 'IBM's Watson Hits Medical School', 5 November. Retrieved 23 December 2012, from Information Week: http://www.informationweek.com/healthcare/clinical-systems/ibms-watson-hits-medical-school/240012800.

Thompson, C. (2012). 'How 3D Printers Are Reshaping Medicine', 10 October. Retrieved 1 August 2013, from TechEdge, CNBC: http://www.cnbc.com/id/49348354.

Wheatley, M. (2007). 'Ten Principles for Creating Healthy Community Change', *NDSQueensland*. http://www.youtube.com/user/NDSQueensland/videos?query=margaret+wheatley.

Wikipedia. (2012). 'Margaret J. Wheatley', 15 December. Retrieved 4 January 2013, from Wikipedia: http://en.wikipedia.org/wiki/Margaret_J._Wheatley.

4　Assess phase

Preconceived notions are locks on the door to wisdom.

Merry Browne

What you will learn

In this chapter you will learn how to conduct the assess phase of an organization design project. This involves taking a series of actions and then producing a business case and/or project charter. During the course of the assess phase certain tools and techniques are used and you will learn how to apply some of these.

Overview of phase

Look at the overview of the phases of an organization design (Figure 4.1) that was first shown in Chapter 1. This provides a roadmap of the sequence of steps in an ideal project. There are very few ideal projects. The majority of projects are messy and iterative and do not proceed predictably from phase to phase. Nevertheless, it is useful to have the organization design roadmap in just the same way as it is to have a road map in a real-life car journey. In this case you know that having the map is not going to stop you getting stuck in traffic, deciding to take a detour, making an accidental wrong turn, having a mechanical breakdown or suddenly deciding to change destination. So it is with design projects. The road map is a guide to move you towards your destination. It is not the interactive, dynamic detail of the journey.

In the majority of cases the project is initiated by a contact from the client. In other cases the organization development or design consultant noticing a piece of work is needed initiates a conversation with the client. Here's how one project got started – by an email from the client, working for a company in the fast-moving consumer goods (FMCG) sector, to the internal organization design consultant:

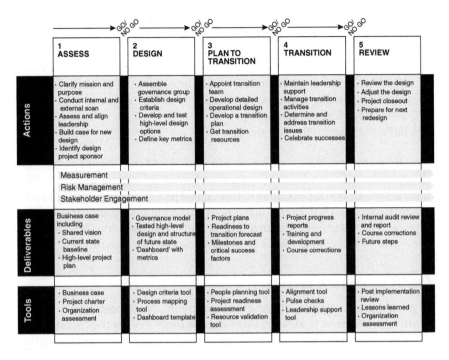

Figure 4.1 Phases of an organization design project

We are having some issues with our packaging function and wonder if you can help us identify what we would look like to be successful, and then how to achieve an effective packaging organizational structure.

People tell me you have done good work in other parts of the organization and I wonder if you have the time and would be willing to discuss the situation with me. I believe that you will have some valuable insights and recommendations, and I'm hoping we can get moving on this as a project.

If we do, we think we would be able to team up our own internal OD consultants (you plus one of our local people, here in Shanghai) and someone with deep expertise within the field of packaging in the FMCG sector so you can get a feel for where the future lies.

Please let me know if you are interested in the discussion and when would be a suitable time for me to call you.

This type of initial contact usually marks the start of the assess phase. Depending on the size of the project, the end of the phase will be marked by the delivery of a business case for continuing and/or a project charter. Even if the project is very small – for example redesigning a 20-person work unit within a larger department – it is sensible to have a document that specifies the rationale for doing the work. During the course of this phase certain actions are taken to:

- clarify the organizational mission and the purpose of the redesign;
- conduct an internal and external scan;
- assess and align the leadership;
- build the case for the new design.

The moment the assess phase begins so should the measurement, risk management and stakeholder engagement (including communications). These three activities should be continued through all phases of the project, and while risk management is not covered in this book as there are many resources available, Chapter 9 covers stakeholder engagement and communication. Meanwhile the remainder of this chapter discusses the four actions listed above.

Clarify mission and purpose

Organizational mission statements are public statements of what the organization aspires to deliver. Look out for them – often they are displayed in the organization's outlets, reception areas and advertising. Here are three examples:

> Pret A Manger, a UK-based food outlet, has a mission statement 'Creating handmade, natural food, avoiding the obscure chemicals, additives and preservatives common to much of the "prepared" and "fast" food on the market today.' (Pret A Manger, 2012)
>
> Walmart, a retailer, states 'Our mission is to save people money so they can live better.' (Walmart, 2012)
>
> Google's mission is 'to organize the world's information and make it universally accessible and useful'. (Google, 2012)

As can be seen from the three examples, the mission statements are declarations of intention. They are not particularly organization-specific. Any restaurant or sandwich supplier could have the same mission statement as Pret A Manger, for example. The differentiation lies in how the organization converts the mission statement into goods and services which are distinctively theirs. The organization design contributes to converting the intention into actions.

Every design project opens by first clarifying the organizational mission and then clarifying the purpose of the design work – what it is aiming to achieve in relation to delivering the mission. Clarifying the mission is critical, because often there is confusion about what it could or should look like in the day-to-day in different operational units. (Note that some organizations and business divisions have visions and missions, and some have one or the other. There are many ways of differentiating the two but for the sake of simplicity this book sticks with the word 'mission' as a catchall for mission and vision.)

With the organizational mission statement defined and agreed, the purpose statement that directs the design work has to be established. Note that a great deal of organization design work is done at the department or business-unit level and not at the whole-organization level. In these instances knowing both the overall mission and the departmental mission helps frame and define the business purpose of the organization design project.

A good purpose statement has a number of characteristics. It must be:

- short, so that it is memorable – 30 words or fewer;
- value-based, so that it clearly expresses the values for which the organization stands;
- declarative, because a purpose should be intentional and indicate action, not just a statement of intent;
- future-oriented, not a statement of what the organization is and does now.

Here are three examples of design project purpose statements:

1 To design and implement an organization structure with appropriately designed jobs that measurably enable efficient and effective delivery of the business strategy.
2 To develop an organization design that is robust enough to meet future demands, including emerging strategy, external market pressures, employee engagement, etc.
3 To meet the public health and financial challenges the department faces in a more consistent, flexible and sustainable way than currently.

The initial contact – as in the case outlined above – is usually followed by a one-to-one meeting between the client and the consultant. In consulting terms this is called the contracting meeting and is well described in the book *Flawless Consulting* by Peter Block mentioned in Chapter 2 (Block, 2011). This meeting aims to establish:

- what the situation, issue or concern is;
- who the client is (it may not be the person the consultant is speaking with);
- the purpose and outcome of any work;
- how this work links to the mission of the organization;
- what timescales the client is working to;
- what level of resources the client has to bring to the project (personnel, expertise, money, equipment, etc.);

Table 4.1 Sample template to gather data before first meeting with client

---

Organization/department name
Date
BASIC BACKGROUND
Financials
Number of employees
FACILITIES
Headquarters
Other locations
RECENT PROJECTS
Planned/proposed
Under way
Completed
CONSULTANTS USED
Internal experience with client
Other consulting firms
ORGANIZATION AND MARKETS
Structure and organization of company
Key markets
Key products/services for each market
LEADERSHIP AND KEY DECISION MAKERS

BUSINESS STRATEGY

BUSINESS GOALS
Revenue growth
Market growth
Geographic growth (US and international)
COMMUNITY AND CHARITABLE INITIATIVES

DEVELOPMENTS IN KEY MARKETS
Acquisitions and divestitures in the last 24 months
Declining markets

- how client and consultant will work with each other – their roles and approaches (discussed in Chapter 2), what access to information and personnel is required and so on;
- next steps.

In the first meeting with the client (or the client's representative) the consultant is also aiming to demonstrate that he/she has the expertise and knowledge to do the work required. This means doing some homework before the meeting takes place. The consultant should go to the meeting armed with background information on: (a) the individual he/she is meeting with; (b) the enterprise; and (c) the industry as a whole. This gives the client confidence that the consultant has the business savvy referred to in Chapter 2. Table 4.1 is a sample template for this pre-meeting data-gathering exercise.

Beyond this essential data be aware that during this first meeting you will be working out how your styles, personalities and characteristics will work together (or not). As Peter Block remarks:

> Pay close attention to your own style and your own feelings as important dimensions to the consulting relationship. Skill in consulting is not only skill in providing a programme, and a process, and procedures that respond to the client's needs but also skill in being able to identify and put into words the issues around trust, feelings, responsibility, and your own needs. (Block, 2011)

After the meeting write up short notes on what you understand the client's needs to be and send them to the client together with the next steps. If you are not sure whether the person you were talking with is the client then ask for clarification on this. Additionally, ask who will be the sponsor. (See 'Executive Engagement: The Role of the Sponsor', from the Project Management Institute, PMI, n.d.)

Here's what one consultant said after an initial meeting with the client.

> The CEO will sponsor the project but in day-to-day work I am to work with the Head of Organization Development as the client. I met with both of them together for this first meeting. The CEO, who's fairly new to the role, describes the company as 'in flight' like a living organism. He thinks the time frame to focus on is three to five years for the redesign longevity.

And here is an example of a write-up of an initial conversation with the chief operating officer of a 10,000-person fast-food company. The redesign focus was the head office group of 300 people.

> Thank you for meeting with me the other day. My understanding is that you are looking for help in completing an exercise to clarify the work that needs to be done to achieve the business mission and strategy and then to group the work into clusters of activities in order to create an appropriate and effective org structure.
>
> High-level project purpose:
>
> • To design and implement an organization structure with appropriately designed jobs that measurably enables efficient and effective delivery of the business strategy within the corporate head office. Outside of the scope are other business units.
>
> Supporting objectives:
>
> • To clarify and streamline the core work processes, identifying decision and handover points.

- To remove role confusion and assign accountabilities in order to eliminate conflict, duplication and mistakes.
- To develop a work-planning process that tracks the business cycle and supports the business strategy.
- To determine metrics/key performance indicators that will demonstrate that work processes are streamlined, efficient and effective and that the new structure supports this workflow.
- To design in co-ordination and linkages between the corporate head office and the business units.

I suggest that the next steps are:

(a) To hold a half-day workshop with your leadership team where we clarify the overall mission in terms of what it means for your part of the business, and get their insights, views and support on the purpose of the project you outlined.
(b) To start the internal and external scan and data-gathering.

Also, after this first meeting evaluate your own performance and note any points learned for any future meetings of this type. A useful prompt-question set is given in Table 4.2.

Once the actions from the initial meeting have been agreed the internal and external scan (data-gathering work) can begin, and a leadership alignment workshop scheduled.

Conduct an internal and external scan

An internal and external scan involves looking in more detail at the triggers (discussed in Chapter 3) that are prompting the request for a new design, prioritizing their impact on the business, seeing the connections between them, interpreting the patterns they present, assessing their meaning and making some recommendations on where the design activity should focus effort in order to achieve the purpose in the current, and predicted future, operating context.

Some clients consider doing an internal and external scan a very valuable exercise, while others think it is a waste of time. One senior manager, in favour of doing a scan, said in the initial interview about his organization:

> In past design work I've learned that it is important to translate abstract issues such as the profile of people, the inspirations of the contextual setting, and the intent of corporate principles into the design. History is also important. While it is important to understand the expectations of the company executives, they are not really the prime 'customers' of the design.
>
> A technique I've found helpful is to understand the profile of the tar-geted customer for each core product/service and, upon understanding

Table 4.2 Consultant evaluation following initial meeting

For each of the following questions ask yourself, 'Did I ...'	Yes	No
1 Do my homework before the meeting?	☐	☐
2 Determine the primary client?	☐	☐
3 Determine the secondary clients and stakeholders?	☐	☐
4 Identify the mission and/or purpose of the effort?	☐	☐
5 Elicit the clients' specific needs and expectations?	☐	☐
6 Identify shared values and differences?	☐	☐
7 Evaluate the client's expertise and ability to support the effort?	☐	☐
8 Discuss my consulting approach?	☐	☐
9 Obtain a sense of client commitment to the effort?	☐	☐

Source: Adapted from Biech, 2007.

that profile, create a design that interprets those profiles. I guess you would call this a customer-focus organization design.

The other layer I look at closely is the corporate values and principles. A company I worked with several years ago had principles around water use, sustainability, community and education. Each of these issues, when layered over the issue customer profiles, added a rich array of design possibilities. I hope you'll find that we have several commitments like this that we can grab on to.

Further issues I am thinking of for this project are understanding the texture of the production facilities and the agricultural landscape of where the food comes from in its original state – example; rice, wheat, tea, etc. A predictive interpretation of these could be very interesting and we need to support your work with someone who has the creativity and subject matter expertise to really pursue these ideas.

A rich source for you could be the corporate archive but you need to check this. However, from a research point of view the above issues will drive the planning and design effort since the archive material may merely give some background.

In another project the response to a recommendation that an internal and external scan was conducted led to the dismissive remark:

It's all well and good suggesting research and assessment activity but it's a time-budget issue. The research consumes a lot of time that will take away from the design hours.

The perspective that assessment and discovery of potentially pertinent information is a time waster reflects the view that research 'takes away' from design and design hours – that it doesn't 'enhance' the end product. This is a risky point of view to have, as failure to invest in research can lead to more expensive mistakes that need to be rectified later. Bear in mind the adage 'good design is expensive, bad design is even more expensive'!

Aim to argue for doing an assessment and do the best possible in the time negotiated. People often ask how long it takes to do an assessment. Obviously, the answer is that it depends on the scope and complexity of the organization. Often a reasonable scan can be done by one consultant within a week using a combination of interviews, focus groups and desk research – which can also pick up on survey information such as customer satisfaction surveys and employee engagement surveys. Doing the scan involves:

1   Making the case for doing the data-gathering. Be clear why data-gathering is necessary to counter opposition from those who want you to just get on and design the organization.
2   Considering the various ways of getting the information you need. Involve a diagonal slice (representatives of all levels) of the organization and have a representative sample of people from each layer of the slice. However, large numbers are not needed. The aim is to get a sense of the situation rather than the detail of it.
3   Involving people who are going to be indirectly affected – other departments, suppliers or customers. They all have a view of the organization and it may be very different from the client's. Having a number of perspectives is very useful and often gives otherwise hidden insights.
4   Assessing the risks of doing the data-gathering. Any intervention of this nature sets hares running. Know how to handle this informal side of the organization and work with the inevitability that people are curious about what is going on and what the implications are for them, and will start rumours going.
5   Knowing how to communicate the fact that this exercise is taking place. This is a crucial part of this stage of the process as it will help to mitigate some of the risks of doing it and it sets the tone for the communication needed as the organization design process gathers pace.
6   Going for the 80:20 rule. The purpose is to get some baseline information to make a decision on whether design should be the focus of the change process or whether there should be some other start point.
7   Analysing the results – not for statistical accuracy but for confidence that findings are relatively reliable, valid and representative.
8   Appropriately communicating the results both to participants in the data capture (for example focus-group members) and to the leadership team.

Table 4.3 summarizes the major methods used for collecting assessment data (McNamara, n.d.). Additionally there are a number of commercially available tools to assess an organization.

Table 4.3 Major methods of collecting assessment data

Method	Overall purpose	Advantages	Challenges
Questionnaires, surveys, checklists	When need to quickly and/or easily get lots of information from people in a non-threatening way	Can complete anonymously; inexpensive to administer; easy to compare and analyse; can administer to many people; can get lots of data; many sample questionnaires already exist	Might not get careful feedback; wording can bias client's responses; are impersonal; in surveys, may need sampling expert; doesn't get full story
Interviews	When want to fully understand someone's impressions or experiences, or learn more about their answers to questionnaires	Get full range and depth of information; develops relationship with client; can be flexible with client	Can take much time; can be hard to analyse and compare; can be costly; interviewer can bias client's responses
Documentation review	When want impression of how programme operates without interrupting the programme; is from review of applications, finances, memos, minutes, etc.	Get comprehensive and historical information; doesn't interrupt programme or client's routine in programme; information already exists; few biases about information	Often takes much time; information may be incomplete; need to be quite clear about what looking for; not flexible means to get data; data restricted to what already exists
Observation	To gather accurate information about how a programme actually operates, particularly about processes	View operations of a programme as they are actually occurring; can adapt to events as they occur	Can be difficult to interpret seen behaviors; can be complex to categorize observations; can influence behaviors of programme participants; can be expensive
Focus groups	Explore a topic in depth through group discussion, e.g., about reactions to an experience or suggestion, understanding common complaints, etc.; useful in evaluation and marketing	Quickly and reliably get common impressions; can be efficient way to get much range and depth of information in short time; can convey key information about programmes	Can be hard to analyse responses; need good facilitator for safety and closure; difficult to schedule 6–8 people together
Case studies	To fully understand or depict client's experiences in a programme, and conduct comprehensive examination through cross-comparison of cases	Fully depicts client's experience in programmeme input, process and results; powerful means to portray programme to outsiders	Usually quite time-consuming to collect, organize and describe; represents depth of information, rather than breadth

Source: McNamara, n.d.

In one organization design project, with a department of a government agency, in the timetable for a week of assessment the consultant aimed to meet with all the operating teams, meet with mixed groups of the department, have one-to-one interviews with business heads, meet the business heads as a group, have a whole-department town hall and do desk research. The week of activity is shown in Table 4.4.

Using a combination of data-collection methods makes for a more robust data set than using either quantitative or qualitative methods alone. The example shown in Table 4.4 shows several methods in use, both qualitative and quantitative. In this particular example the findings of the assessment phase were written up into a report. The summary page noted that:

> The assessment revealed that there is little to no evidence that employees are engaged. Briefly, they feel that:
>
> • They are not given opportunities to improve performance.
> • They are micro-managed against arbitrary, changing and competing priorities.
> • They are not treated with respect, or trusted, by leadership or management.
> • They are not clear about their own roles or the strategy of the organization.
> • They are helpless in pushing the boundaries of regulations, rules and policies.
> • They are unable to use their talents, skills and capabilities to the benefit of the organization.

Following this summary the consultant presented a comprehensive picture of a lack of employee engagement due, in part, to three prior restructurings leaving the workforce very demotivated. Options and a recommended way forward were closing sections of the data-gathering document. The contents page is shown in Table 4.5.

OD short

The first part of the assess phase is about establishing who the client is and what he/she would like as an outcome of the design project. During the early discussion with the client establish what the mission of the organization is and what the purpose of the redesign project is in delivering the mission.

Assuming the go-ahead to proceed, conduct an internal and external scan – basically data-gathering on the operating environment that is triggering the need for a redesign. Compile a report of the assessment findings to present to the client and the leadership team.

Table 4.4 Assessment schedule for one week

When	Purpose and outcome	Who
MONDAY		
9:00–10:00	**Purpose** To introduce myself and to meet business heads To confirm the scope and timescale of the project To present the plan for the week To answer any questions and hear any comments on the project proposal **Outcome** Business heads are clear about the project's intent and comfortable with the Phase 1 approach	Business heads as a group
10:15–11:00 11:15–12:00 12:15–1:00	**Purpose** To meet 1:1 with each business head to hear their views on aspects of the organization, current and future, using semi-structured interview (briefing sheet provided) **Outcome** Consultant will have overview of business heads' challenges, issues, opportunities	Business head Business head Business head
13:00–1:45	Lunch	
2:00–2:45	See above	Business head
3:00–4:00	**Purpose** To introduce myself to all staff To confirm the scope and timescale of the project via PowerPoint presentation To present the plan for the week To answer any questions and hear any comments on the project proposal **Outcome** Employees are clear about the project's intent and comfortable with the Phase 1 approach	All employees in one 'Town Hall' meeting
4:00–5:30	**Purpose** To review documentation that is relevant to the project, e.g. strategic plan, HR plan, annual reports, business unit plans, customer satisfaction survey, employee engagement survey, brand values work, etc. (list sent in advance) **Outcome** Consultant will have greater depth of knowledge of business operation and planned future direction	Consultant will review during the course of the day documents/ intranet, etc. that are provided or referenced in earlier meetings
TUESDAY		
9:00–10:30 10:45–12:15	**Purpose** To facilitate a discussion with up to 10 people from anywhere across the organization on the context, business strategy, challenges and opportunities the enterprise faces **Outcome** Consultant will have representation of views from all staff in the organization	4 × 90 minutes with groups of 10 people (any BU, any level). They can opt for any time slot to maximum of 10 people

Table 4.4 (cont.)

When	Purpose and outcome	Who
12:30–1:15	Lunch	
1:30–3:00	See above	See above
3:15–4:45		

WEDNESDAY

9:00–10:00	**Purpose** To present the proposal outline To discover (high level) how they would like the organization to support them **Outcome** Consultant will have representation of views from the key partners	Conference call with the three key external partners (as a group)
10:15–11:00 11:15:–12:00 12:15–1:00	**Purpose** To talk 1:1 with each key partner to hear his/her views on aspects of the organization, current and future **Outcome** Consultant will have overview of external partner challenges, issues, and opportunities	External partners (1:1)
1:15–2:00	Lunch	
2:15–3:15	**Purpose** To meet with Director of HR and HR To get deeper understanding of HR operation, processes and systems, e.g. talent management, performance management, HRIS, etc. **Outcome** Consultant will have insight into current HR operation	HR team
3:30–4:30	**Purpose** To meet with directorate team To get deeper understanding of directorate operation, processes and systems **Outcome** Consultant will have insight into directorate operation	Directorate team

THURSDAY

9:00–10:00	**Purpose** To meet with budget and procurement To get deeper understanding of budget and procurement operation, processes and systems **Outcome** Consultant will have insight into budget and procurement operation	Budget and procurement team

Table 4.4 (cont.)

When	Purpose and outcome	Who
10:15–11:00	**Purpose** To meet with logistics and event management to get deeper understanding of logistics and event management operation, processes and systems **Outcome** Consultant will have insight into logistics and event management operation	Logistics and event management team
11:15–12:00	**Purpose** To meet with monitoring and performance To get deeper understanding of monitoring and performance operation, processes and systems **Outcome** Consultant will have insight into monitoring and performance operation	Monitoring and performance team
12:15–1:00	**Purpose** To meet with assurance and risk management To get deeper understanding of assurance and risk management operation, processes and systems **Outcome** Consultant will have insight into assurance and risk management operation	Assurance and risk management team
1:00–1:45	Lunch	
2:00–2:45	**Purpose** To meet with corporate knowledge management To get deeper understanding of corporate knowledge management operation, processes and systems **Outcome** Consultant will have insight into corporate knowledge management operation	Corporate knowledge management team
3:00–3:45	**Purpose** To meet with policy support To get deeper understanding of policy support operation, processes and systems **Outcome** Consultant will have insight into policy support operation	Policy support team
4:00–4:45	**Purpose** To meet with cross-partner agenda To get deeper understanding of cross partner agendas operation, processes and systems **Outcome** Consultant will have insight into cross-partner agenda operation	Cross-partner agenda team

Table 4.4 (cont.)

When	Purpose and outcome	Who
4:45–5:30	**Purpose** To meet with learning and good practices To get deeper understanding of learning and good practices operation, processes and systems **Outcome** Consultant will have insight into learning and good practices operation	Learning and good practices team
FRIDAY		
Morning	Consultant will draft a first-thoughts document (not a final document)	Consultant
Afternoon	Discussion of first-thoughts with director	Consultant and director

Table 4.5 Contents page of assessment findings document

Contents
Opening words
Summary findings
Background to organization and project request
Assessment process and rationale
Findings and diagnosis
Thoughts and options on the way forward
Recommended approach and actions
Appendix 1: Documents reviewed
Appendix 2: Alignment principles
Appendix 3: Benchmark organizations to visit

Assess and align the leadership

Whether the design is whole-organization, divisional, business unit or team, make sure that the leadership of the enterprise, or the part of the enterprise you are working in, is collectively committed to organization design work. This collective commitment is described as 'alignment' and is characterized by showing in various ways that leaders have:

- found common ground in ideas, activities and values;
- identified areas of shared responsibility;
- created practices and systems for bridging differences.

This alignment activity usually starts by presenting the findings of the assessment. The assessment highlights areas of current strength and areas which have issues (or may have issues) in delivering the mission in the coming few years. One of the findings of the assessment may well be that the leadership team members are not operating well together and that people are confused by their conflicting messages. One OD consultant commenting on the leadership team of an organization he was working with reported:

> The CEO has recently tightened up and defined the high-level strategic framework and has begun to socialize this into the senior group, though he's not sure how onboard they are and also the detail of the framework has yet to be worked out. He believes that the leadership team can influence the company's destiny if they are aligned about the mission, what they want the company to be and why this is important to customers and clients. That said, he did not say what the mission is. There are some clues on the website and in the marketing brochures but they're pretty generic, like 'to be the best organization for customers to deal with', to be trusted, etc. I need more specificity on this before going too far down the road with this project.

Judging the level of leadership alignment is a key to a successful project, but it is often not that easy to gauge. Leaders are prone to competitive behaviour, territoriality over protecting their turf and so on. One organization vividly described their leaders as 'playing the game of thrones'. This kind of behaviour can militate against starting a project and/or getting a successful outcome.

Helping the leaders get to alignment is one of the tasks of the organization design consultant in this phase. It is best achieved by, first, having a leadership workshop and, second, maintaining engagement and communication with the individual leaders as well as the whole leadership team.

A leadership alignment workshop usually opens with the leader (client or sponsor) outlining the rationale for commissioning the piece of work, and then handing over to the consultant to present the findings of the data-gathering and make recommendations and present options on the way forward. Before the workshop, discuss the content of the presentation with the client and/or sponsor and listen to any ideas on how the information should be presented. Be ready to make amendments to the presentation if that seems appropriate. Table 4.6 gives an example of a leadership alignment workshop.

Following the close of the workshop discuss with the client the questions shown in Table 4.7. If the discussion reveals any cause for concern, agree how these will be handled. It is not a good idea to proceed with organization design work without leadership alignment.

Remember, too, that leaders change their position as circumstances change. Initial support cannot be counted on for the life cycle of the project. During

Table 4.6 Leadership alignment workshop

Time	What	Why	How
09:00 (15 mins)	Introduction to session and purpose. Including: • Purpose of the proposed design project • What has led to the project being commissioned	Attendees know why they are here and the intended outcomes	Client/sponsor to open
09:15 (45 mins)	Presentation of key findings of data-gathering – sticking to the themes, patterns, and areas relevant to the intended project	Participants get a feel for the current state of play	Presentation from HR consultant or line manager
10:00 45 mins (30 mins discussion; 15 mins summarizing and confirming agreement)	Open discussion: What's striking about the analysis? (the working well and the working less well) What's surprising and not surprising? What's important to think about in relation to where you are trying to get to?	To start to move the group towards common ground on their role in leading the design project and how they will demonstrate their alignment and commitment	Skilfully facilitated discussion to keep people on track. Logging key points. Summarizing what is important to think about, divided into 'working well' and 'working less well' buckets. Confirming agreement with the group that this is the list to work with
10:45 45 mins (30 mins discussion; 15 mins summarizing and confirming agreement)	Paired discussion taking the 'what it is important to think about', some pairs taking the 'working well bucket' others the 'working less well bucket'	To identify the basics of what is preventing or driving towards achieving the purpose	Using the 5 Whys (see Glossary) or similar inquiry tool to get to some root causes Capturing the key 'aha's' Confirming collective agreement that these are the critical elements

11:30 (30 mins)	Paired discussion of the checklist given at the end of this chapter '20 characteristics of success/failure in organization design' to ascertain common ground and take comments on what aspects caused people to stop and think	To encourage people to reflect on the conditions for success of an OD project and match these to what they know from the analysis and the critical elements to consider which they have just identified To invite people to identify common ground and to get some feel for where there is a significant disparity of views	Completing the checklist Facilitated discussion of the response to the checklist
12:00 (10 mins)	Are we in shape to go ahead, knowing what we know now?	To get agreement on whether to proceed or whether you need to do some groundwork first	Facilitated discussion using the information you have collected through the session
12:10 (20 mins)	Summary and next steps	To inform and direct people on the next steps	Client/sponsor picks up from what's emerged from the session and summarizes what he/she feels are the next steps, including who, what and by when
12:30	Close		

Table 4.7 Assessment of leadership alignment

Please indicate how much you agree or disagree with each of the statements below using the following 1–5 rating scale:

1 = Strongly disagree; 2 = Disagree; 3 = Neutral; 4 = Agree; 5 = Strongly agree.

1 The leadership team and senior leaders throughout the organization have assessed the organizational strengths and weaknesses and agreed to take actions necessary to address concerns and opportunities.

2 The leadership team and senior leaders share a common vision of the organization's future.

3 The leadership team and senior leaders throughout the organization have discussed, embraced and role-modelled a common set of core values.

4 The leadership team and senior leaders throughout the organization are clearly and obviously agreed on the purpose of the organization design project.

5 The leadership team and senior leaders throughout the organization are agreed on the culture and leadership behaviors required to be successful in the future and are committed to developing these.

6 The leadership team and senior leaders throughout the organization are able to make decisions that will drive the organization design project to success.

7 The leadership team and senior leaders throughout the organization have agreed and support the key metrics that the project will be measured by …

8 The leadership team and senior leaders throughout the organization have agreed and support the key metrics that will demonstrate that the project outcomes are delivering the intended benefits.

Source: Adapted from Center for Creative Leadership, 2005.

this assess phase, determine how to monitor leadership alignment for the duration of the project and what actions need to be built into the project plan to maintain it. Find out if leadership changes are imminent and have a contingency plan for this.

OD short

Developing leadership alignment, that is, the collective commitment to undertaking an organization design project that aims to fulfil a purpose that they all see the need for, is an essential activity in the assess phase. Without the full support of leadership team members, redesigning is likely to be derailed at some point. Achieving leadership alignment is challenging, as circumstances change and with this people's support. Do not assume that initial alignment will mean continuing alignment.

Build case for new design

Out of the data collection and the leadership alignment work comes the business case and/or project charter. Preparing a business case is an integral part of the planning and resourcing process for the organization design project. It becomes more important as the scale and complexity of the project increases.

A business case outlines the business rationale for undertaking the project and defines the parameters and management factors involved in the project itself. It provides the organization design consultant with a tool to guide the planning, management and evaluation of the project.

The business case serves many purposes:

1   It helps the client and consultant think through the project in a systematic, step-by-step manner.
2   It explains to leaders and other stakeholders why the project should be undertaken.
3   It helps stakeholders understand the economic value of the project and the benefits to be realized by undertaking it.
4   It provides a framework for completion of the project on time and to budget.
5   It aims to strongly motivate people to undertake the change and convince them that change is necessary (by reference to hard facts).
6   It helps engage people in the project.
7   It helps build and sustain commitment to the proposed changes.

An effective business case justifies why a project should be undertaken, and why the organization should invest resources (time, money, effort) in it. Many organizations have a standard business-case template but generally certain elements are found in all of them. Table 4.8 is an example of a business-case template.

In some instances a full business case is not required and a project charter stands in its place. A project charter is a formal document with many of the characteristics of a business case. It defines the high-level requirements for the project and links the project to the ongoing work of the organization (Mulcahy, 2009). Figure 4.2 shows a one-page project-charter template. Having the information in this one-page format is convenient and simple. It forms an easy-to-use reference guide for the duration of the project.

OD short

The deliverable from the assessment phase is a business case and/or a project charter. These formal documents guide the project planning and life cycle and aid monitoring the progress of the project. In some cases, such as a very small project, a full business case is not required. In this case the project charter would be the documentary outcome of the assess phase.

Table 4.8 Business-case template

Project title

Draft xx.x Date dd/mm/yy

Contents

Executive summary

- *Specify the end goal (high-level outcome) you are shooting for.*
- *State the compelling reasons why the change is a business imperative, not just a 'nice to have'.*
- *Highlight how the change fits into the overall organizational programme and contributes to achieving the business goals.*
- *Convey a sense of urgency with a clear (but brief) explanation of why the benefits of the proposal make the costs and effort of it worth-while.*

Background *(Use the opportunity to motivate the readers, build commitment and create ownership. Ensure you have sound justification.)*

- *Give an overview of past state, current state and desired state.*
- *Clarify the presenting problem/challenge/dilemma.*
- *State why you are presenting the proposal at this stage and what the high-level outcomes will be.*
- *Balance negative with positive messages. Explain clearly how serious the situation is, the dangers inherent in not supporting the proposal, and articulating the benefits of supporting it.*

Project objectives

- *Describe SMART objectives this project will achieve (stretching, measurable, attainable, relevant, time bound).*
- *Limit the number of objectives to five.*
- *Ensure the objectives are soundly justifiable and positively motivating.*

Scope

- *Define the boundaries and scope of the project.*
- *Include a brief assessment of the implications of these.*
- *Note the exclusions from the project and the methods of addressing interface complexities.*

Methodology/approach

- *Describe how you are going to involve stakeholders.*
- *Clarify the roles of the project sponsors.*
- *Outline the structure and operation that will deliver the proposal (e.g. steering group, programme manager, project co-ordinators, project stream leaders).*
- *State the style and phases of designing and delivering the proposal.*

Key deliverables and milestones/timescale

Deliverable (by objective)	Milestone	Start date	End date

Table 4.8 (cont.)

Success criteria/measures of success

- *State the success criteria or how you will measure success for each deliverable by milestone.*
- *Ensure the measurements are realistic, valid and actually measurable.*
- *Use the measures chosen to support your justification for the project.*
- *Identify measures which will increase motivation and support for the project.*

Issues and risks (including dependencies and assumptions)

- *Note the basis for identifying risks and issues (which usually relate to dependencies and assumptions).*
- *Include the issues which are outstanding at this point and need to be resolved before proceeding.*
- *Identify the key risks at the start-up stage of the process (further risks can be identified as the project proceeds).*
- *Recommend methods of addressing the issues and mitigating the risks (briefly).*

Costs and resources

- *Put a best guess here as things may change as the project is firmed up.*
- *Bid for more than you think rather than less to allow for budget cuts.*
- *Be realistic in the other resources you need (time, people, skills, etc.).*

Benefits to be delivered

- *Clearly state the benefits that will be delivered by this business case.*
- *Identify who will be responsible and accountable for realizing the benefits on an ongoing basis.*
- *Describe the method of evaluating and reporting on the benefit realization after project completion.*

Sign off (as agreement for the project to run and to the content of the business case)

Stakeholder xxxxxx   ....

Stakeholder yyyyyy   ....

Stakeholder zzzzzz   ....

Tool

Twenty characteristics of success/failure in organization design

Use this tool (Table 4.9) as a discussion document with a leadership team or with individual leaders. The 'yes'/'no' answers are less important than the discussion the items generate.

If leaders have answered 'yes' to most of the first ten questions then an organization redesign project is in a good position to move forward. If leaders have answered 'yes' to most of the questions from 11 to 20, then some preparation work is required before contemplating a redesign.

Business Outcome of Successful Project	Project Scope	What has to be in place to have a successful project
Project Objectives	Issues and Risks	Key Project Activities
Steering Group Members	Project Benefits	Project Measures

Figure 4.2 Project charter

Summary

The assess phase sets an organization design project off on the right track. Clarifying the mission of the organization and agreeing the purpose of the organization design in helping to deliver the mission are the first steps in this phase. This is followed by a carefully conducted internal and external scan, together with a leadership alignment exercise giving the information needed to highlight opportunities, risks and issues. The information gained from this phase directs the focus of the organization design. Out of this phase comes the documented business case and/or project charter.

References

Biech, E. (2007). *The Business of Consulting*. San Francisco: Pfeiffer.
Block, P. (2011). *Flawless Consulting*, 3rd edn. San Francisco: Pfeiffer.
Center for Creative Leadership. (2005). 'March Poll Results: Becoming a Strategic Leader', April. Retrieved 29 January 2013, from Center for Creative Leadership Leading Effectively e-Newsletter: http://www.ccl.org/leadership/enewsletter/2005/APRmarpollresults.aspx?pageId=584.
Google. (2012). 'Company'. Retrieved 6 January 2013, from Google: http://www.google.com/about/company.
McNamara, C. (n.d.). 'Selecting Which Business Research Method to Use'. Retrieved 29 January 2013, from Free Managment Library: http://managementhelp.org/businessresearch/selecting-methods.htm#anchor1062017.

Table 4.9 Twenty characteristics of success/failure in organization design

	Yes No
1 There is pressure from the environment (internal or external) for change.	
2 People at the top are demotivated, or disruptive.*	
3 Leadership is provided by a key line executive with a clear goal for change.	
4 There is a collaborative identification of problems.	
5 There is a willingness to take risks in new organizational forms.	
6 There is a realistic long-term perspective.	
7 There is a willingness to face the situation and work on changing it.	
8 The system rewards people for the effort of changing and improvement, not just for short-term results.	
9 Changes made show tangible results and quick wins at all levels in the organization.	
10 There is time and resource available to manage the change as well as do the job.	
11 There is discrepancy between what managers say and what they do.	
12 The organization has a large number of initiatives going simultaneously.	
13 There is confusion between ends and means.	
14 There is conflict between what line people need and want and what staff people think they need and want.	
15 There is a lack of co-ordination among a number of different activities aimed at increasing organizational effectiveness.	
16 There is overdependence on experts and specialists (internal or external).	
17 A large gap exists between commitment to change at the top of the organization and the transfer of this interest to the rest of the organization.	
18 The organization tries to fit a major organizational change into an old organizational structure.	
19 There is a desire for a 'cook book' solution (e.g. 'If we adopt The Balanced Business Scorecard all our problems will be solved').	
20 The organization applies an intervention or strategy inappropriately.	

* NOTE: Question 2 often causes comment. Briefly, leaders need to feel dissatisfied with the current situation otherwise the motivation to support the design changes will not be great. If leaders are satisfied with the current situation, or feel it is 'tolerable', or they have the attitude 'if it's not broken, don't fix it', then further exploration is needed before moving forward.

Mulcahy, R. (2009). 'Project Management Crash Course: What Is a Project Charter?'. Retrieved 29 January 2013, from ciscopress.com: http://www.ciscopress.com/articles/article.asp?p=1400865.

PMI. (n.d.). 'Executive Engagement: The Role of the Sponsor'. Retrieved 30 January 2013, from Project Management Institute: http://www.pmi.org/business-solutions/~/media/PDF/Business-Solutions/Executive%20Engagement_FINAL.ashx.

Pret A Manger. (2012). 'Food for Thought'. Retrieved 6 January 2013, from Pret A Manger: http://www.pret.com/our_food/food_for_thought.htm.

Walmart. (2012). 'Our People'. Retrieved 6 January 2013, from Walmart: http://corporate.walmart.com/global-responsibility/diversity-inclusion/our-people.

5 Design phase

> The roles design team members play during an event alternate between thinking and acting as participants and thinking and acting as a design team.
>
> Jacobs, 1997

What you will learn

This chapter gives you the information you need to develop an organization design (work, people, formal organization, informal organization), aligned to the mission, strategy and values that achieve the design purpose. You will learn how to set up the governance of the design work, develop design criteria, map the workflow, come up with two or three high-level design options and test them in order to recommend which to take forward. Additionally you will learn to establish measures – both of project success and the organizational performance in the new design.

Overview of phase

The project charter and/or business case that is delivered at the end of the assess phase is the blueprint for the work of the design phase. Look at the overview of the phases (Figure 5.1) and see that the design phase involves four specific actions:

1   assemble governance group;
2   develop design criteria;
3   develop and test high-level design options;
4   define key metrics.

Each of these is discussed in the course of this chapter. The outcome of this phase is a high-level organization design (including structure). In the next phase – planning to transition – work is done to take the high-level design into the detailed operational design which intentionally:

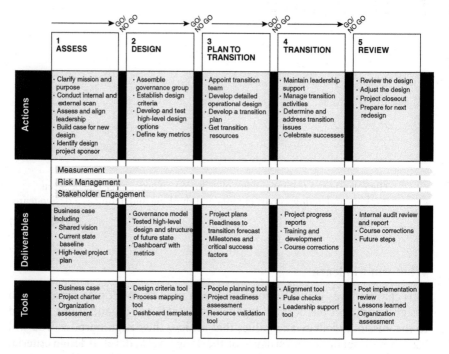

	1 ASSESS	2 DESIGN	3 PLAN TO TRANSITION	4 TRANSITION	5 REVIEW
Actions	· Clarify mission and purpose · Conduct internal and external scan · Assess and align leadership · Build case for new design · Identify design project sponsor	· Assemble governance group · Establish design criteria · Develop and test high-level design options · Define key metrics	· Appoint transition team · Develop detailed operational design · Develop a transition plan · Get transition resources	· Maintain leadership support · Manage transition activities · Determine and address transition issues · Celebrate successes	· Review the design · Adjust the design · Project closeout · Prepare for next redesign
	Measurement				
	Risk Management				
	Stakeholder Engagement				
Deliverables	Business case including · Shared vision · Current state baseline · High-level project plan	· Governance model · Tested high-level design and structure of future state · 'Dashboard' with metrics	· Project plans · Readiness to transition forecast · Milestones and critical success factors	· Project progress reports · Training and development · Course corrections	· Internal audit review and report · Course corrections · Future steps
Tools	· Business case · Project charter · Organization assessment	· Design criteria tool · Process mapping tool · Dashboard template	· People planning tool · Project readiness assessment · Resource validation tool	· Alignment tool · Pulse checks · Leadership support tool	· Post implementation review · Lessons learned · Organization assessment

Figure 5.1 Phases of an organization design project

- makes transparent how high-level functions and tasks are delegated to different work units and individuals;
- clarifies the vertical and lateral relationships between work units and individuals in terms of processes, communications, flow of information and chain of command;
- identifies the location of authority in the organization in terms of decision-making and control (McLean and Co., 2012);
- ensures work processes are streamlined and flow smoothly through the organization;
- aligns people and skills with the roles;
- builds individual and organizational capability.

There is always more than one design possibility and deciding on the way to go inevitably means making tradeoffs of one type or another. Note that 'the best designs emerge from the widest possible range of alternatives' (Oliver Wyman Delta, n.d.). Evaluating the options against the design criteria, the outcomes desired, 'walk-throughs' (see Glossary) and the various tests of a good design help make the recommended choice.

Some powerful technologies are becoming available for organizational visualization, modelling, scenario-planning and testing. In much the same way that architects design buildings via increasingly sophisticated software, these organization design technologies both shortcut the traditional ways of designing and offer exciting new possibilities for OD. Some of these technologies are discussed later in this chapter.

Assemble governance group

Before starting the design work determine how it will be governed, monitored and kept on track. Establishing robust governance is critical for several reasons:

- to set out lines of responsibility and accountability for the delivery of the project;
- to give the stakeholders the ability to manage their interest in the project;
- to support the project team to deliver the required outcomes by providing resources, giving direction and enabling tradeoffs and timely decision-taking;
- to provide a forum for issue resolution;
- to provide access to best practice and independent expert advice;
- to disseminate information by reporting to stakeholders so that they can effectively fulfil their roles;
- to provide a framework for project disclosures.

Even if the project is small, it is best done by people working within a formal governance structure. This means a steering group (one of whose members is likely to be the sponsor), a project manager, the organization design consultant and a design team. One organization, of 240 people, set up the design phase of the project with the structure shown in Figure 5.2. (The 'core team' was their name for the steering group.) This project involved a move to a new building for 100 of the staff. The move provided the opportunity for a radical review of the whole organization, which was spread across five sites. Note that there were parallel initiatives outside the scope of the redesign project but which had a significant interdependence with it. The co-ordination group was charged with ensuring that things stayed in alignment across the various pieces of work. In the example the two consultants involved (one organization design consultant and one project manager) were present at the meetings of each of the teams shown on the chart.

The teams each had a specific charge. The co-ordination team, for example, was charged with:

- translating a transition schedule (to the new building) into assignable work and tasks;

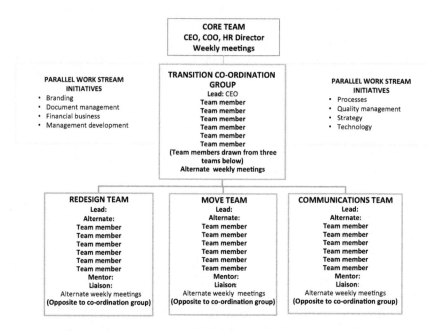

Figure 5.2 Design team governance structure example

- delegating to various project teams, work groups, personnel;
- co-ordinating and integrating transition plans, tasks and activities;
- resolving issues brought forward by work teams;
- creating alignment between entities;
- managing expectations of various constituents;
- managing the work according to the timeline and budget;
- facilitating project communication/pacing the project;
- providing resource guidance;
- supporting and guiding work team members while holding them accountable.

As shown in Figure 5.2 regular meetings were scheduled to keep things on track. All project documentation, discussions, additional materials and schedules were kept on an open access SharePoint site. This meant full transparency to all employees of the status of the organization redesign.

In this organization, the redesign team was doing the high-level design work but had to keep the move schedule front of mind as the new organization had to be introduced synchronously with the move. In other redesigns a move may not be involved and the governance structure may look somewhat different. The key point is that redesign projects need good governance.

A question that often comes up in relation to governance and team membership is who should be on the teams. To achieve a good high-level design enrol organizational members from various levels and job roles to systematically develop design criteria, design options and recommendations on which option is best fitted to meet the purpose. The 'best design processes involve people who fully understand the organization and its work. In large corporations the third and fourth level managers are positioned better than either the senior team or outside consultants to understand how the organization works both formally and informally' (Oliver Wyman Delta, n.d.). Grade and job role are less important in design work than an inquiring frame of mind, good influencing skills and an ability to hold off proposing solutions too early in the process. Below is a generic role description of a design team member.

Organization design team member profile

Note: This is a generic profile that needs to be adapted for each organization. Broadly speaking an organization design team needs to represent a 'diagonal slice' of the organization both in grade/level and in organizational business units.

The initial design team should be between five and eight people who are **selected** for the attributes below and recognized and rewarded for participation. Design team members need to represent the various levels of the organization and be willing and able to speak up for that level in the design team.

It is good practice to put work on the design team in the staff member's performance objectives and/or development plan.

Each team member must agree participation with their managers and be allowed time (usually in the ball park of one-third of the job for the duration of the design phase) to work as a project team member. The work is demanding and not an add-on to an existing work load.

Personal

- Recognized informal and/or formal leader with authority and scope to influence change.
- Natural leader respected for his/her collaborative nature, work ethic, honesty and trustworthiness.
- A 'doer' who see things through and is accountable.
- Enthusiastic about developing and designing effective, efficient and agile ways of operating the business.
- Wide knowledge of the organization's business, organization and culture.
- Strong influencing skills:
  - ability to operate at senior levels
  - ability to tailor approach so that it is accessible to people at different levels.
- Creative thinker, not daunted by new ideas.

Business

- Knowledgeable about the organization's mission, processes, protocols and challenges.
- Understanding of the trends and forecasts that are shaping and changing organizations and work.
- Clear view of the competitive environment in which the organization is operating.

Technical

- Experience of project/programme management or working in a project environment.
- Strong written and oral communications skills:
  - presentation skills
  - ability to create compelling messages using images and words
  - ability to use PowerPoint, SharePoint, social media and other communication channels.

Include someone from each level of the organization in each team but aim to keep the teams small. As stated, up to eight people are enough and fewer is better. This 'diagonal slice' means the consultant is working to the tested principle that those who do the work should redesign it. This makes it easier to understand and to influence and change work patterns at a day-to-day level. Usually one member of the higher-level team (in the example shown in Figure 5.2 it was a member of the co-ordination team) leads each work stream.

Train all team members to perform their OD roles effectively. This includes explaining the OD theories, methods and approaches, building awareness on handling change and clarifying the way the governance structure works. Getting the balance right on this requires thought, as one OD consultant explains:

> I have worked on a number of OD initiatives in the past; however, the approach has tended to be reactive and tactical. I realized last year when I started my current intervention that there were theories and models that I could explore to provide a more strategic approach – hence my enrolment on the CIPD course.
>
> I have discovered over the years that creativity needs a framework, and OD is no different. A big learning for me in my current initiative is the importance of contracting in the initial stage. With hindsight, I should have spent more time on this, outlining the road map, clarifying the different roles, perhaps explaining the change-management model that we might use, and factoring in the right time to introduce and explore

relevant theories, e.g. different organization structures, as the initiative develops.

The difficulty is getting the balance right; the team I am working with are action-oriented and desperate to get to the implementation phase, and in reality I am not sure how much theory they would have let me introduce them to up-front, so I have resorted to introducing theory as we go along. Perhaps I could have given top-line concepts so they could have been aware of what we would be considering along the way. Being a pragmatist myself, in their position how much would I tolerate before I wanted to 'get on with the job'? I do think I should have put more consideration into what and how I introduce underpinning theory.

Hand in hand with the governance structure goes project management, as organization design work should be run as a project with a skilled project manager. Both the Project Management Institute (PMI) and the Association for Project Management (APM) have tools, white papers and advice on how to run projects. Whatever its size and scope the design project requires expert use of project management disciplines to keep it moving and on track. It is in the next phase – planning to transition – that project management skills and disciplines become critical, but setting up the work as a project in the design phase is recommended.

OD short

Regardless of the scale and complexity of a redesign it needs to be managed systematically. A strong governance structure is the keystone for this. Members of the governance group comprise steering group and design team members who have the attributes, skills and capabilities to work with the demands the project makes on them. Beyond strong governance, a standard project management approach to running the project makes it more likely to stay on track.

Establish design criteria

In any organization design project stakeholders need to agree on the design criteria. Essentially, design criteria:

- clarify what the new organization design must do well;
- identify problems that must be solved or opportunities that should be capitalized on in the new design;
- develop the 'benchmark profile' to guide the design and use in evaluating the design alternatives;
- take the emotion out of organization design and provide evidence-based data with which to assess options;
- provide focus for design or redesign that improves performance;

- lay the foundation for tradeoff decisions – they articulate priorities that guide the design through conflicting needs;
- keep members focused on the same outcomes of designing;
- enable differences to be surfaced and discussed;
- are used to evaluate different design solutions.

The organization design criteria are developed from the phase-one assessment of things that will have to change to implement the new strategy, purpose and vision and achieve the new performance requirements, together with an analysis of the strengths and weaknesses of the organization. They need to be a balanced set, not all focused on one aspect of the business. Use the systems model as a guide to thinking carefully about the criteria. For example, the model shown in Figure 1.3 could generate five criteria, one each related to strategy, informal organization, formal organization, work and people.

Design criteria comprise five or six statements of what the design should accomplish in terms of observable/measurable operating features/outcomes. For example:

- Move decision making out to those interfacing with customers to speed up decision making.
- Enable effective information exchange between ABC and 123 to increase innovative problem solving.
- Maintain strategic global/regional presence with capacity to capture greater global market share and future business growth.

The criteria are *not*:

- A description of how to organize, such as 'Centralize Support Services' or 'Create an Architecture Group'.
- A directive goal statement, such as 'Implement Lean'.

In his book *Change by Design*, Tim Brown, CEO IDEO, a design company, talks about innovation, design constraints and boundaries – essentially synonymous with design criteria (Brown, 2009). With this in mind, organization designers would do well to follow Brown's guidance:

> To an artist in pursuit of beauty or a scientist in search of truth, the bounds of a project may appear as unwelcome constraints. But the mark of a designer, as the legendary Charles Eames said often, is a willing embrace of constraints.
>
> Without constraints design cannot happen, and the best design – a precision medical device or emergency shelter for disaster victims – is often carried out within quite severe constraints. For less extreme cases we need only look at Target's success in bringing design within the reach of a broader population for significantly less cost than had previously been

achieved. It is actually much more difficult for an accomplished designer such as Michael Graves to create a collection of low-cost kitchen implements or Isaac Mizrahi a line of ready-to-wear clothing than it is to design a teakettle that will sell in a museum store for hundreds of dollars or a dress that will sell in a boutique for thousands.

The willing and even enthusiastic acceptance of competing constraints is the foundation of design thinking. The first stage of the design process is often about discovering which constraints are important and establishing a framework for evaluating them.

Constraints can be visualized in terms of three overlapping criteria for successful ideas: feasibility (what is functionally possible within the foreseeable future); viability (what is likely to become part of a sustainable business model); and desirability (what makes sense to people and for people).

A competent designer will resolve each of these three constraints, but a *design thinker* will bring them into a harmonious balance... (This is not to say) that all constraints are created equal; a given project may be driven disproportionately by technology, budget, or a volatile mix of human factors. Different types of organizations may push one or another of them to the fore. Nor is it a simple linear process. Design teams will cycle back throughout the life of a project, but the emphasis on fundamental human needs – as distinct from fleeting or artificially manipulated desires – is what drives design thinking to depart from the status quo.

Designers, then, have learned to excel at resolving one or another or even all three of these constraints. *Design thinkers*, by contrast, are learning to navigate between and among them in creative ways. They do so because they have shifted their thinking from *problem* to *project*. (Brown, 2009)

Organization design team members often find difficulty in generating design criteria. They can be helped if they are given a practical example. Here are the instructions that one organization designer gave to a colleague:

1   In the workshop draw an analogy of a journey by car from start point to destination. Explain design criteria in this instance as, for example: journey not to exceed eight hours of driving per day, everyone in the car must take a turn at driving, rest stops will be at three-hour intervals, costs will be equally shared, etc. Design criteria for organization design are similar. You're specifying the criteria which the design must meet – if you like, the boundaries within which it falls.
2   You can have very specific criteria (which tend to limit options) or you can have very general criteria (which offer many possibilities). We recommend fewer rather than more criteria. Up to six work well.
3   Determine the criteria which your design project has to meet in the future state.

Table 5.1 Template for logging design criteria and constraints

Design criteria and constraints	
Design criteria	The design should:
Design constraints (any boundaries or stakes in the ground limiting the design)	The design cannot: The most critical criteria or
Ranking of criteria and constraints	constraints are (say why):

4   Check that the criteria meet the MECE principle. That is, they are mutually exclusive and collectively exhaustive. Or at least avoid the situation where conformance with one of the criteria means non-conformance with another.

An alternate method is to use a template such as the one shown in Table 5.1.

OD short

No design should proceed without clear design criteria: the specific requirements that the redesign is supposed to meet. These form the 'guide rails' for the design. Aim for a smaller (five or six) rather than a larger number. More criteria mean less room to design. Criteria should be short and action-oriented. Check that they complement and support each other (following the MECE principle).

Develop design options: high-level design of ideal state

Developing design options is the nub of the organization design work and takes time and effort. It is done in two parts.

Part 1: in the **design phase** the work is focused on the higher levels of the organization: the high-level business processes, the macro-level groupings of work and the top layers of the hierarchies. Think of it as the umbrella or macro design.

Part 2: the more detailed design work comes in the **planning-to-transition** phase. It is at this point that attention shifts to the granularity of the work-flows and business process, the allocation of resources, job roles and responsibilities, and the detail of policies and procedures – all of which may need to be changed or developed if the macro design points to this.

The high-level design, the focus of this chapter, is developed in seven steps:

1   Identify the three or so core business processes of the enterprise or part of the enterprise being redesigned. Map their **ideal** state. Do not map the current state at this point but the state they would be in if they were working perfectly.

2   Review the core business processes and look for sensible and appropriate groupings of the work activities in the core processes. Then group or cluster the work, paying attention to the design criteria, the business purpose of the redesign and the likelihood that work will flow effectively through the groupings. Develop at least five different sets of groupings. Generally, grouping can be formed by:
- function
- work process
- knowledge/skills/discipline
- product
- service
- project, market segment
- user/customer need
- geography
- any combination of activity/output/user.

3   Evaluate each set of groupings in terms of design criteria, business purpose and workflow. Make any grouping adjustments or refinements. Eliminate those that do not meet the design criteria.

4   For those two or three sets that remain consider linking mechanisms that enable effective:
- co-ordination
- decision making and control
- multi-directional movement of information
- chains of command
- delegation of functions and tasks.

The linking mechanisms can be on a scale of informal to formal and shown both laterally (across the groupings) and vertically (up and down the groupings).

5   With the remaining grouped sets conduct an impact analysis and eliminate, blend and/or amend each of the grouped sets to arrive at two options with the pros and cons of each.

6   For each option develop a high-level organization chart (top two or three levels only) but consider what the lower levels could look like. Include reference to the linking mechanisms and where/how they will appear. Note that most organizations are not a single-structure form – different forms appear at different levels or within different business units. Often there is a hierarchy at the top of the organization, with perhaps project teams below this. Newer organizational forms are beginning to look different from more traditional organizations. Some are rejecting the notion of an organization chart altogether. Valve, a computer games company, is an example of this.

We've been boss-free since 1996.

Imagine working with super-smart, super-talented colleagues in a free-wheeling, innovative environment – no bosses, no middle management, no bureaucracy. Just highly motivated peers coming together to make cool stuff. It's amazing what creative people can come up with when there's nobody there telling them what to do. (Valve, 2013)

7   Test against workflow, walk-throughs, design criteria, and purpose. Once satisfied, hand over to the planning-to-transition team to take the design to the operational level, i.e. the detailed plan to transition.

Each of these steps is discussed in more detail below.

1   Identify the core business processes

Business processes are the end-to-end major sets of steps or tasks which when completed convert an input into an output (Input → Process → Output).

Core processes are those that create sustainable competitive advantage, create long-term benefit and tie directly with the business strategy. They are the 'heartbeat' of an organization, and they include those processes that are strategic in nature. In most cases (at an organizational level and within departments and business units) there are only about three business processes that are core.

Essential processes are those that must be performed for the business to operate, they support the core processes and create disadvantage if done poorly. But they can afford to be at par with competitors. They may potentially be outsourced if, for example, they are transactional or support functions.

Non-essential processes do not add value. These should be eliminated or adjusted to minimize the time/resource spent on these activities. Excessive internal reporting is an example of a non-essential core process.

Identification of the core processes causes debate and is not necessarily straightforward. Look at the organization chart shown in Figure 5.3. It shows a divisional HR function, organized around HR processes (HR service areas × 7). Each of the other divisions had a similarly organized function. Although this may have served a purpose at some point, the new group HR director was of the view that there was a lot of repeated work. He commissioned a project to streamline and professionalize the function. A leadership team developed design criteria as follows:

1   Operate a 'light-touch' centralized group HR function with a common core of HR products and services across the group.
2   Maximize the synergies between the divisional HR functions.
3   Enable each divisional HR function to meet its customers' needs.
4   Allow for divisional flexibility and scalability.
5   Deliver a compelling employee value proposition across the group's HR workforce.
6   Use consistent and transparent metrics that reveal HR's value-added contribution to business performance.

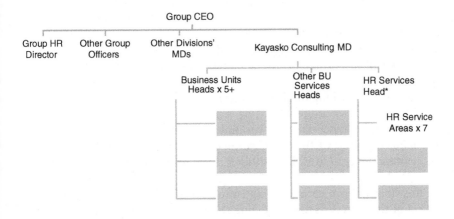

*HR Services** = Resourcing, Learning and Development, Organization Development, Talent Management, Health and Benefits, Mobility, Employment Law and Compliance.
+ **Kayasko Consulting Business Units** = UK Central Government, UK Public Sector, UK Commercial Business, Nordic and Asia, MEA

Figure 5.3 Kayasko Consulting organization chart

Several discussions took place on both group-level purpose of the HR function and the divisional-level purpose(s). They arrived at a final purpose statement:

> The purpose of the Human Resource function within Kayasko Group and each of the divisions is to forecast staff requirements and advise managers on employee sourcing and individual and organizational development options to deliver their business strategies.

With this purpose statement in mind the team identified four core processes at group and divisional levels – workforce planning, employee sourcing, individual learning and organizational development – and ran a workshop with ten participants from HR and client departments who, jointly, worked to answer the following questions – generic in relation to any workflow – and map the ideal flows of the four processes:

- What in the flow would establish and sustain competitive advantage?
- What is the best order or sequence for the activities?
- What are important interfaces in the workflow that facilitate effective operation?
- Where can activities be eliminated, streamlined or done in parallel?
- How shall we eliminate repetition, redundancies, unnecessary delays, rework or unnecessary costs?

- How could the decision-making processes be improved?
- How could the processes be changed to prevent gaps in information or conflict in priorities?
- What are key interfaces and handoffs?
- How will we ensure effective and efficient interfaces and handoffs?

The objective in asking these questions is to:

- eliminate fragmentation in workflows;
- focus the effort of the organization on the most critical work processes;
- enhance overall workflow within the organization.

At this stage it is not necessary to go into a lot of process-mapping detail. The object of the exercise is to learn enough about the flows to identify where there could be synergies/streamlining opportunities and efficiency gains across the core processes. The appropriate level of detail is shown in Figure 5.4.

Once the core processes have been mapped – preferably on one long sheet of paper with the activities/tasks on sticky notes that can be easily moved around – arrange the process flows one under the other, scan across them looking for appropriate groupings that conform to the design criteria and deliver the business purpose. Take a photo of the workflows before taking them down in case the notes drop off. Remember to zoom sufficiently to be able to read the tasks and activities.

For those unfamiliar with process mapping an excellent, simple book on the topic is *The Basics of Process Mapping*, 2nd edn, by Robert Damelio (CRC Press, 2011).

2   Group the work activity

Grouping the activity is necessary as it defines the strategic groups that will deliver the work, provides a framework for the more detailed design and illustrates how the organization might operate. In the Kayasko example, design workshop participants looked at the workflows, the design criteria and the business purpose of the HR function and developed four possible options of work groupings that fitted. Table 5.2 shows these at a high level.

3   Evaluate each option

Evaluate each option against the design criteria, the business purpose the design is intended to achieve and the workflow mapping. In the Kayasko case the four core processes were agreed to be workforce planning, employee sourcing, individual learning and organizational development, so the team was assessing how well these processes could be delivered in each of the four options. At this stage aim to assess the options in an objective way. Avoid worrying about the people and personalities that may be involved when it

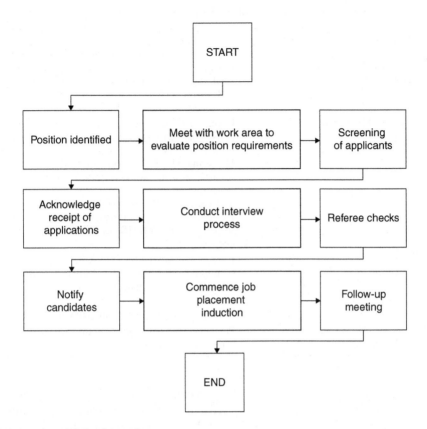

Figure 5.4 High-level recruitment process

comes to implementing any of them. (This is difficult in practice, requiring tact, sensitivity and diplomacy.)

Often through this exercise some further options emerge which can be blends of those already on the table or new ones. Go through the same evaluation process with these. Eliminate the options which do not deliver against the criteria, or which might result in workflow bottlenecks. In the options shown in Table 5.1, option 3, for example – the largely centralized function – is unlikely to meet the design criteria of 'light touch' or 'divisional scalability and flexibility'. Aim to end the evaluation with two possible options to continue working on.

4 Develop linking mechanisms

Linking mechanisms are those that connect various people, teams and units of work enabling them to share and act on information that will keep their part of the work flowing. Linking mechanisms take a variety of forms that

Table 5.2 Four process groupings of work options

Grouping	Description
Kayasko HR Services: option 1 See Figure 5.5	Group HR level does strategy and planning Each division has four functional teams HR business partners work within each division Largely decentralized HR
Kayasko HR Services: option 2 See Figure 5.6	Group HR focuses on areas for synergy and consistency with concept that managers are a group resource Divisional HR focuses on specific divisional requirements including technical career development There are no HR business partner roles Designated managers have a local responsibility to co-ordinate with HR (divisional or group) as needed
Kayasko HR Services: option 3 See Figure 5.7	Largely centralized function with all but strategy/planning and consulting outsourced No HR business partners but skilled internal consultants Managers doing talent management
Kayasko HR Services: option 4 See Figure 5.8	Partly centralized group function with key aspects decentralized

can be formal and/or informal. Those that are established within boundaries, for example within an operating division, are easier to maintain than those that are established across boundaries. Across-boundary linking may require more formal mechanisms than within-boundary linking.

Formal linking mechanisms include:

- Liaison roles – someone has the specific job of working between or across work groups. Often these are formal roles and may include the word 'co-ordinator' or 'liaison' in the job title.
- Cross unit groups – for example, standing monthly meetings, committees set up for a specific purpose or project teams.
- Integrator departments – these are established to ensure that the parts of the work process (for example if the process crosses two organizational units) are working together effectively. The International Labour Organization has a policy integration department that takes on this role, describing its work as:

Supporting the ILO's agenda for decent work for a fair globalization. Its central objective is to further greater policy coherence of social and economic policies at the international and national level. To this end, it

Kayasko Group HR Level: HR Strategy+Workforce Planning

Kayasko Divisional HR Level:

OD + D, L & D, Talent Management Resourcing, Health/Benefit, Employment Law + Compliance

HR Business Partner Role

Figure 5.5 Kayasko HR Services: option 1

Kayasko Group HR Level: HR Strategy and Workforce Planning, Employment Law, Compliance, Health and Benefit, Management L & D, OD, D

Kayasko Divisional HR Level: Technical L & D, Resourcing and Talent Management

Geography based line manager co-ordinators to HR (divisional and group)

Figure 5.6 Kayasko HR Services: option 2

Kayasko Group HR Level: HR Strategy and Workforce planning, OD & D Consulting, SLA + purchasing team for (outsourced) resourcing, L & D, Health & Benefits, Employment Laws + Compliance + Legal aspect of mobility

Pool of internal consultants

Within each division and geography line managers trained to do talent management

Figure 5.7 Kayasko HR Services: option 3

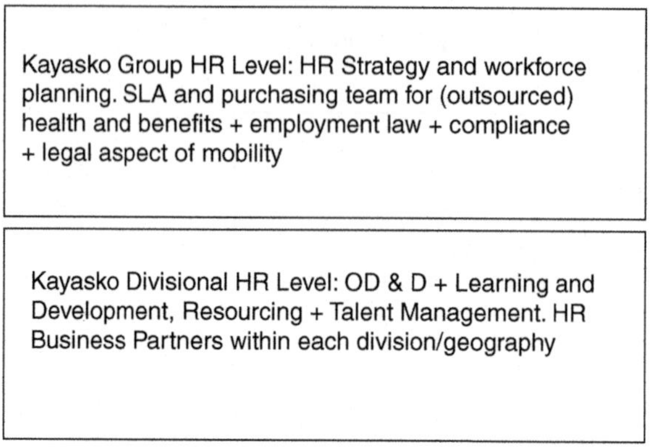

Kayasko Group HR Level: HR Strategy and workforce planning. SLA and purchasing team for (outsourced) health and benefits + employment law + compliance + legal aspect of mobility

Kayasko Divisional HR Level: OD & D + Learning and Development, Resourcing + Talent Management. HR Business Partners within each division/geography

Figure 5.8 Kayasko HR Services: option 4

works closely with other multilateral agencies and Governments, workers' and employers' organizations. It also reaches out to civil society organizations and the academic world. Through its policy-oriented agenda, it explores the complementarities and interdependencies between employment, working conditions, social protection, social dialogue and labour standards using research, policy advice, dialogue and technical cooperation as means of action. (International Labour Organization, 2013)

- Matrix structures – these formalize linkages through the organizational hierarchies but can be difficult and costly to operate.
- Service-level agreements – for example between an IT function, other organizations' functional areas and third parties.

Informal linking mechanisms include:

- Technology-based collaboration channels – for example, SharePoint, where employees, customers and partners can share documents, work on them jointly, have discussions, organize projects and teams and discover people and information (Sharepoint, 2012).
- Informal networks of people – for example, those who gather outside to smoke a cigarette (in locations where smoking in the building is banned) often discover information and insights through this casual, informal interaction that they would not run across in the normal course of events. Informal networks can also be formally established, for example a group of people with a shared interest in a topic might be encouraged to form a 'community of practice' (see Glossary).

- Social media channels – for example, Yammer (a form of Facebook for organizations). It is described as 'a popular collaboration tool used by thousands of companies to communicate within the firewall. Though it is somewhat of a simplification, think of Yammer as Facebook meets Instant Messaging' (Ragan, 2011).
- Ad hoc meetings – often called at short notice to discuss a particular issue or opportunity that has suddenly come to light.

Note that the choice of linking mechanisms depends on a number of factors, including cost and/or difficulty of introducing and maintaining them, decision-making speed and authority required, degree of co-ordination necessary to achieve results, organizational culture and expectations and so on.

With most groupings it is easy to come up with a range of possible lateral and vertical linking mechanisms, so, again, aim to have more than one set of linking possibilities for each of the two groupings options. Evaluate the linking mechanisms in the same way that the options were evaluated.

5   *Conduct an impact analysis*

Conduct an impact analysis on the selected options with their linking mechanisms. Doing this provides a structured approach for looking at them in order to identify as many of the negative and positive impacts or consequences of each as possible. This makes it an important tool for evaluating whether to go ahead with either project. And once the go-ahead has been given it helps to prepare for and manage any serious issues that may arise (Impact Analysis, 2013).

A common format is on a 2 × 2 matrix (Table 5.3) – one for each option – where judgments are made as follows:

(a) High/low impact: make judgments based on achievement of objectives, fit to boundaries, assessment of the amount of savings achieved and/or revenue increased, streamlining process, shortening timescales, etc.
(b) Easy/hard to achieve: make judgments based on the degree of possible disruption, the HR implications, the impact on operations and/ or customer service, the amount of time likely to achieve the required changes, etc.

Using the systems model introduced in Chapter 1 (see Figure 1.3) helps identify areas of impact. Once they are identified with related actions, plot them on the chart. In the Kayasko example, option 3 suggested introducing a pool of internal consultants. This might be a high-impact action but be hard to achieve in terms of cost and time to retrain people, communicating the work of the newly formed consulting group, time to get them up to speed, etc. and so this would be plotted in the bottom right-hand cell.

Table 5.3 Impact analysis template

Low impact/easy to achieve	High impact/easy to achieve
Low impact/hard to achieve	High impact/hard to achieve

This form of impact analysis creates a visual that aids decisions and choices around the option to take to the next step of the process. There are many methods of conducting an impact analysis, but all too often organizations do not undertake one. This is one reason that so many designs do not work as well as they might, 'as unforeseen consequences wreak havoc' (Impact Analysis, 2013).

Once the impact analysis is complete and the implications assessed, eliminate, blend and/or amend each of the grouped sets to arrive at the final two design options with the pros and cons of each in terms of their operational design implications and implementation implications. Now take the two options to the client and/or steering group for discussion, feedback and input, and finally sign off to one of the options that will then be taken forward to convert into a structure chart. What often happens at this point is that when the relative merits of the two options are discussed amendments are made and on occasion a whole alternate proposal is put forward. The aim is to get sign off for the design.

6   Develop a high-level organization chart

Based on the service-delivery model of the chosen option, i.e. product-focused, customer-focused, etc. and the grouping of the activity, develop a high-level organization chart, starting with the top two or three levels, and then working down the next few levels until there is a fairly complete structure. While doing this consider:

- how high-level functions and tasks could be delegated to different work units and individuals;
- the vertical and lateral relationships between work units and individuals in terms of processes;
- communications, flow of information and decision making;
- chain of command;
- span of control;
- location of authority, accountability and control;

- volume of work and level of effort required to do the work (this may require specialists);
- the types of position within each group (this may require specialists).

Be aware that there are a number of ways to structure the workflow but people can work within any structure. Some structures are more efficient than others. There is no one structure that is 'right', and any structure chosen will always be mobile, i.e. changing as people leave, change roles and so on.

Think about the pros and cons of each type of structure in terms of the business purpose, design criteria and ideal workflow. Some of the currently common structures are described in Table 5.4. Other structures are less commonly seen, including the back-to-front organization, hollow organization, modular organization and virtual organization. As organization visualization techniques become commonplace it is likely that other forms of organizing will emerge. (See the section below on 'Organization design technologies'.)

As mentioned earlier, be aware too that organizations are never 'pure' in their structure. They may have functional structures in the top levels that then become customer or product structures within which there are project teams or matrix structures. So aim to convert the chosen grouping option into more than one structure possibility: two or three structure options enable testing, comparison and selection of best fit.

7   Test the chosen structure

With the high-level organization chart in hand and the ideal work processes, see whether the design meets certain tests of good design. There are several available. One commonly used is known as nine tests of a good design (described in Chapter 8). Another is a 20-item checklist, the organization design quality check, shown below:

Ask the question: does the new design ...

1   speed up decision-making;
2   eliminate bottlenecks;
3   enable solutions to be found and decisions made at the lowest level;
4   support empowerment of workers;
5   operate efficiently;
6   allow for global standardization with flexibility for appropriate local variation;
7   align across all elements of the organization design;
8   make it easier to do a task (than currently);
9   identify handover points;
10   highlight decision points;
11   map to interdependent departments, business units, etc.;

Table 5.4 Organization structures: pros and cons

Structure	Description	Pros and cons
Functional structure See Figure 5.9	Typically there are heads of finance, marketing, human resources, sales, product development and so on. Each department has a specific function and is usually managed in a self-contained way giving rise to senior management statements like 'We must break down the silo mentality.' Co-ordination of the departments takes place at a senior level.	**Pros** Common expertise/community of practice/critical mass Flexibility of deployment Ease of supervision, development Ease of development of common functional processes **Cons** Disconnected from value chain and big picture Processes cut across functions – white spaces problem Narrow perspective – functional, not business metrics and criteria for decision-making Difficulty of developing general management capability Motivation – may not have line of sight for contribution to the business
Process structure See Figure 5.10	Processes cut across an organization and represent the flow and transformation of information, decisions, materials or resources to serve customers Structure is defined by whole processes that deliver value to customer, or sub-processes, each of which has a clear product, system or service as their output.	**Pros** Cross-functional collaboration and integration: connects white spaces between functional contributions Focus on customer, business outputs and clear metrics – line of sight to business Speed, customer responsiveness Broad knowledge and perspectives **Cons** Internal focus of process teams Divergence of practice – difficulty achieving common processes Difficulty of sharing learning, developing functional skills Difficulty of supervision of multiple functions

Structure	Description	Pros / Cons
Product or market or geographical structure See Figure 5.11	These evolve as a result of trying to get better cross-organizational working. Business units are formed around a product, service and/or geography (for example Commercial Banking in Hong Kong, Retail Banking in the Americas) and there may be a sharing of corporate supports services like HR, IT and finance.	**Pros** Can address regional customer bases, and regional requirements and differences Proximity and cultural kinship Ease of access/distribution Distance from HQ enables local adaptation and innovation If purely customer-focused can present one integrated face to the customer Ability to customize, tailor for the customer Customer response capability Deep understanding of customer requirements **Cons** Difficulty of development of common functional processes Redundancy Local perspective predominates – suboptimization Difficulty of co-ordination and learning across regions Motivation – may not have line of sight for contribution to the overall business Internal focus of customer teams Divergence of practice – difficulty achieving common processes Difficulty of sharing learnings, developing functional skills Difficulty of supervision of multiple functions
Matrix or project structure See Figure 5.12	Combine aspects of both the functional and product structures. Typically employees deploy their technical skills on a project either full- or part-time and report to a project manager on this while reporting to a line manager for the non-project aspects of their work. Some organizations are wholly structured on a matrix basis. In this case there may be 'embedded' functional/product staff who report to the business unit head and to the functional head.	**Pros** Cross functional business focus and integration and emphasis on functional excellence Efficiency of staffing of businesses Functional learning carried between businesses **Cons** Contention between businesses and functions over methods, resources, priorities Matrixed individuals experience role and priority conflict Shadow organizations develop in businesses

Table 5.4 (cont.)

Structure	Description	Pros and cons
Network structure See Figure 5.13	Those which co-ordinate a range of suppliers whose products or services are integral to the end-product. So, for example, Dell computers have Intel chips and Microsoft software. Airline catering is another example, where the meals provided are integral to the service passengers get on airlines, but are not usually part of the core airline business – they are outsourced or sub-contracted. This type of organization has a certain designed-in flexibility which can be advantageous. Adopting this structure requires close attention to be paid to service level agreements and delivering on these.	**Pros** Highly flexible Quick response to markets Empowered employees, decentralized decisions, freed up management Enables fast development and rapid response to market changes **Cons** Can turn into chaos without appropriate corporate culture and successful management controls Lack of deep functional expertise Difficulty with co-ordination between groups Accountability needs to be thought through and made clear

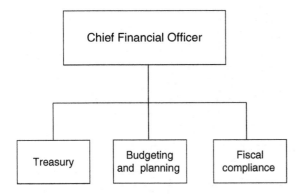

Figure 5.9 Functional structure

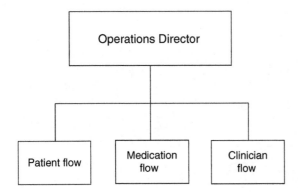

Figure 5.10 Process structure

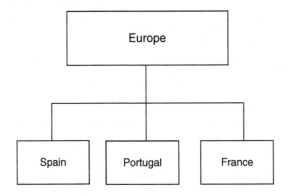

Figure 5.11 Product or market or geographic structure

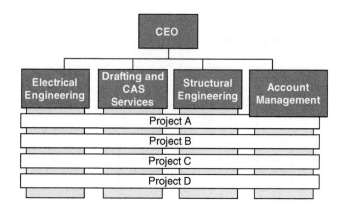

Figure 5.12 Matrix or project structure

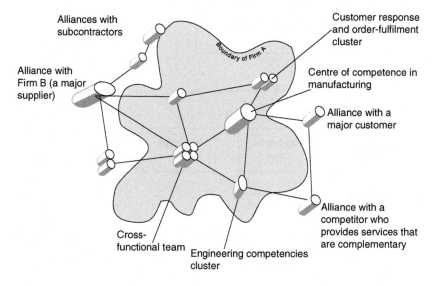

Figure 5.13 Network structure

12 eliminate non-value-added work;
13 eliminate repetition, redundancies, unnecessary delays, rework and unnecessary costs;
14 have the best order or sequence for the activities;
15 have effective interface points that facilitate effective operation;
16 enable good and swift information flow (prevent information gaps);
17 stop conflicts arising over prioritization;
18 make prioritization points clear;

19 help develop trust and respect;
20 allow for incremental and quantum leap improvements over time?

A third test is shown in Table 5.5, the ten tests of organization design (Morgan, 2006). Use more than one test to check whether the organization design meets needs.

OD short

The method for designing the final structure (organization chart) is a systematic seven-step one that builds on information gained in the assess phase of the project. The objective is to design an organization that is fit to deliver the business purpose and strategy but working from the perspective that there is no one right design, and that by developing options and selecting, via comparison and testing, the design best fitted for purpose will emerge.

Organization design technology

Post-2010, several technologies became available that show great promise for revolutionizing the way organizations are visualized and designed. Broadly they each pull data from a range of organizational data sources, for example HR, IT, finance, property, customer and employee surveys, and key performance indicators. These are used to visually 'model the impact of reprioritizing resources, juggling lease breaks, deploying technologies, changing HR practices and more – and immediately see the Net Present Value cost controls, resource impacts, and timelines for your organization' (Quora Consulting, 2012).

The value of these technologies lies in the swift modelling capability and the range of data that can be visually presented to show the impact of structure (or other change choices) on the organization as a whole. With the software it is easy to:

- Drag and drop what-if scenarios with headcount, costs, and skills.
- Build business cases.
- Design and link connected hierarchies, e.g. processes vs. accountabilities vs. people vs. skills to build a system view, track actuals versus scenario. (Concentra.co.uk, 2012)

Assuming reliable organization data, the time taken to model, visualize and select appropriate groupings and structures based on design criteria is likely to be significantly less using the technology than doing the design work the traditional way. It also has the potential to be much more successful (and innovative) as it is built on a range and volume of hard information.

Table 5.5 Ten tests of organization design

Customer-focused	Enabling sets of people working together to produce and deliver products and services that meet customer requirements in the context of changing environments.
Empowered and autonomous units	Units should be designed around whole pieces of work – complete products, services or processes. The goal is to maximize interdependence within the work unit and minimize interdependence among work units. Where there is interdependence among work units linking mechanisms must be consciously thought through and designed in.
Clear direction and goals	Units need to have a very clear purpose, defined output requirements and agreed-on performance measures.
Control of variance at source	Work processes and units should be designed so that variances (errors) can be detected and controlled at source. This implies that the work unit is provided with the information and tools to detect and prevent error.
Social and technical integration	The social and technical systems are seen as interlinked. (Technical systems include workflow, movement of information, work processes.)
Accessible information flow	The flow of information must be designed so that work-unit members can create, receive and transmit information as needed.
Enriched and shared jobs	Broader jobs increase autonomy, learning and individual motivation.
Good people management practices	The design of the department should foster the good people management practices and the achievement of the Inspired People goal.
Management structure, processes and culture that support high performance	Typically high performance is achieved in open and flexible management systems where management is concerned with achieving alignment and 'good fit'. Structures are likely to be matrix- or team-based.
Capacity to reconfigure	In an environment that is changing at an increasing pace there is advantage for those who can anticipate and respond to those changes quickly. Departments should be designed to be adaptive and adaptable.

Source: Morgan, 2006.

Be aware, though, that this almost purely quantitative approach to organization design will not work as a stand-alone process. The 'what-if' scenarios and the information gained from the visualization form the basis for dialogue, collaboration and engagement in reaching a solution that is not only supported by the numbers but also supported by the culture.

Define key metrics

During the design phase, measures of success of both project progress and the benefits the design is intended to realize need to be developed and put into play. Each design will have different benefits to be realized, but generally they will all be aiming towards organizational high performance. Areas covered by bodies like the Baldrige Performance Excellence Program and the European Foundation for Quality Management's (EFQM) model are good start points from which to develop appropriate metrics (if they do not already exist in the organization). Table 5.6 is an adaptation of the EFQM model illustrating areas for metric development.

Measures for tracking project progress are usually a standard part of a project management methodology that builds in milestones, review points, critical success factors and so on. For a book that covers the topic in great detail consider *Project Management Metrics, KPIs, and Dashboards: A Guide to Measuring and Monitoring Project Performance*, by Harold Kerzner (Kerzner, 2011).

The organization design technologies mentioned previously support tracking and monitoring.

OD short

Measuring both OD project progress and the realization of the benefits it is intended to deliver is a critical part of organization design success. There are various ways appropriate metrics for benefits realization can be developed: the use of external frameworks such as the EFQM is one approach. Generally, skilled project managers are well versed in tracking and monitoring the progress of a project.

Tool

When managers think about structure they are generally thinking about 'their' organization and not the interrelationships their departments have with other parts of the organization and with external entities. To be effective the structural choices made in one part of the organization must recognize the consequences both in that part and also in other parts of the wider system.

To help make good structural choices, ask and answer questions related to the following points:

1   **Ensure the structure delivers the strategic goals of the organization**
    - How does the structure enable the required combination of products, services and customer relationships to be delivered?
    - How does the structure minimize costs?
    - How does the structure enable the organization to create added value (e.g. combinations)?
2   **Clarify departmental accountabilities**
    - Each element has clearly articulated responsibilities, accountabilities and performance measures.

Table 5.6 Areas for development of metrics

Organization element	What success looks like
Leadership	Managers are willing to let go and empower people to become involved in improvement teams between departments and with customers and suppliers.
Policy and strategy	Strategic direction is understood by all stakeholders. Visibility championed by top team. Key success indicators (e.g. customer needs) are reviewed at every level in the organization.
People management	Employees are allowed to implement improvement activity without reference to management. A climate conducive to personal development and continuous improvement exists.
Resources	All areas of waste are measured and form part of the improvement plan. Data are gathered to form an accurate view of competitors and used in business planning. Financial plans meet stakeholders' needs.
Processes	Meeting customers' needs is seen as the purpose of the system. Procedures and operating standards are owned by the operators, managers and suppliers.
Customer satisfaction	Continuous research exists to identify and meet individual customer needs. This research is fully integrated into the business planning, improvement and innovation processes.
People satisfaction	Business changes that may adversely affect staff are jointly worked on. Data available to show that all employees feel responsible for both their jobs and improving the organization capability.
Impact on society	Data show that the organization 'betters' legal requirements. Encouragement is given for employees to become involved with supporting local community activities. The public are aware of the environmental strategy.
Business results	Benchmarking is used to compare results with industry and 'best in class' trends. Differences between targets and results are always published and available to stakeholders on request.

Source: Adapted from EFQM Excellence Model.

- Are there strategic deliverables which do not have a clear owner?
- Where there is shared ownership for a strategic deliverable, how will the structure maximize co-ordination?

3 **Make structures as flat as possible**
- Structures are designed to a minimum number of organization levels, e.g. how can the number of layers be reduced and what would be the impact?
- Spans of control guidelines.

4 **Avoid unnecessary duplication**
- Do other parts of the company perform this service? Could it be combined?

- Activities are located together to create economies of scale and centres of expertise.
- Expertise and resource is located where it has optimal impact.
- How much duplication do customers (external or internal) experience?
- Are activities that most need to be co-ordinated located together?

5 **Test that structures are flexible and responsive to change**
- Structures are designed to cope with workload fluctuations and variations in customer demand.
- Consideration of contract staff to cope with peaks.
- In what ways can the structure support predicted future growth and innovation?

6 **Ensure that structure demonstrates appropriate governance and risk standards**
- The organization complies with the regulatory and financial governance framework within which it operates.
- Are there clearly documented risk and governance accountabilities?
- How fast can issues be escalated?

7 **Check structures will support the development of key capabilities**
- The business critical career paths are clearly visible within the structure.
- How are the capability gaps created by the new structures to be resolved (build/buy)?

8 **Remember the organization design process should be consistent between departments**
- Consider roles not people.

Summary

The organization design phase is one that must not be skimped. To get to an appropriate design that will deliver the business strategy, go systematically through each one of seven steps. Involve people who know the work at various levels of the organization in design discussions and decisions. Investigate the use of organization design visualization technologies to improve the efficiency and effectiveness of the design process. Ensure that good metrics are developed and put to use for project tracking and for the benefits realization of the new design.

References

Brown, T. (2009). *Change by Design*. New York: HarperCollins.
Campbell, A. and Goold, M. (2002). 'Nine Tests of Organization Design', *Ashridge Journal*, Summer, 4–9.
Concentra.co.uk. (2012). *OrgVue: Visualize, Design, Deliver*. London: Concentra.
Impact Analysis. (2013). Retrieved 13 February 2013, from Mind Tools: http://www.mindtools.com/pages/article/newTED_96.htm.

International Labour Organization. (2013). 'Policy Integration Department'. Retrieved 13 February 2013, from International Labour Organization: http://www.ilo.org/integration/lang – en/index.htm.

Jacobs, R. (1997). *Real-Time Strategic Change: How to Involve an Entire Organization in Fast and Far-Reaching Change.* San Francisco: Berrett Koehler Publishers Inc.

Kerzner, H. (2011). *Project Management Metrics, KPIs, and Dashboards: A Guide to Measuring and Monitoring Project Performance.* Hoboken, NJ: John Wiley and Sons, Inc.

McLean & Co. (2012). *Determine the Degree of Structural Centralization.* Toronto: McLean & Co.

Morgan, G. (2006). *Images of Organization.* Thousand Oaks, CA: Sage Publications.

Oliver Wyman Delta. (n.d.). *Strategic Organization Design: An Integrated Approach.* New York: Oliver Wyman.

Quora Consulting. (2012). *Workplace Excellence Platform.* Henley-on-Thames, UK: Quora Consulting.

Ragan, M. (2011). 'How NOT to use Yammer: Ragan Offers Prime Example', 23 December. Retrieved 13 February 2013, from Ragan.com: http://www.ragan.com/Main/Articles/How_NOT_to_use_Yammer_Ragan_offers_prime_example_42669.aspx#.

Sharepoint. (2012). 'Benefits'. Retrieved 13 February 2013, from Sharepoint: http://sharepoint.microsoft.com/en-us/Pages/Overview.aspx#.

Valve. (2013). 'Our People'. Retrieved 18 May 2013, from Valve: http://www.valvesoftware.com/company/people.html.

6 Planning to transition

Plans are of little importance, but planning is essential.

Winston Churchill

What you will learn

In this chapter you will learn how to take the high-level organization design to the detailed operational level through four key activities: appointing the transition team, developing a detailed operational design, developing a transition plan and getting the tangible and intangible resources needed to make the transition to the new design smooth and effective.

Overview of phase

In this phase the high-level design is converted into the detailed operational design and from this a project plan with implementation schedule is developed. The plan states specifically what actions and decisions have to be taken to transition from the current to the new design and who is accountable for these.

Another way of seeing this phase is as a detailed gap analysis between the current organization design and the planned one. It requires identifying and listing everything needed to bridge the gap in a logical order – a critical path – with dependencies and time estimates.

This phase takes time and concentrated effort and there is the inherent danger of sacrificing business continuity and performance while focusing on the OD project. One of the main tasks of the leadership team is to handle the balance between getting the new design ready to go whilst keeping the business running effectively.

Key actions in this phase are to:

* Appoint a transition team.
* Develop the detailed operational design.
* Develop a transition plan to deliver the operational design.

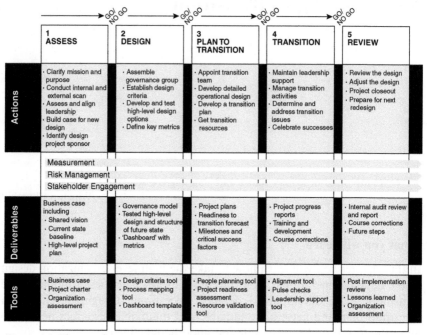

Figure 6.1 Phases of an organization design project

- Get transition resources to ensure the move from current to planned design is smooth.

These four actions are discussed in the course of this chapter. The deliverables from this phase are project plans with milestones and critical success factors, together with a readiness to transition forecast. Useful tools in this phase are the people-planning tool, the project-readiness assessment and the resource-validation tool.

Appoint a transition team

In the design phase, one team of five to eight people worked on developing the high-level design. In this planning-to-transition phase, the work is usually divided between several teams, each focused on an aspect of the work that needs to be done to take the organization from the current design to the redesign. These work streams vary depending on the scope, nature and purpose of the design. It is likely that during the design phase much of the detailed work needed to realize the final redesign will have been identified. The work of detailed operational design is rather different from the work of high-level design and for this reason those who worked on the design team may or may not be involved in this transition planning phase of the work,

Table 6.1 Examples of work streams for two different projects

Work streams: Project 1 – new department setup	Work streams: Project 2 – redesign of call centre
Market proposition	Infrastructure
Management structure	Team-working
Stakeholder work	Performance measurement
People matters	Manpower planning
Culture	Communications and union negotiations
Communications	Equipment requirements
Practicalities/logistics	

although it is good practice to keep some team members engaged as they have the history of how the high-level design was chosen.

Typically, planning-to-transition work streams include one team working on communication/engagement and another on the people aspects of the new design. Table 6.1 shows the work streams for two different projects, one a new department setup and the other the redesign of a call centre.

As with the design team, appoint a representative from each level of the organization to each work stream but, as before, aim to keep the teams small: between four and six people is enough. Remember this 'diagonal slice' of organizational members conforms to the tested principle that those who do the work should redesign it. Without this level of knowledge it is hard to understand, influence or change work patterns at a day-to-day level. Often one member of the original high-level design team leads each work stream. In smaller-scale initiatives, fewer work streams are appropriate: sometimes just one or two are appropriate. In these instances the organization designer is likely to be working with the team leader and two or three team members to develop the detail.

Refer back to the design team member profile presented in Chapter 5. This profile is equally applicable for the selection of transition-planning team members. Bear in mind that people, not surprisingly, find it difficult to remain objective in doing this work – particularly if they see that their role could be under threat. Selecting the right team members requires thought and sensitivity. Individuals selected for the work streams must be capable of influencing colleagues, acting as change agents, being proactive in doing the required work and staying emotionally fit.

Instruct managers nominating team members to give them time to work on the OD project and to be recognized for this work. One organization, in selecting design team members, requested that line managers nominate people they thought would be suitable (in line with the role profile). These people then attended a briefing that included explaining the methods and approaches they would be using, building awareness of handling changes of the type the new design required and clarifying the way the project would be run. At this point nominees were able to opt in or out of project participation: there was no obligation or expectation that nominees had to work as planning team members.

Once the team members were finalized the department heads sent out a note to all staff communicating names of design team members and asking for support for their work, as follows:

> Message from [Organizational Leader's Name]
>
> In a time of budget and climate uncertainty, our redesign moonshot is a unique opportunity to leverage sustainability to achieve cost savings, create jobs, grow the clean energy economy, and improve quality of life. Our goal around the zero environmental footprint gives us a backdrop to frame new approaches to business operations, customer intimacy, and innovations. In that spirit, we are thinking differently about how we set up our workplaces, choose our work styles, and manage our work. As you know we are redesigning our organization and have reached the point of having a high-level design and asked for nominees to help us with the detailed operational design work.
>
> We have now selected members of the various planning-to-transition work streams and I am pleased to let you know that the following people will be working on these.
>
> [Names and work streams here]
>
> This redesign programme will help our organization capitalize on our current challenges to innovate and drive critical business outcomes while working to achieve our goal of zero environmental footprint.
>
> Please support team members by constructively engaging in, contributing your unique perspective to, and actively participating in the programme. Attached you will find an informational one-pager that provides additional details on the work of the planning-to-transition team and your colleagues' new roles and responsibilities.
>
> If you have questions or would like more information on this please contact me.
>
> All the best,
>
> [Organizational Leader]

If the project is a large or complex one consider appointing additional 'change agents' or 'change champions'. Their role is less concerned with the detailed operational planning and more with employee engagement and communication (which should be ramped up in this phase). Look back to Chapter 3 for a bit more on change management. If change champions are appointed it is good practice to consider them as an additional work stream and to manage them as such.

OD short

Those who have worked on the high-level design are not always the best people to take the design into the development of the operational design and implementation plan. For this detailed work select people from a 'diagonal slice' of the organization to have representation from the various levels and types of work.

Develop the detailed operational design

Developing the detailed operational design generally starts with a 'kick-off' meeting with both high-level and operational-level team members present. Think of it as a meeting to 'pass the baton' as in a relay race between one team and the next. Each team's objective is to design, for their part of the whole system, the conditions for peak performance workflow as specified by the high-level design. Their work must align with the work of each of the other teams to deliver something that is more than the sum of the individual parts.

The transition-to-planning kick-off meeting is generally sequenced as follows:

• review and orientation to the work that has happened to this point;
• analysis of the chosen high-level design option (participants retest the design for workability and capability to deliver the future state);
• logging of any amendments, new ideas, issues and concerns;
• identification of obvious areas of work to close the gap between current and new design;
• setup of teams to work on each aspect with team lead designated;
• initial scoping of each team's work and development of broad-brush types of actions and outputs envisaged by each work stream (see Table 6.2 for an example) on an activity card;
• scheduling of design meetings for the life cycle of the planning-to-transition phase.

Working through this gap-closing exercise to arrive at all the tasks and activities required and logging them on activity cards takes anything from four to eight weeks or more, depending on the scale of the project. Each team reports weekly to the project manager, who co-ordinates and monitors their activity. A straightforward and useful way of capturing weekly progress is through ABCD reports, where A = achieved this week; B = the benefit this activity has brought to the project implementation planning; C = any concerns or issues that surfaced during the week; and D = the planned activity for the coming week.

This is a simple format for keeping the transition-planning teams on track. Each team lead completes it for his/her team. The team leads circulate their update to one another for discussion at a weekly face-to-face or telephone meeting with the project manager and organization design consultant. Following the meeting (when actions have been agreed) the project manager consolidates the information in one document and circulates it to the project steering group members. On p. 139 is a worked example extracted from one such report:

Table 6.2 Activity card extract from initial scoping activity in kick-off meeting for culture work stream

Culture work stream

Transition gap	Activity to bridge gap	Why is this activity important?	Success measures of bridging activity	Tools or resources needed to get to outcome, i.e. bridge the gap	Issues or opportunities for decision, clarification, etc. to ensure gap closed	Accountable
Territorialism and 'my patch' thinking	Leaders role model joint problem-solving and sharing of resources	To set a positive example that others will notice and emulate	Scores on culture survey show movement from 'silo' organization to 'collaborative organization'	Review of rewards and recognition to discourage territorialism Better use of collaborative technologies	Leaders may be unwilling to role model What will it cost to adjust reward and recognition system?	RGW

Achieved

- engagement of affected staff started;
- gaps in process design identified (following walk-throughs);
- project teams in place, with team leads appointed;
- high-level implementation plan outlined.

Benefits

- clarity on roles in implementation team;
- alignment around big milestones;
- implementation plan fine-tuned with inputs from team.

Concerns

- need to refine granular, bottom-up activity plan in line with high-level milestones;
- need to ensure more integration working teams;
- concerns regarding resourcing timelines.

Do next week

- refine and simplify bottom-up activity plan with different team leads;
- start consultation process.

As this detailed planning work proceeds, the project manager's focus is on each work stream delivering to target. Weekly status reporting, using the ABCD approach or similar (a more formal weekly reporting approach is shown in Table 6.3), helps the project manager see what is going on across the portfolio of work and in discussion with the organization design consultant and/or the steering group make the adjustments necessary to keep all work streams aligned, focused in the same direction and on track.

Keeping alignment and focus can be a difficult task if there are parallel initiatives or other work going on in the organization that will affect the new design but are outside its scope. Take a look again at Figure 5.2 – reproduced in this chapter as Figure 6.2. It shows eight organizational projects running parallel to the redesign project and several of these were interdependent with the organization redesign but involved different consultants, different steering groups and so on. The project manager on this redesign project noted:

This is a very complex and somewhat frustrating thing to orchestrate. I'm really surprised that some of the co-ordination group members are also participants in one or more of the parallel initiatives but are not making the connections between them. A prime example was the discussion the redesign team had about measuring the quality of customer

Table 6.3 Work stream weekly report form

Work stream:
Key work stream achievements and highlights:
Key questions (tasks in progress):

1 Has scope of the tasks changed?	Yes/No
2 Will target dates be hit?	Yes/No
3 Any technical problems?	Yes/No
4 Any review and approval problems?	Yes/No
5 Any alignment and integration concerns?	Yes/No

Last week's work stream tasks and activities:

Task	Activity	Progress

Work stream tasks and activities for this week:

Task	Activity

Summary from resource schedule:

Previous week (31)	Org.	Consultants	Current week (32)	Org.	Consultants
Planned			Planned		
Actual			Actual		

Milestone status:

Milestone	Agreed date	Delivered date	Reason for revision (as per scope change request)	Revised Date

---

experience as an outcome of the workflow. There was a redesign team member who was also a co-ordination team member and a quality management team member. The quality team is explicitly working on measuring the quality of customer experience yet she did not mention this in the redesign meeting nor appear to recognize that information-sharing across the two initiatives would be immensely helpful and reduce duplication and/or rework.

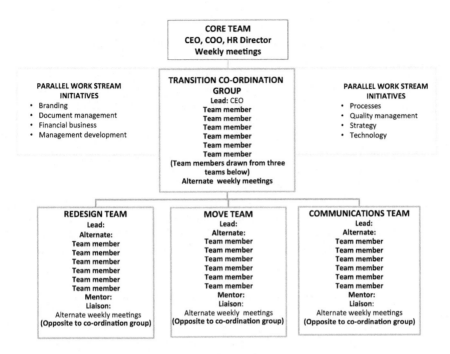

Figure 6.2 Phases of an organization design project

One method of addressing this type of difficulty is to orchestrate collaboration and transparency across the organization, and help those working on the various initiatives to keep asking questions, for example: 'Are we making the connections?' 'What are we missing?' 'What are the possible impacts of what I am doing on other aspects of work I know about?' Also ask employees less closely involved in the projects to raise an alert if they see a 'join the dots' opportunity that may be being missed.

Another method is to follow a more formal eight-step process to align the range of initiatives that are happening outside the scope of the redesign with the redesign. This acts to highlight areas for close co-ordination. The eight steps are:

1   Identify other planned or happening changes whose implementation will make an impact on the redesign project and stakeholders.
2   List the purpose and objectives of each of the other projects, looking for conflicts and overlaps with the redesign.
3   Run workshops or focus groups for the sponsors of existing initiatives in which they collectively review the initiatives, remove conflicts, minimize duplication and co-ordinate implementation.

4   Review implementation timetables for each initiative and produce a matrix that shows when they will affect particular groups or locations. Where the timetables are unknown, make some assumptions and plan for best- and worst-case impacts.
5   Look for instances of potential overload or things being delivered in the wrong order. For example, national installation of new procedures preceding some locations having the equipment installed to make these work.
6   Recommend ways of aligning, channelling or integrating activity in the interests of the whole organization.
7   Log and circulate the overall implementation timetable, highlighting any assumptions of critical dates.
8   Review this timetable regularly.

The act of thinking through and completing the activity cards, mentioned earlier, identifies the gap-closing needed between the current and required design state and reveals the detailed design, which must include the following:

- a developed, articulated and communicable vision of the new organization;
- clearly described and agreed business objectives;
- the detailed organization structure (levels, layers, spans, linkages, co-ordination mechanisms);
- mapped core business processes/workflows with interdependencies and handoff points;
- defined units of work that feed into roles and jobs;
- descriptions of the jobs and person specifications with decision and authority levels.

Once the detailed design is available, do some 'walk-throughs' of the design by taking typical pieces of work or work processes (ones that represent what will be done when the design has been implemented) and testing them in the new state. This shows up obstacles or bottlenecks or unintended consequences of the operational design. Additionally it acts as a check to see if the new design achieves its objectives and conforms to the design criteria. Below is an example of one of the walk-throughs tested by an engineering company (Engco).

Purpose

The purpose of the walk-through is to 'test' the new design (goals, metrics, processes, structure, roles/responsibilities, communication) and demonstrate the design itself is workable and works to achieve the vision of 'Constantly using our ingenuity to improve how we do maintenance'.

What we will do is use two of the three scenarios below to walk-through the new processes, structure, metrics, etc. seeing whether this type of issue is swiftly, effectively, and efficiently resolved in the new design. We'll be checking for a number of things but in the broad sense the day will be about identifying anything that needs to be addressed before we start the implementation run-up.

Use the scenarios to trace paths through the business processes, structures, roles, responsibilities, metrics, communication, and look out for issues of usability, consistency or deviation from items on the checklist. The aim is to identify and log problems, but not to solve them.

The team lead (who may also be an observer) will log the issues.

Issues will be raised for any problems relating to the vision, objectives, and checklist items. For example:

- the business processes fail to provide logical, step-by-step activities to perform the desired tasks;
- for a stage in the process, the inputs (information, resource) are not available at the right time, in the right place to complete the task.

Scenario 1

In the past two weeks retailers have been complaining about the refrigeration and freezer contractor. It seems that the lump sum contract is not working and that the work/repairs are not being completed on time. The retailers are demanding compensation from Engco for their frozen goods that went bad. The retailers also complained that their freezers and chillers needed to be repaired several times (repeat work orders), compounding their losses.

The refrigeration contractor in turn complained to Engco that some of the chillers and freezers that broke down are aged and needed replacing but have not yet provided data to prove that. The contractor also noted that a lot of spare parts for the refrigerators are not available locally and that the hot summer and frequent breakdowns in the industry have led to depletion of spares in the industry. Similar refrigerators are shared with competitors.

Assumptions

Terms and Responsibilities process was done for the year (done in prior year, by January you have the approval).

Refrigeration was identified in the asset plan to be replaced. The refrigerators have not been replaced as yet. Contract was negotiated by the supply chain team. Contract specifications included only equipment list. Monthly service meetings were conducted and KPIs [Key Performance Indicators] were reviewed. Action was to address the problems.

Points to think about

- Is there a plan put in place by Engco for replacing refrigerators and freezers as per Terms and Responsibilities?
- Who do you think is responsible for this breakdown in system?
- Does an on-the-ground retailer have to provide data to prove what he is saying? What other ways were there to predict the failure?

- Isn't summer an annual event? Do we have spare parts within the country in spring?
- Why did this happen? Where is the breakdown? Does the new design mean that this does not happen?
- What makes the new approach better/easier/more streamlined than the current approach?
- How was the review conducted? What tools were used?
- What information and instructions should have been given to the suppliers as part of the bid process?
- What was the accreditation process?

As well as doing some walk-throughs, do an alignment diagnosis. This requires thinking logically about each element of the redesign in relation to each other element. Look for consistency and coherence. Check that all the elements combine to generate the outcomes that are critical to design success. Often this exercise uncovers misalignments (sometimes substantial ones) to address before proceeding. An unaligned system is not robust. Do the exercise with all team members present. An alignment diagnosis tool is given at the end of this chapter.

OD short

Use activity cards for each work stream to list what is needed to take the design from high-level to detailed operational design. Ensure that each work stream is aware of what others are doing so that all the work is proceeding in the same direction. It is the job of the project manager to monitor alignment of this stage of the work. Once all activities are listed conduct 'walk-throughs' of the workflow through the operational design to test its viability.

Develop a transition plan to deliver the operational design

As mentioned in Chapter 5, it is in this planning to transition that project management skills and disciplines become critical. Project management is a well-established discipline and as many books and training programmes plumb the depths of project management, discussing it here would be redundant. Both the Association for Project Managers (www.apm.org.uk) and the Project Management Institute (www.pmi.org) are valuable sources of further information. The Mind Tools and Businessballs websites also have project management information.

The time to flesh out the plan is once all activity cards (Table 6.2) have been developed and the detailed design tested. Careful transition planning makes or breaks transition success. Following the seven steps listed below guides the planning process for those unfamiliar with it.

Seven steps to project planning:

1   For each project work stream, list that work stream's deliverables.
2   Think through the main tasks involved in delivering each.
3   For each task, identify what activities (units of work) are needed to complete the task. While doing this consider:
  (a) complexity of the activity
  (b) skills, experience and attitude required to carry out the activity
  (c) availability of people to carry out the activity
  (d) tools available to make the job easier
  (e) general working environment
  (f) past experience/learning in carrying out this (or similar) activity.
4   Factor in the dependencies that affect completion of the activity. These fall into three categories:
  (a) Mandatory inter-activity dependency. That is, activities within the project which cannot possibly start until another activity within the same project has completed.
  (b) Optional inter-activity dependency. That is, activities within the project which could start at any time but which the project manager would prefer to undertake in a particular sequence.
  (c) Inter-project dependency. That is, the activity within the project which cannot possibly start until an activity within another project has completed.
5   If the project is large enough to warrant it, draw a critical path to get the activities in logical order (www.mindtools.com has a critical path analysis tool).
6   Estimate the time it will take to do the work.
7   Document the work breakdown using a chosen software package.

It is good practice to appoint a skilled project manager to an organization design project but in some cases this is not feasible. Whether there is a specialist project manager or not, there is no need to go overboard on overly sophisticated planning tools – the aim is to use appropriate planning techniques that will deliver an efficient and effective transition plan. For the most part this means including activities by work stream, completion dates for each, milestones, critical dependencies and person accountable for that element. Using a standard project planning software – Wikipedia has a good comparison of these (Wikipedia, 2013) – is almost a necessity, but failing that an Excel spreadsheet does a perfectly good job. Figure 6.3 illustrates a project plan that was constructed in Excel.

One of the questions organization design consultants ask is whether use of project planning techniques and skills is a necessity. Good practice and experience suggest that they are a critical component of project success. But, as stated, they require judicious selection and use. Table 6.4 suggests appropriate approaches to project management by size of OD project. Be aware, though, that size of project is not the only factor to consider when determining what

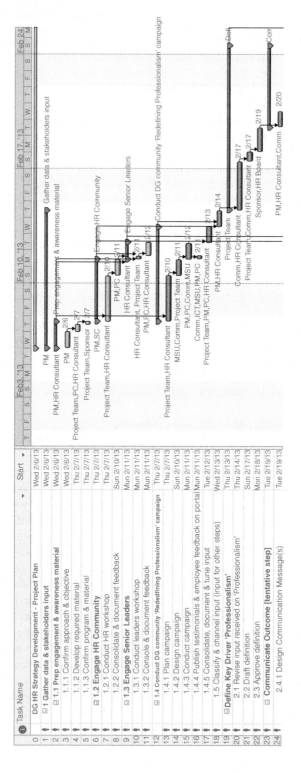

Figure 6.3 Project plan example

Table 6.4 Appropriate aspects of project management by size of OD project

Project size	Characteristics	Approach	Example project
Small	No high-level team (just line and **HR** manager), one small detail-level team Up to 20 days' effort Up to 6 weeks elapsed time from start to finish	Project file set up Line or HR manager takes on project management responsibilities Terms of reference/business plan informally agreed Prioritized to do list as a plan Progress monitored informally Verbal agreement at stage reviews Written de-brief at end	Redesign of part of a department
Medium	Small high-level team 2–5 detail-level teams Up to 40 days' effort Up to 12 weeks elapsed time from start to finish	Project file set up Project manager appointed (likely to be full-time) Terms of reference/business plan formally agreed Written approval/sign-off Written progress reporting Written agreement at milestone reviews Written review at end	Departmental or small business unit redesign (around 250–300 people)
Large	Steering group High-level team of up to 7 people Between 5 and 8 detail-level teams Up to 90 days' effort Up to 9 months elapsed time from start to finish	Programme office set up Programme manager plus project managers appointed Terms of reference/business plan formally agreed Written approval/sign-off Written progress reporting Written agreement at milestone reviews Formal post-implementation review by external team (e.g. internal audit)	Large departmental or whole-organization restructuring (up to 1,000 people)

Table 6.4 (cont.)

Project size	Characteristics	Approach	Example project
Very large	Steering group reporting to board High-level team of up to 7 people Between 8 and 10 detail-level teams Up to 180 days' effort Up to 2 years elapsed time from start to finish	Programme office set up Programme manager plus project managers appointed Terms of reference/business plan formally agreed at highest level of organization Written approval/sign-off Written progress reporting Written agreement at milestone reviews Formal post-implementation review by external team (e.g. internal audit)	Several departments restructuring across the organization or whole-organization restructuring (more than 1,000 people involved)

project management approaches are appropriate. For example, a small but complex redesign may require formal gate reviews and sign-offs.

Regardless of the size of the project, make sure there is:

- a named sponsor commissioning the work and tracking the benefits;
- a skilful project manager to lead the project plan development, and be accountable for its delivery;
- a well-thought-through plan with targets for both costs and benefits;
- thoughtful use of project management techniques;
- clarity about the governance, roles and responsibilities of the project delivery organization;
- an auditable documentary record of the project progress;
- a process for change control and quality assurance;
- a schedule of regular reviews of project progress;
- adequate resource to achieve the plan development.

Note that any organization design project has an impact on employees, and project success is largely dependent on people's effective transition from the current design to the new design. Whether changes in job role form part of the new design or not, supporting people through any transition demands sensitivity, empathy and support from leaders and managers. But it is not always an easy task to action and demonstrate this. In a workshop discussing staff responses to a redesign, one head of division asked:

> How do we address the different ways people accept and/or respond to change? We have to present this reorganization as an inevitability and face the fact that there are different ideas on whether this approach will take us to where we want to get to. I know I will have to address the multiple levels of emotions around change: organization, team, and individual. I'm wondering how we work with the reality that many of us directors in the room today are *not fine* with this redesign. How can we act authentically and lead our teams through it when we are so ambivalent ourselves?

All transition plans should include activity that addresses employees' engagement with the process and responses to it. If the redesign involves role changes, turn to the Appendix for an outline of a typical people-transition process from which a people-transition plan can be developed.

OD short

Developing an appropriate transition plan takes project management skills and techniques. These need not be overly sophisticated but must be focused on ensuring an efficient and effective transition to the new state. It helps to have a professional project manager working on the project. Regardless of

Table 6.5 Example list of transition resources required

Tangible resources required	Intangible resources required
Equipment	Time
Software	Goodwill
Furniture	The right politics
Money	Readiness
People	'The moment'
Workspace	Skills
Data	Trust

whether this is the case, development and then tracking of a transition plan is essential to organization redesign implementation.

Get transition resources to ensure the move from current to planned is smooth

A group of divisional leaders (the high-level organization design team) were asked to list the resources required to move from the current to the planned redesign. Their responses are shown in Table 6.5.

It seems like an eclectic list, but for their project it made sense. What is interesting about it is that it specifies intangibles that are needed: things that the project team felt could be derailers and that needed intentional activity to obtain. Sometimes it is difficult to work out what resources, either tangible or intangible, are needed, and if this is the case try out the 'premortem exercise'. Gary Klein, its author, explains it as follows:

> A premortem is the hypothetical opposite of a postmortem. A postmortem in a medical setting allows health professionals and the family to learn what caused a patient's death. Everyone benefits except, of course, the patient. A premortem in a business setting comes at the beginning of a project rather than the end, so that the project can be improved rather than autopsied. Unlike a typical critiquing session, in which project team members are asked what might go wrong, the premortem operates on the assumption that the patient has died, and so asks what did go wrong. The team members' task is to generate plausible reasons for the project's failure.
>
> A typical premortem begins after the team has been briefed on the plan. The leader starts the exercise by informing everyone that the project has failed spectacularly. Over the next few minutes those in the room independently write down every reason they can think of for the failure – especially the kinds of things they ordinarily wouldn't mention as potential problems, for fear of being impolite. For example, in a session held at one Fortune 500-size company, an executive suggested that a billion-

dollar environmental sustainability project had failed because interest waned when the CEO retired. Another pinned the failure on a dilution of the business case after a government agency revised its policies.

Next the leader asks each team member, starting with the project manager, to read one reason from his or her list; everyone states a different reason until all have been recorded. After the session is over, the project manager reviews the list, looking for ways to strengthen the plan.

...

In a session assessing a research project in a different organization, a senior executive suggested that the project's failure occurred because there had been insufficient time to prepare a business case prior to an upcoming corporate review of product initiatives. During the entire 90-minute kickoff meeting, no one had even mentioned any time constraints. The project manager quickly revised the plan to take the corporate decision cycle into account.

Although many project teams engage in prelaunch risk analysis, the premortem's prospective hindsight approach offers benefits that other methods don't. Indeed, the premortem doesn't just help teams to identify potential problems early on. It also reduces the kind of damn-the-torpedoes attitude often assumed by people who are over-invested in a project. Moreover, in describing weaknesses that no one else has mentioned, team members feel valued for their intelligence and experience, and others learn from them. The exercise also sensitizes the team to pick up early signs of trouble once the project gets under way. In the end, a premortem may be the best way to circumvent any need for a painful postmortem. (Klein, 2007)

However it is done, focusing on what resources are needed to achieve a successful transition is an essential step in the planning process. It may be that in some cases a work stream devoted to obtaining resources would be appropriate, while in other cases each work stream might be responsible for obtaining specific resources. In any event, for each of the resources required in a particular project, ask five questions:

1 Why is this resource necessary – can we do without it?
2 Have we already got this resource and if so where is it?
3 Can/should we obtain it internally and if so how?
4 Can/should we obtain it externally and if so how?
5 How do we mobilize the resource once we have acquired it?

One of the issues around obtaining resources is that control of them is often tied to an organizational power base, or bases. Leaders and others can choose to give or withhold resources depending on their view of the benefits or dis-benefits of the organization design. This organization design consultant reported an example of such an issue that can arise around obtaining resources:

The success of our new organization design depends, in large measure, on obtaining the go-ahead to invest in a new patient scheduling system. We have to have this if we are to operate the new patient flow and organization structure that supports it. Our current system simply doesn't do the job. But the IT Director is not convinced that this is a priority and is arguing in favour of putting resources into wifi capability in the new building. This would help staff keep in touch with each other and does benefit the patient flow but it isn't the priority as far as the frontline medical providers, nurses and medical assistants are concerned. At this point it seems to be whoever can get the ear of the COO wins. It's not a good situation to be in. Ideally we would have both but with the budget the way it is there's only one winner here.

Working with this 'shadow side' of the organization takes awareness of and ability to operate within five dimensions (Rodgers, 2007):

1   The impact of real-life messiness and informality on a planned organization design which confounds the idea of how a plan should work.
2   The perspectives and idiosyncrasies of individuals that can run counter to organizational expectations or wants.
3   The operation of the organization as a social system 'with its in-groups, out-groups, social routines and rituals', all of which distort the interrelationships and decision-making processes implicit in a transition plan.
4   The organization as a political system which recognizes that the organization reflects a diverse range of viewpoints, motivations and self-interests leading to competing coalitions of people, each seeking to define the organization's agenda and to shape its course of action.
5   The cultural assumptions of the organization through which many of the above characteristics become embedded and taken-for-granted ways of operating – whether these are outside people's awareness or known but undiscussable.

Peter Senge describes these aspects of the organization in terms of ten key challenges for organization consultants and designers that manifest in statements like:

'We don't have time for this stuff.'
'We have no help.'
'This stuff isn't relevant.'
'You're not walking the talk.'
'This stuff is ****.'
'This stuff isn't working.'
'You don't understand what we do.'
'Who's in charge of doing this?'
'We keep re-inventing the wheel.'
'Where are we going and what are we here for?' (Senge, 1999)

Asked to identify what the key resource shortage and requirement is, many leaders will say that it is the time to work on the organization design whilst maintaining business continuity. This is a very real resource issue and one that Peter Senge writes on with insight. He points out that a design project will fail if people do not commit time to it and makes a number of suggestions on how to think differently about time in order to make it more flexible and available. Here are eight of the many strategies he presents that have proved effective to those managing and working on OD projects.

Integrate initiatives: combine several different initiatives, even if they started with different champions and participants. The goal is to share the resources, enable progress on key issues and mitigate risks associated with interfaces, overlap and duplication.

Block off time for focus and concentration: organize working and design sessions in blocks of time. A one-day workshop is far more intense and productive than two half-days. Time blocks encourage people to reflect and concentrate. A block of time makes better use of this scarce resource than short bursts of time.

Trust people to control their own use of time: those asked to work on the project have to manage their own resource balance of keeping their 'day job' going and doing the design work. Allow people to schedule themselves and reward them on results. Letting people schedule their own time builds motivation and trust.

Recognize the value of unstructured time: people who work on design projects must keep the pace up. They have to meet deadlines and targets. Too tight a focus on this is counter-productive. People's productivity increases if they meet one another casually to compare notes, see how things are going and discuss concerns or issues. Without the pressure to rush into a decision or produce immediate results they can sometimes solve problems and gain insights to the benefit of the project.

Build the capability to eliminate unnecessary tasks: this not only saves resource it frees up resource for other purposes. Encouraging people to stop doing things may seem counter-intuitive but many tasks are done because they always have been, not because they serve a useful purpose at this point. For example, stop the generation of reports that no one reads. Cancel regularly scheduled meetings that have no specific purpose or decision-making role.

Say 'no' to political game playing: lobbying and influencing stakeholders to support the project might involve politics and game-playing but keep focus on the interests of the organization and the customer. Maintain integrity and demonstrate openness and fairness in dealings. (Unfortunately, in some organizations, this approach may be a 'career limiter'.)

Say 'no' to non-essential demands: check that what is done makes the best use of people's time. If something non-essential is in the schedule, does it need doing? Distinguish between urgent and important. Cut out the non-essentials to give people more unstructured time.

> **Experiment with time**: ask questions about time use in your organiza-
> tion. (Senge, 1999)

In his useful book *QBQ! The Question behind the Question: Practicing Personal Accountability at Work and in Life* (Miller, 2004), the author suggests that personal accountability begins with asking a 'what' or 'how 'question', contains an 'I' and focuses on action. Try this with questions about time use. Answer the questions 'What if our purpose is vital, how can I avoid wasting the time we have to get there?' Assess the problems with time flexibility – what controls the amount of time availability in the organization? (Adapted from Miller, 2004.)

Since obtaining resources for organization design work is challenging in a number of ways organization designers are often in the position of working out how to deliver a project with fewer resources than required, with a shifting context in terms of potential resource allocation and a potential political minefield around the whole resource issue. This calls for workarounds, creative thinking and judicious deployment of the resources that are forthcoming. Although it may feel easier to focus on the explicit, tangible resources required and aim to get these, the implicit, intangible resources are often more useful in driving to a smooth transition. These intangible resources sit in what Chris Rodgers calls 'informal coalitions', and he describes the arena as:

> Power-laden and political. It involves the coming together of people with differing and often competing interpretations, interests, ideologies, and identities. Much of the process takes place informally, 'in the shadows' of the formal structures, systems and procedures. And it is influenced by taken-for-granted patterns of assumptions that have arisen over time as a result of past sense-making-cum-action-taking interactions. All of these factors, and others, arise because organizations are dynamic networks of *people* interacting with each other.

Rodgers continues by making the point that 'it seems to me that an understanding of these dynamics, and how they impact upon business change and performance, should be at the heart of HR practice. Sadly, it isn't' (Rodgers 2013).

OD short

Working out what resources are needed, identifying where to find them and then working with both the 'legitimate' and the shadow side of the organization to actually get the resources requires a range of skills, techniques and intentional application of these. Any organization design project requires a variety of resources to take the organization from current to new design. Consider whether the intangible, shadow-side resources are more valuable to project success than the tangible, 'legitimate'-side organizational resources.

Table 6.6 Project readiness to transition

Business case

The reasons for launching the project are clearly defined.	1□□□□□5
The impact to the business is clear.	1□□□□□5
Leaders of the initiatives are supportive of and committed to the project.	1□□□□□5
The priority of this project with respect to other projects is clear.	1□□□□□5
The business case for this project creates a sense of urgency or priority for everyone involved.	1□□□□□5
We are confident that we are 'on the same page' with this project.	1□□□□□5

Vision clarity

Leaders have a compelling vision of the benefits of this project.	1□□□□□5
The vision is specific enough to give people a good indication of how they will be doing things differently.	1□□□□□5
People affected by the project are able to answer the question, 'What's in it for me?'	1□□□□□5
It is clear how this initiative links to the overall strategy and LRP.	1□□□□□5
The vision creates understanding and excitement about the change.	1□□□□□5

Change leadership and accountability

Leaders personally demonstrate the commitment to achieving the project objectives through public and private actions.	1□□□□□5
Leaders are accountable for the expected results of the project.	1□□□□□5
Leaders are actively involved in the communication process and are helping to create energy and enthusiasm around the change.	1□□□□□5
Leaders are helping to remove barriers and allocate the resources needed to accomplish the change (time, best people and funds).	1□□□□□5
Leaders are staying focused on this initiative even when other problems or issues are competing for their attention.	1□□□□□5

Change-specific communication

The internal messages we have planned are informative and credible and will address the questions of most employees.	1□□□□□5
We have a consistent and agreed message to deliver to our employees.	1□□□□□5
The messages we have planned for our other stakeholders (franchisees, suppliers, etc.) are informative and credible and will address the questions they have.	1□□□□□5
We have a consistent and agreed message to deliver to our stakeholders.	1□□□□□5
We have plans to communicate in a timely and open fashion and have contingency plans if functional or departmental boundaries become obstacles.	1□□□□□5
We are planning to achieve a dialogue rather than a one-way stream of information.	1□□□□□5

Stakeholder commitment

We have given careful thought to how this project affects groups both within and outside the company, and how they might respond.	1□□□□□5
We are clear on the people issues, as well as the technical and financial issues.	1□□□□□5

Table 6.6 (cont.)

We are planning to monitor people's reactions and address any issues as they arise.	1☐☐☐☐☐5
We are planning opportunities to involve people or groups of people as soon as we announce.	1☐☐☐☐☐5
We will be encouraging people who are affected by the change to voice their concerns.	1☐☐☐☐☐5

Increasing change capability

We recognize that this major change puts extra stress on people, and have planned steps to help people cope.	1☐☐☐☐☐5
We recognize that this major change requires special management skills and techniques and have plans to develop these skills rapidly if needed.	1☐☐☐☐☐5
Our plans for this change include attention to technical and financial issues as well as people issues.	1☐☐☐☐☐5
We have taken the time to identify and share lessons learned from past change-implementation efforts.	1☐☐☐☐☐5
We are not assuming that people in our organization accept that change has become a way of life for us, and are planning to help them reach this acceptance.	1☐☐☐☐☐5

Project planning and resourcing

We are ensuring that effective project management policies and procedures are established and consistently followed.	1☐☐☐☐☐5
We will request (if necessary) that the right resources, based on knowledge and skills, are allocated to the initiatives.	1☐☐☐☐☐5
We have confirmed that people, process and technology issues are integrated and addressed throughout the project implementation plan.	1☐☐☐☐☐5
We have set clear expectations for the project team(s) regarding roles, responsibilities and scope.	1☐☐☐☐☐5
We show obvious evidence of an overall motivation and drive to make the project work.	1☐☐☐☐☐5
We have a realistic view of the financial resource allocation and emotional commitment level we will be required to contribute in order to make the project work.	1☐☐☐☐☐5
We have the technical capacity and change-management skills to marshal our workforce behind the project.	1☐☐☐☐☐5
We have identified any potentially significant/imminent derailers to project development and delivery.	1☐☐☐☐☐5
We are confident that we have the staying power to handle the scope and pace of the project over the long haul.	1☐☐☐☐☐5

Tool

Project readiness to transition

This assessment addresses readiness to implement a project. The checklist in Table 6.6 covers a broad range of project-readiness issues for consideration when considering implementation. Use it at the end of this planning-to-transition phase. It can also be used at the end of the assess and design phases as an ongoing checklist.

Score:

5	We are ready to go.
4	We still have a few things to do before we are ready.
3	We have a significant amount of work to do before we are ready.
2	We are only beginning to work on this.
1	We haven't begun to think about this yet.
N/A	Not applicable or do not know.

Summary

It is essential to carry out the planning-to-transition phase of an organization design project in an intentional manner using tested project management techniques to develop a robust transition plan. Conduct this phase by establishing work streams to plan out each part of the organization design transition. Each work stream should comprise between four and eight members with the personality and skillset to represent the various levels of the organization. During this phase a number of resource challenges are likely to emerge – both for tangible and intangible resources. Recognizing and working with the tension between the 'legitimate' and 'shadow side' of the organization is paramount in this phase.

References

Klein, G. (2007). 'Performing a Project Premortem', September. Retrieved 1 March 2013, from Applied Research Associates, Inc: http://www.ara.com/Newsroom_Whatsnew/press_releases/pr_harvard_business_review.html.

Miller, J. G. (2004). *QBQ! The Question behind the Question: Practicing Personal Accountability at Work and in Life.* New York: Penguin Group.

Rodgers, C. (2007). *Informal Coalitions: Mastering the Hidden Dynamics of Organizational Change.* New York: Palgrave Macmillan.

Rodgers, C. (2013). 'Thoughts on "Soft Power" and the Dynamics of Informal Coalitions in Organizations', 13 January. Retrieved 2 March 2013, from Informal Coalitions: http://informalcoalitions.typepad.com/informal_coalitions/2013/01/soft-power-and-informal-coalitions.html.

Senge, P. E. (1999). *The Dance of Change: The Challenges to Sustaining Momentum in Learning Organizations.* New York: Doubleday/Currency.

Wikipedia. (2013). 'Comparison of Project Management Software'. Retrieved 28 February 2013, from Wikipedia: http://en.wikipedia.org/wiki/Comparison_of_project-management_software.

7 Transition

Not in his goals but in his transitions is man great.

Ralph Waldo Emerson

What you will learn

This chapter considers the transition phase of an organization design project. It discusses the role of leaders during this phase. Keeping transition momentum going in the face of day-to-day work during this phase is discussed along with a number of commonly emerging issues and the suggestion is made that celebrating successes can help.

Overview of phase

The transition phase – see Figure 7.1 – of an OD project is when things are most likely to go wrong. People have lived through the excitement of creating the design and the detail of planning its implementation, and now have to get to grips with transitioning to the new design and the new ways of working it brings. They find this much easier said than done.

However, if the transition has been thoroughly planned it will be easier to deal with the usual problems that arise during the transition than if there had been no, or sketchy, planning. Transition is usually about placing people into new jobs or changing aspects of their current jobs, putting new processes into place, making sure systems are aligned to deliver the outcomes specified and so on.

How the transition is initiated is dependent on various factors including the type of design project, cost of transitioning, risk to business continuity, reliability of any new IT systems, availability of skilled staff resources and context of the design. There are three common ways of transitioning:

- 'Big bang', where there is a given date when everything starts anew. A hospital move is an example of this 'big bang' transition, as the following description illustrates:

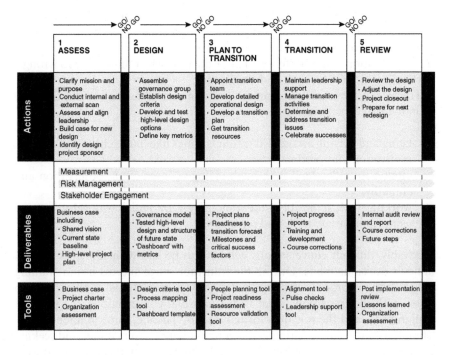

	1 **ASSESS**	2 **DESIGN**	3 **PLAN TO TRANSITION**	4 **TRANSITION**	5 **REVIEW**
Actions	· Clarify mission and purpose · Conduct internal and external scan · Assess and align leadership · Build case for new design · Identify design project sponsor	· Assemble governance group · Establish design criteria · Develop and test high-level design options · Define key metrics	· Appoint transition team · Develop detailed operational design · Develop a transition plan · Get transition resources	· Maintain leadership support · Manage transition activities · Determine and address transition issues · Celebrate successes	· Review the design · Adjust the design · Project closeout · Prepare for next redesign
	Measurement				
	Risk Management				
	Stakeholder Engagement				
Deliverables	Business case including · Shared vision · Current state baseline · High-level project plan	· Governance model · Tested high-level design and structure of future state · 'Dashboard' with metrics	· Project plans · Readiness to transition forecast · Milestones and critical success factors	· Project progress reports · Training and development · Course corrections	· Internal audit review and report · Course corrections · Future steps
Tools	· Business case · Project charter · Organization assessment	· Design criteria tool · Process mapping tool · Dashboard template	· People planning tool · Project readiness assessment · Resource validation tool	· Alignment tool · Pulse checks · Leadership support tool	· Post implementation review · Lessons learned · Organization assessment

Figure 7.1 Phases of an organization design project

We moved on May 15. The process was not about moving furniture and fixtures. It was about moving living, breathing hospital patients from one location to another with no interruption in care or sacrifice in service. We planned and executed it over months with military precision.

The move to the new location meant changing the way we work and we put a great deal of time and effort into better understanding how patients move through treatment, redesigning the process from their perspective. We've made changes to make sure all activities are as efficient as possible and add real value to patient care. (Adapted from McRae, 2012)

- Rolling/phased programme. This is where the transition starts with some groups, or with pilot units, or in one location or operating area and then rolls through others. This is a useful approach if things like consulting with staff forums take longer in one place than in another. It also allows for learning from each rollout to be tracked and adjustments made to the rollout plan as things proceed.
- Parallel tracks. This is where the new design is initiated alongside the current design. The danger in this approach is that there will be no cut-over to the new and close-down of the old. Nevertheless it can be useful as a risk-mitigation strategy, particularly where computer software is involved.

Remember, as the transition progresses, for everyone who sees the changes as beneficial there will be someone who sees the changes as detrimental. Simultaneously some will see a muddle erupt and others will see clarity emerge. Everyone's experience of what is happening to change the design of the organization will be different. This is the time when things can go wrong – particularly if staff feel lost and confused.

The role of the transition team is to recognize and respond to this diversity of individual experience by:

- being and staying aware of it through things like 'pulse checks' of morale, motivation and productivity;
- aiming to understand it through dialogue, interaction, observation and empathy;
- working with it flexibly and responsively by judiciously selecting and using appropriate tools and techniques.

Inevitably, difficult conversations will have to be had with some people and difficult decisions made. During the transition stage success lies in 'valuing the continuous process of people's day-to-day interactions' as they come to terms with the transition – that is, the informal conversations, the political realignments and the role of informal leaders. There is value in intentionally 'stimulating and participating in meaning-making conversations, and seeking to mobilize the actions of people around important emerging themes during this period' (Rodgers, 2012a).

Regardless of set-piece events of communications involving senior people who are communicating 'on message', employees are interpreting and evaluating what is going on 'continuously and mundanely' and relating it to their expectations and needs (Rodgers, 2012a). Working with this informal organizational meaning-making is a thread that runs through the four main activities of this phase:

1   maintaining leadership support;
2   managing transition activities;
3   determining and addressing transition issues;
4   celebrating successes.

Each of these is discussed in this chapter.

Maintaining leadership support

Leadership is a slippery topic. Although there has been a huge amount of research on it, for the most part this has created competing theories and none-too-actionable information. In 1985 three researchers summed up the leadership research position, saying: 'We have been unable to generate an understanding of leadership that is both intellectually compelling and emotionally satisfying. The concept of leadership remains largely elusive and enigmatic' (Meindel *et al.*, 1985), and this statement holds true today.

This makes the notion of 'maintaining leadership support' equally challenging for the organization design team, as there are several types of leaders: formal and informal; managerial and technical; thought leaders; and influencers. In the radical change that organization design usually implies various types and levels of leadership emerge – often at unexpected times and in unexpected places.

Typically organization designers focus on maintaining support of the formal leaders: those in recognized authority and/or hierarchical positions, whose 'legitimate' power is overtly recognized and/or reinforced through formal authority networks and codified in the formal organization charts. This focus is insufficient, because although organizations are designed to be power networks, through which influence is exerted and results achieved, there are sources of power in organizations other than formal authority, many of these having more power than 'legitimate' power holders.

Organizations are a minefield of informal systems, processes and interactions that frequently contravene, sometimes contradict, and often overrule the formal policies, instructions, organization charts and control mechanisms. The fact that this is the case is widely known but not often acknowledged or brought out into the open by people and rarely is it tackled in a standard organization design or change-management methodology. More often than not, these realities remain publicly undiscussed and undiscussable, but everyone is aware of them. They are the unwritten rules of the game and immensely powerful ones.

Anyone who works in an enterprise involving people and interactions knows that despite the way things are 'supposed' to be, in practice people continually jockey for power, position, turf and resources. It is an organizational fact that organizations consist of competing groups of people engaged in legitimate and illegitimate conflicts to define the agenda of the organization and in doing so shape its course of action.

Success in design projects depends on gaining and then maintaining the support of both the leaders in the legitimate side of the organization and the leaders in this 'shadow side' – the part of an organization described as those 'realities that often disrupt, and sometimes benefit the business but are not dealt with in the formal settings of the organization' (Egan, 1994). Both aspects are shown on the systems model (Figure 1.3) as the formal (legitimate) and informal (shadow) organization.

Once the power of both the formal and informal organization is recognized it is possible to reassess how organizational members think and talk about leadership, allowing project team members to include in their alignment activity the informal leaders and influencers as well as the formal leaders (who may or may not be influencers). Reframing notions of leadership is not that easy, but Chris Rodgers offers seven ways of doing so. He makes the point that 'These reflect radically different assumptions about how organizations work from those that currently inform mainstream descriptions of, and prescriptions for, leadership practice. But they accord much more closely with today's experienced realities of organizational life – including what leaders and others do in practice.'

1   **From elite practice to emergent property** Leadership would be recognized as an emergent property of people in relationship, not as an elite practice confined to *individuals* at senior levels in organizations. That is, it would be understood as a complex social process enacted by many people in the normal course of their everyday interactions; rather than as a rational, scientific endeavour practised by a few gifted and formally appointed leaders.

2   **From individual dynamism to interactional dynamics** The approaches to selecting, developing and recognizing the contributions of formal leaders would shift considerably. The focus would be on the complex dynamics of interaction and the implications of these for leadership practice (i.e. on organizational dynamics), rather than on the current preoccupation with the traits, styles, competencies and so on of individuals who occupy formal leadership positions (i.e. on the so-called 'best practice' attributes of individual actors).

3   **From controlling to contributing** Those in formal leadership positions (as well as others who prescribe leadership behaviours or commentate upon their performance) would accept that they were not in control of organizational outcomes. As powerful participants in the ongoing process of social interaction, they would of course be contributing to those dynamics and outcomes in important and influential ways – whether intentionally or not. But they would not be *in control* of them. The concept of leadership and the expectations of others about the nature and omnipotence of the role would thus be substantially different from those which shape today's understanding and rhetoric.

4   **From diagnosis to dialogue** The currently dominant view on leadership, based on a rational-scientific model of organizational dynamics, assumes that strategic and operational challenges can be dealt with by expert diagnosis – whether a leader's own or that offered by specialist advisers. In contrast, an *informal coalitions* perspective would see it as inappropriate to look at organizations through a scientific lens; with its evidence-based explanations, rigorous analytical methods and claims of predictability and certainty of outcome. Instead, it would recognize that knowledge in a social process is co-created through the everyday conversations and interactions that take place locally – between *specific people*, at *specific times* and in *specific circumstances*. Ongoing dialogue, focusing on joint sense-making-cum-action-taking, and seeking to tap into people's collective wisdom, would therefore be seen as the essence of strategic and operational leadership.

5 **From standing out to standing in** Today's conception of organizational leadership assumes that this is provided by someone (or a cadre of people) with outstanding ability – *individuals* who 'stand out from the crowd' in terms of their intellectual capacity, charisma, vision, courage, risk appetite and so on. It is seen as being exercised by standing apart from the minutiae of the action to see and address the 'big picture' from a position of objectivity. Instead, from an *informal coalitions* viewpoint, a central element of the formal leadership role would be one of 'standing in' – that is, *actively participating* in the conversations around important emerging issues. This means paying attention to what's going on in the day-to-day conversations and interactions *that comprise the organization*; seeking to shift the patterns and content of interactions in organizationally beneficial ways.

6 **From certainty to curiosity** The search for, and expectancy of, certainty and predictability would be replaced by the valuing and practice of curiosity. That is, there would be a preference for leading through questions, rather than a presumption that the leader's role is to provide all of the answers; a capacity to embrace uncertainty and to accept a position of 'not knowing'; a focus on noticing and exploring underlying patterns of thinking, feeling and behaving; and an ability to articulate these in ways that resonate with staff.

7 **From colluding to confronting** Realizing the above shifts in thinking and practice would bring with it an increasing tendency for people (and particularly leaders) to confront – rather than collude with – the basic myths that sustain current management orthodoxy. This tendency for people to confront rather than collude with policies and practices that run counter to their lived experience would also extend to the exposure and exploration of other shadow-side themes and behaviours, where previously these would have remained hidden and undiscussable. (Rodgers, 2012b)

These seven points take some reflecting on before they lead to actions and activities that would sensitively maintain, attract and co-opt the formal and informal leadership support needed in this phase. But several possibilities are hinted at – all focused on encouraging a level of engagement in the process that is central to maintaining support. Table 7.1 lists some of these possible actions.

Informal and formal leadership support can be strengthened 'when conversations and interactions break out of existing channels and novel conversational themes arise'. Acting on some of the seven reframing activities is a step in this direction.

OD short

Maintaining leadership support through the transition stage is critical to redesign success. It is important to bear in mind that leaders in this situation are not

Table 7.1 Reframing leadership and suggested actions to gain support

Reframing leadership	Action
From elite practice to emergent property	Encourage active engagement in the design process from a diversity of stakeholders. Identify where the influencers are, listen attentively to their point of view and ask what they can offer in the way of support.
From individual dynamism to interactional dynamics	Look for formal and informal leaders who have demonstrated interest in the future of the organization and the part they can play in it, see where suggestions and experiments are happening and invite these initiators to support.
From controlling to contributing	Initiate forums for discussion on where and how people can contribute to transition success. One organization instituted the idea of the 'Giraffe Award' for 'sticking your neck out' – in the redesign transition many ideas were put forward and actioned for making the transition smooth.
From diagnosis to dialogue	Interact with the gossip and grapevine. Be an authentic part of the conversations providing trustworthy perspectives and insights.
From standing out to standing in	Participate in shifting and nudging the conversations and interactions in a way that empowers individuals to support and engage positively.
From certainty to curiosity	Communicate the unknown and the uncertain as well as the known. Within the communications ask 'what if?' questions that foster interaction and engagement.
From colluding to confronting	Open up discussions on matters that are relevant but not usually brought up – leadership 'entitlement' to a particular size of office is an example.

just the formal leaders in the hierarchy representing the legitimate power in the organization. Equally important, and in some circumstances more important, are the informal leaders and influencers who emerge at various points in the transition process. Intentionally acting to obtain and maintain the support of both legitimate and informal leaders is a key activity in the transition phase.

Managing transition activities

As implied in the previous section, successful transition from current state to planned state requires aligning the unwritten rules of the game with the written rules. This means having the courage to put on the table what one organization called 'the bleeding rhinoceros head'. Unless this happens defensive behaviour, blocking, non-compliance and other potential showstoppers are likely to emerge. Although it is possible to force through a change, the consequences are usually punitive. It is in the transition phase that the shadow side of the organization is the most powerful, and attracting this to work on-side is a key activity to focus on. It becomes critical because in this phase the reality of the redesign becomes apparent to people, their roles and patterns of work and interactions change and they feel an emotional impact that they may not have been able to predict in advance. In many instances the original employee value proposition that drew them to the organization is fractured.

Although there is a tendency to concentrate on the problems arising and the negative side of a transition, consider instead (or, at least, as well) looking at the things that are going well and the positive side of transition. Here the field of positive psychology – the scientific study of what goes right in life and makes life worth living – offers sound and tested methods for 'enabling institutions' in the domains of work, love, play and service that are applicable in this transition phase (Peterson, 2006).

> The scientific base of positive psychology offers organizations an understanding of human growth and change that challenges the prevailing view of people as 'resistant to change'. It recognizes people as resourceful and adaptive, and sees the ability to change behaviour as an inherent growth and survival skill. A practical methodology that has grown up in parallel with positive psychology and that we consider to be part of this emerging field is appreciative inquiry. (Lewis *et al.*, 2008)

Appreciative inquiry is perhaps the best known of the systematic approaches to changing business performance through a phased approach (Figure 7.2) but the evolving neuroscience field is resulting in more systemic ways of using insights from positive psychology.

There is a wealth of material on the topic of positive psychology. Founders of the field include Martin Seligman, Barbara Frederickson, Mihaly Csikszentmihalyi and Ed Diener. The University of Pennsylvania's Authentic Happiness site is a good place to look for further information and resources. Making a choice to manage transition activities from a mindset of 'what's going well' is more energizing (and effective) than approaching the transition management from a mindset of 'what are the problems'.

In brief, managing the transition requires:

- implementing the plan developed in the planning-to-transition phase;
- managing the risks in this phase;
- doing both in a way that uses a positive psychology mindset and showing consideration (kindness and fairness) and support (concern and encouragement) towards employees.

Each is discussed in more detail below.

Implementing the plan involves maintaining the project or programme office and sticking to disciplines around project management techniques. (Look back at Chapter 6 for more on project management.)

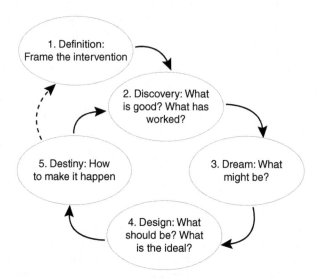

Figure 7.2 Phases of appreciative inquiry work
Source: Sette, 2008.

Critical at this point is to confirm once again that there are clear performance goals in mind and to know why, when and how the new design is intended to achieve these. Assessors of change projects suggest that unless measurable results are delivered quickly a project is likely fail or have 'ambivalent success' (Pettigrew, 1998). Key to good transition is tracking exactly what impact it is having on business performance in terms of things like customer service, increase in sales or revenue, increase in employee satisfaction, decrease in waste or rework. Completion of a simple matrix (Table 7.2) is a useful way of recording what is aimed for. It is important to make regular checks on the impact the transition is having on performance. (*Note*: there may not be a direct cause/effect, but it provides a good indicator.)

Achieving transition-plan milestones and results is crucial to maintaining momentum and avoiding cynicism. The old adage holds true – nothing succeeds like success. Plan to have quick wins within the first two weeks of the start of the transition. A tracking template like Table 7.3 keeps tabs on progress, issues and achievements.

Managing the risks. Success in aligning the informal and shadow side of the organization with the formal side, goals and plans is not of itself sufficient to bring quick wins, engagement and early results. Even given optimum conditions, a project is not necessarily going to be successful. The unforeseen might strike – a sudden change at the top, a crisis that hits the whole organization or something else that diverts attention. The risk-assessment and mitigation planning done in earlier phases of the organization design work must continue during this transition phase.

Table 7.2 Example of transition deliverables

Performance area (percentages)	Current performance	Target performance	What impact is the transition having (±)	Action required
Cost of sales				
Market share				
Customer complaints				
Employee absence rates				
Call-handling				
Employee satisfaction				

Table 7.3 Transition plan tracking template

Project delivery status	Key status indicators
STATUS SUMMARY [one-line summary of overall status]	Progress Scope Resources Comms Issues Costs IT
Status for each element current period (INDICATE AS Red, Green or Amber)	
STATUS RATIONALE [rationale for each non-green indicator]	
Status for each element previous period (INDICATE AS Red, Green or Amber)	
KEY ACHIEVEMENTS/QUICK WINS/WHAT'S GOING WELL THIS WEEK	
SLIPPAGE AGAINST PLAN THIS WEEK: IMPACT AND ACTIONS	

Indeed, it is worth ramping up the risk-management aspect of the project at this point because, as noted, people have emotional reactions to changes that affect them and the form these reactions will take is hard to predict in advance of the change actually happening. This increases the risk in transition if the plan does not deliver the intended benefit, or if the new state begins to seriously disrupt normal business operations or if relationships are fractured or broken because of the change. (These risks may have been mitigated in the design phase but this does not always happen.)

Because risk management is covered in many books, training courses and events on programme and project management this book does not go into any detail. But there are three specific aspects of risk management it is useful to be aware of in transitioning to a new organization design:

1　As the transition proceeds, risks will bubble to the top and then fall in an unpredictable way. Because the environment is dynamic, what might be an acceptable risk today will be unacceptable tomorrow. Ensure regular reassessment.

2　Different stakeholders have different attitudes to risk. Surfacing and acknowledging these different perspectives is helpful. As transition proceeds aim to come to shared understanding of which risks are acceptable and which are unacceptable to the project. For example, is it acceptable that turnover increases as people experience the reality of the new design?

3　There is a tendency to focus risk identification and assessment on the formal parts of the organization. During transition more of the risks lie in the informal organization. So identify risks in all four aspects of the organization shown in the systems model (Figure 1.3) – work, people, informal organization, formal organization – as well as risks in the operational context/external environment that could have an impact on the transition.

One example of the informal organization at work in what was probably a somewhat predictable risk in the transition of the BBC's office was published in the *London Evening Standard*:

> Signs seem to be proliferating at the BBC's revamped Broadcasting House. Last week the Londoner reported that a notice had been put above a kitchen sink in the current affairs department asking staff to refrain from washing their feet there. Another sign has appeared in the ladies' lavatories. It reads 'Senior Management Hotdesks'.
>
> It had obviously been dumped there by someone who is less than impressed by staff directives at the BBC's new corporate cathedral.
>
> 'Is it the first act of vandalism?' my BBC mole asks. Or is it perhaps a cry for help? (*London Evening Standard*, 2013)

Showing consideration and support. The type of behaviour illustrated in the BBC offices can be alleviated by the principles that underpin the way that the transition is managed. During the previous three organization design phases the reality of what it means in practice is not experienced. Although pilot runs, experimentation and try-outs can help they are just that and not the real thing. Everyone involved in the transition activity, and particularly its leadership, can expect better outcomes if they show, as mentioned above, consideration (kindness and fairness) and support (concern and encouragement) towards employees. In the day-to-day this is demonstrated by doing the right thing, which translates as 'having a strong commitment to the welfare of all, and clear – and enforced – guidelines on what are acceptable actions' (Peterson, 2013).

Margaret Wheatley's 'Ten Principles for Creating Healthy Organizational and Community Change' – the tool at the end of Chapter 3 – offers principles that will underpin the approach of consideration and support. Additionally, using some of the insights derived from the science of positive psychology fosters helpful attitudes and behaviours.

OD short

Managing the transition requires intentional activity around implementing the transition plan. It means keeping track of and mitigating emerging risks, knowing that those related to the informal (shadow side) organization are likely to be at the forefront in this phase. And it requires demonstrating through the transition consideration and support for employees and other stakeholders as they move from the current to the new design.

Determining and addressing transition issues

Transition issues are found in all four categories of the organization systems model (Figure 1.3): people, work, informal organization and formal organization. In most issues that arise these elements are interrelated, for example someone finding that he/she now has to desk-share may not be able to work in the accustomed way, which leads to indignation and a call to colleagues for a move to end desk-sharing and then a meeting with a 'higher-up' to resolve the issue.

The people implications of transitioning are significant. Briefly, in the transition stage the issue is twofold: first, to help people manage any changes in their work roles, and second, to ensure that collectively they reach high performance – to achieve the intended benefits of the new design – as quickly as possible. (Remember that in nearly all cases, one of the objectives of redesign is to improve performance.)

But beware of the phrase 'high performance'. It is a phrase often used without first defining it for a specific organization. High performance in one organization will have a different focus and manifestation from high performance in another. As one researcher in the field noted:

> When reviewing the articles and books written on high performance organizations (HPOs), it is conspicuous that many different characteristics are found. It seems it depends on the angle of research or on the personal views and interests of the researchers what type of characteristics are found. This makes it difficult to distinguish an overall set of characteristics which describe a High Performing Organization (HPO) in general. (DeWaal, 2010)

Nevertheless, drawing on his research, DeWaal suggests that the success factors that determine what makes an HPO, i.e. an organization that achieves better financial and non-financial results than comparable organizations over a period of at least five to ten years, are in brief:

Quality of management

The management of an HPO is of high quality, builds relationships based on trust by combining integrity and coaching leadership with highly exemplary behavior, is quick to make decisions (also regarding non-performers), is results-oriented and committed to a long-term vision.

Quality of employees

The employees of an HPO are diverse, complementary and well able to work together. They are flexible and resilient when it comes to achieving results. They are busy every day answering the question: 'How can I make our organization more successful?'

Openness and action orientation

The culture of an HPO is an open one in which everyone is involved in important processes through shared dialogue, continuous knowledge-sharing and learning from mistakes, where change is encouraged and actions are taken to improve performance.

Continuous improvement and innovation

An HPO is aware of its distinctive (strategic) characteristics and has all employees continuously contributing to improving, simplifying, aligning and renewing processes, services and products.

Long-term orientation

To an HPO, continuity in the long term always takes precedence over profit in the short term. The long-term orientation of an HPO applies to clients, collaboration partners, as well as relationships with employees. Management positions are filled by employees rising from the ranks.

These five factors each point to several clues where transition issues arise.

Managers often lack the skills, ability and confidence to help their staff handle the transition to the new state: they need the skills to hold difficult conversations and answer honestly all the questions that arise, the ability to role model any new behaviours or values required and the confidence (and back-up) to take swift action if necessary.

Employees want to know what's in it (the new design) for them. Difficulties may be headed off by engaging in continuous discussion and dialogue on the point of the change, and negotiating with employees to a point where they agree with it – at least enough to give it a try. Additionally, they must see people they respect actively supporting the new design.

Issues can also arise if insufficient attention has been paid in earlier phases to aligning surrounding structures (reward and recognition systems or policies, for example) to facilitate the new ways of working and if there has been inadequate employee training to do the work differently.

Transparency and openness in the transition with a positive psychology bent on looking for what's working well and encouraging feedback is the way to go. Hiding mistakes, covering up what is not going so well and failing to take quick action to adjust the new design all lead to issues. Cyrus Massoumi, CEO ZocDoc – a constantly redesigning online company that connects doctors and patients – says that:

> It is every single person at ZocDoc's duty to speak up if they feel that the company is making a mistake or could be doing something better. The only way to ensure that anyone in the company, regardless of title, team or seniority, feels comfortable speaking up is to create an environment of collaboration and openness. (Massoumi, 2013)

No redesign is perfect. Again issues arise when conscious reflection, learning and readjustments are not taking place through the transition process. Reaching for innovation and improvement as part of the transition and using collaborative forums like SharePoint, Yammer, Jabber or Salesforce's work.com to post and discuss design improvements all help to smooth process.

Issues arise when people expect instant performance improvements. Taking a long-term view – longer than one quarter's results – that the redesign could take time to see benefits being realized is realistic. Things take time to bed down. United Airlines' merger with Continental in 2010 is a case in point.

> The world's biggest airline, created after United merged with Continental Airlines in 2010, promised an unparalleled global network, with eight major hubs and 5,500 daily flights serving nearly 400 destinations. As an added benefit, the new airline would be led by Mr. Smisek of Continental, which was known for its attention to customer service.
>
> But two years on, United still grapples with myriad problems in integrating the two airlines. The result has been hobbled operations, angry passengers and soured relations with employees.
>
> 'United remains at a challenging point,' analysts from Barclays wrote last month, and they forecast that the carrier would not begin to see the benefits of its merger until late in 2013 and into 2014.
>
> Mr. Smisek … acknowledged that things were not going as fast as expected, particularly given the aggressive targets he set two years ago. Back then, Mr. Smisek said the merger would be wrapped up in 12 to 18 months. He has since learned to be patient, he said. (Mouawad, 2012)

The United Airlines experience highlights the common experience of a transition phase: the feeling that 'wheels are spinning' and progress is getting bogged down.

This is often the reality rather than a feeling, and although there are many reasons for getting bogged down one of the most common is that people lose energy and enthusiasm. Liken it to moving house – buyers arrive at the new location having spent months planning the move, packing their goods and now it is time to start living in the new place. They look around at everything boxed up, heaped rather randomly and quail at the task that lies ahead. Often only some stuff is unpacked and years later other stuff is still boxed up as it was on moving day.

Like a house move, a design transition is a start point not an end point. Employees have to galvanize themselves into the unpacking, rearranging and getting to know the new location (real and/or metaphorical). New and effective routines have to be built up and confidence generated – confidence that the change was the right thing, or at least is liveable with. The role of the organization design consultant and the transition team is to foster a new wave of energy and enthusiasm in stakeholders.

A second common reason for getting bogged down is that formal leadership attention gets diverted. Their effort has been in the initial generation of support and, possibly, enthusiasm and then 'selling' the project in the right places. Once they have achieved this, many formal leaders feel their role is complete. However, as noted, successful redesign projects require their commitment and focus from the start and then right through all phases. If other things in the transition phase divert leadership attention, the project is very likely to flag.

A third common reason for the project to flag is the sheer weight of legacy, custom and practice, which can drag down the redesign in the transition to the new model. In spite of contingency planning and risk management, unexpected barriers surface. This is often because insufficient work has been done with the interface departments, systems and processes – and the time and effort needed to overcome these means that there is a slow reversion to business as usual.

To repeat a point made earlier, in order to avoid getting stuck, plan regular and systematic progress checks (Table 7.2). Back up this form of progress assessment with more qualitative and anecdotal assessments – asking people how things are going, listening carefully and 'taking the temperature' of the project. Often consultants get a good feel for project status simply by being curious, observant, picking up on clues and making connections.

Robert Shaw's list of issues evident in the transition phase is useful to consider. He suggests that there are leadership/management issues of:

Priority stress:

- Leaders/managers have too many things to do, with no clear view of the top items versus the other 40, or whatever number. (They do not know what to do.)
- The redesign conflicts with other strategic initiatives. (There are competing and conflicting priorities.)

- There are insufficient resources to do everything. (There is too much to do and not enough to do all of it with.)

Going for activity rather than results:

- The transition work focuses more on processes than results.
- The activity focuses on tasks that drive current measurements, not the new measurements.
- Activity sticks with the known rather than the new, showing risk averseness.

Feeling powerless to implement the plan because there is:

- Unclear accountability.
- Over-control by others in the chain.
- Inadequate skill and capability. (Shaw, 1992)

Clearly, if these issues are evident in an organization design transition then take specific actions to address them using an appropriate range of tactics and responses. Beyond the suggestions for these already put forward in this section consider:

1   Avoiding exclusive transition project team membership – cycling people through brings new thinking and extends participation. Although there are some risks in bringing new people into project teams the 'fresh eyes' generally outweigh the risk of newness. A greater risk is sticking with the same team all the way through. Members can form a silo which acts to sideline the project rather than keeping it mainstream.
2   Minimizing bureaucratic support structures around the transition to the new design whilst ensuring good project governance.
3   Cascading transition work to the lowest possible level to get maximum involvement and ownership. Involving people who do the frontline work in the organization in the project design teams provides a reality check to the new design.
4   Balancing tradeoffs between quantity, quality and pace in achieving results. Aim for 'good enough' and what works rather than getting things perfectly right. A pragmatist stands a better chance of success in organization design than a perfectionist.
5   Demonstrating how the redesign works with other change projects. Clarify how these work to develop the business and are part of a coherent strategy to keep the organization moving effectively into a planned future. Too often people have a cynical view of 'change for change's sake'.
6   Adjusting the design if it becomes apparent that this would be the best course of action. It may well be as transition proceeds that a gap between planned design and design in practice emerges. In this case aim to understand why and then review the design. Use the design criteria to guide any changes to retain the overall integrity of the project.

OD short

A raft of issues usually emerges in the transition phase. Determining what these are and how to address them swiftly is essential. A prescription for addressing issues is unavailable. Rather it is a case of being aware that issues will arise in any one, or all four, of the organizational elements of people, work, informal organization and formal organization, and taking swift action to address these. Working from an optimistic bias helps.

Celebrate successes (daily)

All too frequently the transition phase feels like hard going, with scant attention paid to celebrating successes, telling stories of what's going well and publicly recognizing small progress. It is easy to be cynical of this type of thing but moving transition activity from the typical to the notable – doing it with enthusiasm, engagement, meaning and purpose is not a waste of time, rather it is a genuine builder of more likely success. Simple expressions of cheerfulness, recognition and random acts of kindness make a big difference in engendering well-being and community, necessary while going through stressful times.

Although some projects have formal methods of celebrating success, this is often more spasmodic than regular. Transitions in general benefit from ramping up the everyday fun aspects of what is going on rather than dwelling on the 'issues', on what's not working and the drudge aspects.

One organization, with lots of people working off-site, and going through a redesign, set up a Yammer group with the express purpose of building a social support network based around positive attitudes. A helpdesk home-worker said:

> I was sceptical about this when we set it up. But it's been great. This week, for example, we've celebrated two birthdays, I've got the update on some-one recovering from leg surgery, I 'participated' via a webcam and Skype at a retirement party for someone back at the office, and a team member who was leaving after 16 years told us some lovely stories about his time here and how much he's enjoyed it. Now we're thinking about the annual wu-hu egg hunt – how can we do it remotely and on-site? We're going through difficult times and this just brings camaraderie into our lives as we struggle to get to grips with the new process.

This type of online social media community-building works well if there is a facilitator who keeps things going – questions, comments, jokes and discussion of the latest football game or soap opera – all light-hearted social glue that, whether the employee is on- or off-site, build connection to the organization, pride in what it is aiming to achieve and a sense of shared purpose and values.

In some organizations this attribute of fun is deliberately designed in – and not just in the transition phase of a redesign. ZocDoc, mentioned earlier, is one example. The CEO says:

Find ways to make work fun. While the occasional happy hour or Ping-Pong tournament certainly doesn't hurt, there is a distinction between having fun at work and making work fun. Whether it's including a funny Easter egg on our 404-page or rewarding success with a victory lap (cape and all) around the office, I'm always impressed by how innovative our team is at bringing happiness to their experience at ZocDoc. If the work you do brings a smile to your face and the faces of your colleagues, it's a pleasure to contribute in person every day. (Massoumi, 2013)

Before cringing at that paragraph, think about how an intention to make a workplace an engaging, happy and productive one could translate into different cultures and settings.

Google aims to do that across its global operation. In an article about the company's Manhattan office, the spokesperson made the point that 'Google's various offices and campuses around the globe reflect the company's overarching philosophy, which is nothing less than "to create the happiest, most productive workplace in the world"' (Stewart, 2013).

Interestingly, creating that positive, supportive workplace is not so much a 'nice to have' but a necessity even when not going through a redesign transition. Why? Because research has shown that 'positive emotions and interventions can bolster health, achievement, and resilience and can buffer against depression and anxiety' (Seligman, n.d.).

However, celebrating successes during transition is not just about designing in community fun to encourage positive emotions and therefore make success more likely. It is also about intentional individual, team and organizational reward and recognition. Again this does not need to be spasmodic or ponderous. Various social media platforms enable reward and recognition to be an ongoing dynamic process. Salesforce's work.com is one example of this:

Work.com is a social performance management platform that revolutionizes the way companies align around social goals, motivate their people with real-time recognition and rewards and drive performance with continuous feedback and relevant performance reviews.

Work.com focuses on the inherent social nature of performance management – goal setting, feedback, recognition and continuous dialogue – to help companies align, motivate and drive performance. Work.com liberates performance management from a top-down, once-a-year process into an integrated daily solution that makes a meaningful impact on business performance. (Salesforce, 2012)

An additional feature of work.com is that a partnership with Amazon.com empowers work.com customers to reward and motivate their people directly from within work.com.

Even easier than invoking social media is a straightforward 'thank you', or 'well done' or 'you did a good job there'. It can come from managers and/or colleagues and works towards a happy workplace. A good workplace that is fun to be in and engenders employee emotional well-being (aka happiness) is not Utopian or non-achievable. It can be designed in and should be designed in to the transition phase of an organization design. Peterson (2013) is firm in saying, 'The good life can be taught.' He says that this point is 'especially important because it means that happiness is not simply the result of a fortunate spin of the genetic roulette wheel. There are things people can do to lead better lives, although I hasten to say that all require that we live (behave) differently ... permanently. The good life is hard work and there are no shortcuts to sustained happiness.'

OD short

Generally speaking, transitions to a new design are experienced as chaotic, demoralizing and disconnecting. In having to get to grips with new routines, new work styles and sometimes new workplaces people lose the capacity for fun. It is important to underpin an organization design transition with fun, irreverence, good humour and a very strong orientation that people matter. Formal, intermittent 'celebrate success' ways are good, but not as good as everyday demonstration of positive attitudes and characteristics. Social media-style performance management gives a formal dimension to the informality of building strong community.

Tool 1

Team audit

Use Table 7.4 with the transition implementation team(s) and/or with the employees in the new design.

Tool 2

How are we doing on change?

Use this tool (Table 7.5) to measure the success of the transition. Administer it at the start of the transition phase and at intervals as it proceeds. Use it with various stakeholder groups and/or across the whole population.

Summary

The transition phase is a time of anxiety and sometimes frustration. Disruptive currents are felt and there is a likelihood that the redesign implementation will stall. To minimize the risk of this take a range of actions that will maintain

Table 7.4 Team audit: how are we doing?

Use this audit periodically to gather data from each team member to create a group profile the team can use as a focal point for discussion about 'How well are we doing as a team?'. The discussion provides an opportunity to compare points of view objectively and, if need be, to get back on track and move forward more productively. Each team member can complete the audit. Individual responses should be kept confidential. Compile the individual responses into a group profile for the team to share in a team meeting.

Team's goals/purpose

Rate your opinion of the team's effectiveness on the dimensions listed below with '1' being an ineffective area in need of improvement and '5' being an area of effectiveness and strength.

Aspect/dimension	Rating					Comments/ examples
	1	2	3	4	5	
Goals/purpose						
Meetings						
Ground rules and norms						
Communication						
Leadership						
Workload						
Distribution of work						
Energy level						
Commitment level						
Adequacy of resources						
Availability of resources						
Management of stress						
Decision-making						
Respect for differences						
Management of conflict						
Level of participation						
Comments						

The biggest challenge we face as a team is:

Our greatest strength as a team is:

The one thing I would most like to see the team do is:

Source: ©1999 by the President and Fellows of Harvard College and its licensors. All rights reserved.

a high level of trust and co-operation, foster a fun spirit of community and engagement and keep people feeling connected with what is going on. This requires visible/obvious leadership support, planning for contingencies and taking regular soundings on progress. It is often wise and appropriate to adapt plans as the transition proceeds. This phase requires alertness to all aspects of the organizational system: work, people, informal organization and formal organization.

Table 7.5 How are we doing on change?

Success of the transition	1	2	3	4	5	6
Focus and clarity of direction and communication. Everyone understands where we are going, how and why.						
Clarity of objectives, roles and accountability. Everyone understands and owns what they are expected to do.						
Team-working across the business is based on trust and support. Everyone feels able to share ideas and work with other groups and functions.						
Motivation, confidence and commitment are obvious and aligned with reward. People want to come to work and feel proud to be here.						
Customer focus and meeting customer needs is the driver of everything we do.						
HR policy and process is consistent and clear, creating a leading-standards working environment.						
People feel willing to challenge, to be open and honest and demonstrate a 'can do' attitude.						
We are measurably and increasingly successful. People are determined to deliver results.						

References

DeWaal, A. A. (2010). *The Characteristics of a High Performance Organization.* Hilversum, the Netherlands: Centre for Organizational Performance.

Egan, G. (1994). *Working the Shadow Side: A Guide to Positive behind-the-scenes Management.* San Francisco: Jossey-Bass.

Lewis, S., Passmore, J. and Cantore, S. (2008). 'Positive Psychology and Managing Change', *The Psychologist*, **21**(11), 932–4.

London Evening Standard. (2013). 'Sign Warfare Breaks Out at the Beeb', 7 February. Retrieved 15 March 2013, from *London Evening Standard*: http://www.standard.co.uk/news/londoners-diary/sign-warfare-breaks-out-at-the-beeb-8485199.html.

McRae, A. (2012). 'Moving a Hospital More Than Moving Furniture; Patients Are First Priority', 15 January. Retrieved 14 March 2013, from *Times Herald*: http://www.times-herald.com/Local/A-new-Piedmont-Newnan–Moving-a-hospital-more-than-moving-furniture–patients-first-priority-2029816.

Massoumi, C. (2013). 'Go Ahead, Work from Home (But You Shouldn't Want To)', 15 March. Retrieved 18 March 2013, from LinkedIn: http://www.linkedin.com/today/post/article/20130315135013-766323-go-ahead-work-from-home-but-i-bet-you-won-t-want-to.

Meindel, J., Ehrlich, S. B. and Dukerich, J. M. (1985). 'The Romance of Leadership', *Administrative Science Quarterly*, **30**(1), 78–102.

Mouawad, J. (2012). 'For United, Big Problems at Biggest Airline', 28 November. Retrieved 16 March 2013, from *The New York Times*: http://www.nytimes. com/2012/11/29/business/united-is-struggling-two-years-after-its-merger-with-continental.html?pagewanted=all.

Peterson, C. (2006). *A Primer in Positive Psychology*. New York: Oxford University Press.

Peterson, C. (2013). *Pursuing the Good Life*. New York: Oxford University Press.

Pettigrew, A. (1998). 'Success and Failure in Corporate Transformation Initiatives', in *Information Technology and Organizational Transformation*. R. D. Galliers and W. J. Baets (eds). Chichester: John Wiley & Sons Ltd.

Rodgers, C. (2012a). 'Making the Most of "the Leader as Host"', 12 November. Retrieved 2 March 2013, from Informal Coalitions: http://informalcoalitions. typepad.com/informal_coalitions/2012/11/making-the-most-of-the-leader-as-host. html.

Rodgers, C. (2012b). 'Reframing Leadership – Seven Would-Be Shifts in How We Think and Talk about Leadership Practice', 26 January. Retrieved 14 March 2013, from Informal Coalitions: http://informalcoalitions.typepad.com/informal_ coalitions/2012/01/reframing-leadership-seven-shifts.html.

Salesforce. (2012). 'Salesforce.com Launches work.com – Transforming Human Resources for the Social Era', 19 September. Retrieved 18 March 2013, from Salesforce: http://www.salesforce.com/company/news-press/press-releases/2012/09/120919-5. jsp.

Seligman, M. (n.d.). 'Positive Neuroscience'. Retrieved 18 March 2013, from Authentic Happiness: http://www.authentichappiness.sas.upenn.edu/newsletter.aspx?id=1545.

Sette, C. (2008). 'Appreciative Inquiry: An Approach for Learning and Change Based on Our Own Best Practices', 9 December. Retrieved 18 May 2013, from Institutional Learning and Change: http://www.cgiar-ilac.org/content/chapter-19-appreciative-inquiry.

Shaw, B. (1992). 'The Capacity to Act: Creating a Context for Empowerment', in *Organizational Architecture: Designs for Changing Organizations*. D. Nadler, M. Gerstein and B. Shaw (eds). San Francisco: Jossey-Bass.

Stewart, J. B. (2013). 'Looking for a Lesson in Google's Perks', 15 March. Retrieved 18 March 2013, from *The New York Times*: http://www.nytimes.com/2013/03/16/ business/at-google-a-place-to-work-and-play.html?_r=2&.

8 Reviewing the design

One of the most common reasons that redesigns fail is the all too common assumption that the job essentially ends with the announcement of the new design.

Nadler and Tushman, 1997

What you will learn

This chapter covers methods of embedding the organization design, evaluating its effectiveness and learning the lessons of the design and implementation that can be carried forward into the next iteration of the design.

Overview of phase

Reviewing the redesign project is typically an overlooked part of the project plan – if, indeed, it ever appeared as part of the plan. However, neglect this phase and the risk is that the project will be one that appears in the often quoted statistic that '75 per cent of change projects fail'. This happens because unless a review is commissioned, systematic and intentional course correction is unlikely to be triggered.

The point of a review is fivefold:

1   To verify and validate that the design will achieve its purpose within the boundaries established.
2   To assess whether the information on which the design was based was reliable (in case data-gathering techniques need to be adjusted on future projects).
3   To capture the experience and learning to pass on to future organization design teams.
4   To find out where to take action to keep the new design delivering to target.
5   To see where there are opportunities for taking things further and delivering greater benefit than originally thought.

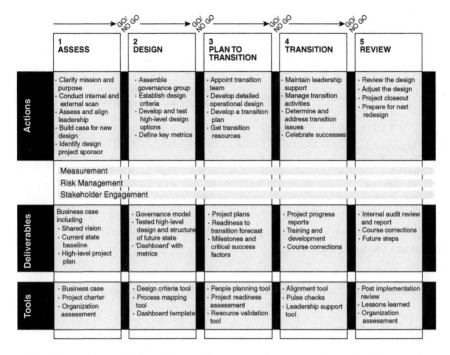

Figure 8.1 Phases of an organization design project

However, as one report remarks:

> Exercise common sense in deciding how much time and resources should
> be devoted to a review – the costs of conducting one should not outweigh
> the perceived benefits. There will be occasions when the review will be no
> more than a short report on file. On other occasions it will be a minor
> project in itself. The most important thing is that a review is conducted
> and that it is used for learning and improvement and not for apportioning
> blame. (Efficiency Unit, 2009)

Reviewing project progress should have been going on throughout the life
cycle of the project to date. At this point following the transition (implementation) the post-implementation review is intended less to see whether the
project was managed and run effectively – this is the content of the project
closeout discussed later in this chapter – and more to see if its intended benefits are being realized. Figure 8.2 shows the sequence for reviewing.

Following the review of the design comes activity to make any adjustments
required that have been highlighted in the review, closing out the project and
then preparing for the next phase of the redesign cycle.

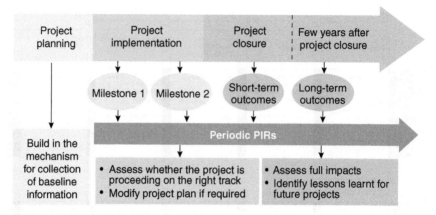

Figure 8.2 Sequence for conducting post-implementation reviews (PIRs)
Source: Efficiency Unit, 2009.

Each of these aspects is covered in more detail in this chapter.

Review the design

There is merit in conducting two fairly formal reviews. The first should come about four to eight weeks after the transition is more or less accomplished. This is likely to be with the project team and immediate stakeholders and will cover quick wins and immediately obvious areas for course corrections. The second is further out – between six months and a year after project closeout – and looks more at the benefits realization and the lessons learned in the period between closeout and this point (Figure 8.1).

The first task in the post-implementation review (PIR) process is to plan how it will be conducted. A four-step approach is helpful here (Table 8.1).

The website Mind Tools has some useful tips on conducting PIRs. The advice given there is to:

- Ask for openness. Emphasize the importance of being open and honest in the assessment, and make sure that people are not in any way punished, blamed or scapegoated for being open.
- Be objective. Describe what has happened in objective terms, and then focus on improvements.
- Document success. Document practices and procedures that led to project successes, and make recommendations for applying them to similar future projects.

Table 8.1 PIR tasks, activities and questions

Step	Tasks	Questions
Define review objectives and scope	Conduct preliminary research on the project under review Identify special areas that need to be addressed Finalize review objectives and scope. The PIR will usually assess: • the achievement (to date) of business case objectives • costs and benefits to date against forecast, and other benefits realized and expected • continued alignment to the business strategy • the effectiveness of revised business operations (functions, processes, staff numbers etc.) • ways of maximizing benefits and minimizing cost and risk • the sensitivity of the business service to expected business change • business, user and employee satisfaction	Are there any obvious issues or opportunities that need to be addressed? Are there resources to complete the review to time and budget?
Determine review methodology	Identify project outcomes to be assessed Develop assessment method Design data collection approach	What project outcomes should be addressed? (Refer back to the project charter, Chapter 4.) Are pre-project data available? Are there any agreed performance measures, and are they still relevant and adequate? (Refer back to the project charter, Chapter 4.) What are the most effective and efficient ways to collect the information required?

Table 8.1 (cont.)

Step	Tasks	Questions
Collect and analyse data	Collect the data. Common sources include: • the business case • information kept to track costs and benefits • any previous **PIR** report(s) • data collected on a regular basis as part of the normal business operation • questionnaires directed at a pre-determined audience, or a sample Interpret the data: analysis of the information gathered involves comparing what actually happened against that predicted to happen (for example in a business case). It will examine what went well and what went less well; this forms the basis for recommendations Compare actual project outcomes against intended project outcomes	Can the pre project data and current project data be reliably compared on a like-for-like basis? Have there been any changes in project parameters and assumptions? Are there any external factors that may have affected project outcomes, e.g. merger announced?
Identify issues and opportunities, lessons learned, and agree report back method	Identify lessons learned Surface causes of issues raised and/or opportunities gained/lost Develop recommendations for improvement: they should cover both of the organization design and the project management and be coherent, useful, evidence based and actionable Document and circulate the **PIR** findings	What happened as things unrolled? Why did they happen? How should we do it differently next time? What should we do about things now? Do the project outcomes meet the actual needs?

Source: Adapted from Efficiency Unit, 2009.

- Look with hindsight. Pay attention to the 'unknowns' (now known!) that may have increased implementation risks. Develop a way of looking out for these in future projects.
- Be future-focused. Remember, the purpose is to focus on the future, not to assign blame for what happened in the past. This is not the time to focus on any one person or team.
- Look both at positives and negatives. Identify positive as well as negative lessons. (Mind Tools, 2013)

A short-term PIR provides the opportunity for project-team-member personal learning (style of operation, strengths and weaknesses), team learning and learning for the organization. It also gives the opportunity to debrief and disband the implementation team(s) and closeout the project. People who have worked on it are likely to view its closure with mixed feelings. They may look forward to future opportunities or they may face their own job loss because of the new design.

This short-term PIR may take the form of a fairly informal debriefing aimed at:

- identifying any planned or emerging tasks still to be completed;
- highlighting the impact of change so far – using the measures and metrics in place to track success;
- agreeing the method of transfer of ownership from project manager to line managers;
- providing the opportunity to recognize and reward the achievement of project team members and others involved.

A longer-term PIR takes a much more in-depth look at the success or otherwise of the redesign. In large organizations an internal audit team using a standard reporting format (see Table 8.2) can be asked to conduct the PIR. If there is no internal audit team invite an objective third party to do it. A member of the project team is likely to have conscious and unconscious biases and thus is not best suited to review.

Selecting the right people to conduct the PIR (in the absence of an internal audit department) involves finding those who are some or all of the following:

- members of the department/consultancy conducting the review;
- people with working knowledge of the business area under review and its processes;
- people with relevant technical knowledge;
- strategy planners with knowledge of the organization's business strategy and the organization design contribution to it;
- people involved in meeting the objectives of the project but not directly involved in its design and planning.

Table 8.2 PIR template

Check list item   Description

Reference:
Project title/reference: *Project name*
Project manager: *Project manager(s) of the project*
Project sponsor: *The sponsor for the project*
Review conducted by: *Who conducted the review? (Usually it is someone independent of the project team.)*
Review dates: *When was the review actually conducted?*
Date project completed: *When was the project completed or terminated?*

Outcomes:
Outcomes of the project: *Were the objectives of the project clearly defined and measurable? Were the objectives of the project met overall? If so, where is the proof? If not, why not? Were the objectives met in terms of quality? If so, where is the proof? If not, why not?*
Were the objectives met in terms of cost? If so, where is the proof? If not, why not? Were the objectives met in terms of time? If so, where is the proof? If not, why not?
Reason for variance: *What were the main reasons for not meeting the project objectives? What can be learnt from this for the future?*

Scope:
Scope of the project: *Was the scope of the project clearly documented and agreed? Were changes to the original scope clearly documented and approved?*
Scope delivered: *Was the planned scope actually delivered by the project? If so, where is the proof? If not, why not?*

Benefits:
Expected benefits of the project: *The project financial case included values and measures for financial benefits. Was this accurately completed?*
Were the benefits adequately described, bought in to by the sponsor and measures adequately defined?
Direct – financial: *Were the latest agreed estimates of direct financial benefits the project would deliver achieved? If so, where is the proof? If not, why not?*
Direct – intangible: *Were the latest agreed estimates of direct intangible benefits the project would deliver achieved? If so, where is the proof? If not, why not?*
Indirect: *Were the latest agreed estimates of indirect benefits the project would deliver achieved? If so, where is the proof? If not, why not?*
Unexpected: *Were there any unexpected benefits arising from the project? If so, where is the proof and why were they not identified earlier? Did any unexpected negative impacts to the business occur?*
Reasons for variances: *What were the main reasons for not delivering the project benefits? What can be learnt from this for the future? Was the justification or benefit review process ineffective or given adequate attention?*

Costs:
Costs review: *Was a project budget established at the start of the project accurate? Were costs adequately reviewed throughout the project?*
Were changes to costs adequately controlled and authorized?

Table 8.2 (cont.)

Check list item	Description

Financial summary:
Project costs (£k)

Authorized	Actual	Over-/underspend

Capital revenue total
Project benefits (£k)

Original	Revised	Variance
Income staff costs	Other costs	Total

Project returns

Original	Revised	Increase/decrease
IRR (%)	NPV (£k)	

Project time scales

Authorized	Actual	Variance (± mths)	Start date

Completion date

Customer comments:
Customer satisfaction   *Is the customer satisfied with the project outcome? If not, why not?*

Team performance:
(PDRs)   *Please confirm that all team members have had a development review (PDR) before leaving the project.*

External consultants or other professional advisers:
Did they perform to expected standards? Were agreed benefits delivered? Were costs and time constraints met? Would you recommend them for future work? What were their main strengths and weaknesses? If there was a partnership agreement, how successful was it?

Lessons learnt:
Things that worked: *What went well with regard to managing the business benefits and why?*
Things that did not work: *What did not go well and why?*

Further actions:
Are there any actions arising from the review which need to be addressed? Who needs to address them and when?

Agreement:
Sponsor:
Project manager: Customer: Finance:

An organization-design PIR needs to assess each of the four elements of the system (Figure 1.3) in relation to the business purpose outlined in the project charter (Figure 4.2). Typically, the PIR includes:

- checking whether everyone understands the purpose of his/her job and where it fits in and has sufficient information to do it effectively (work);
- finding out whether everyone has felt involved appropriately in the redesign process (people);

- assessing how well each person is able to establish an effective dialogue with his/her customers and suppliers (formal organization);
- determining how well the work is flowing and how effective the decision-making process is;
- evaluating whether an appropriate culture and management style is being supported and maintained (informal organization).

Reviewing in both the short and longer term provides different types of information and knowledge to share with other project teams and with stakeholders. Many large organizations describe themselves as 'siloed' or 'smoke-stacked' and have difficulty learning from their own members. And many are much better at benchmarking other companies than learning from their own experiences. Having the skills, will and ability to share project learning effectively avoids reinventing the wheel and other people making the same mistakes. Publishing what has been learned and what changes and adjustments are being made to the redesign helps spread good practice and develop common values and consistent approaches.

There are some common problems that may be encountered in carrying out PIRs, and the review team needs to be aware of these and work around them. These include:

- More than one department/business unit involved, where there is no common standard for measuring and recording the benefits and costs.
- Lack of documentation. Much factual information will come from project documentation, especially the business case.
- Lack or inadequacy of baseline measures. For a PIR, measures of success can only be made accurately by comparing the level of performance before the project implementation against that at the time of the PIR.
- Sensitivities. Examining the performance of project teams or current operations against a predicted level may lead to feelings of insecurity or grievance for those who were involved with the project, or in the business area supported by the change.
- Management of expectations. Although the use of reviews will improve the effectiveness of the organization, the review team should ensure that they do not raise expectations of system enhancements or business change. They may cost more to implement than the value of the benefits they would deliver.
- The organization is too busy to do a PIR and never gets it done. There should be policies to ensure that reviews are carried out as part of the organization's normal practice.
- Lack of co-operation from the service provider.

Organization design teams can take some action to avoid or reduce these problems in the earlier phases of the project by:

- harmonizing the measurements across business units (preferably in the assessment phase);
- establishing protocols for filing and warehousing project documentation (when the project is formally established);
- making formal agreements with departments/BUs to participate in the review process (as part of the business case).

To repeat a point made earlier, carefully select the members of the review team to ensure as far as possible independence and objectivity.

OD short

The post-implementation review is often left out of the original business case and project plan. This is a mistake: there is value in conducting more than one review – one soon after transition and one later. Do not neglect or skimp on the review phase, as both informal and formal reviews pick up operational and behavioural issues that are an essential part of design success. Done systematically, the review will yield actionable information on things that must be addressed to optimize the new organization design. Note that reviews tend to highlight deficiencies rather than good work, so take steps to ensure that the review is balanced in its assessment of what is working well and what is working less well.

Adjust the design

All reviews find issues and concerns to be addressed. The most common transition and implementation findings include:

Implementation taking more time than originally allocated: if a phased transition is carried out it is sometimes difficult to know when the new design is 'there'. Phased transitions often drift towards their goal rather than march to it decisively, reaching agreed milestones as they go. To avoid drift have clear markers of the end point the project is planned to reach so that there is clarity on when to 'stop the clock'. Even with these markers, projects often take longer than anticipated. Build reasonable contingency time into the plans.

Major problems surfacing during implementation that were not identified beforehand: these can be internal or external, and either way will have an adverse impact on implementation. However good the risk analysis, things difficult to anticipate will have been omitted. Catastrophes and about-turns occur out of the blue. If this happens, redo the risk planning, be flexible enough to change course and respond appropriately. Derailing is extremely traumatic for people, so remember to address emotional responses sensitively.

Co-ordination of implementation activities was not effective enough: this talks to project and programme management abilities. Good skills here are essential. Where there are a number of streams of work progressing simultaneously, a governance structure that keeps clear oversight of all of them and provides a coherent framework for them to operate within is essential (see Chapter 5). Reminders about collaboration, boundaries and principles all help the project teams stay in touch with one another's progress.

Key implementation tasks and activities were not defined in enough detail: check the detail of the project plan. The test of having enough detail is that a newcomer could pick up and run with the project without a hitch. The cliché 'the devil is in the detail' holds true in redesign projects. However, the trick is to get enough detail without becoming bureaucratic and prescriptive.

Competing activities and crises distracted attention from implementing this decision: day-to-day running of the business has to continue even through the redesign process. People's tendency is to work on the urgent rather than the important. Design work usually falls into their 'important' category. To offset this, have at least one person (depending on the size of the project) who is charged with working on it full-time or with full focus. This person must have the authority to keep people on track with the project timescales and milestones.

Capabilities of employees involved were not enough: where people move to new roles or responsibilities they must have the skills to deliver quickly in these. Make sure training and development activity is timed to match the milestones of the project. This is particularly important if it is technology training. Too often people try to do new things without adequate preparation and instruction. Budget enough time and money at the start of the project for the training aspects.

Training and instruction given to lower-level employees was not adequate: remember, front-line staff are the people delivering for the business. Unfortunately, they often come last in the pecking order of communication, training and support in new processes. Put them as much in the spotlight as other grades of staff to ensure parity of treatment. Where lower levels of staff need more help, give it to them or customers will suffer.

Leadership and direction provided by departmental managers was not adequate: in a useful white paper, 'Transition into Business as Usual', the author makes the point that 'Leaders who have some understanding of the human psyche are crucial. These leaders can apply intelligence to emotions to create and harness energy in individuals, groups and the organization, and so gaining trust is key' (Pyne, 2013). This is not easy, as previous failed initiatives will tend to drive the organizational energy into corrosive, passive or resigned states. So change leaders also need to fight the lost battle of history. Pyne's suggestion is that a leadership strategy based in some of the precepts of neuro-leadership (see Glossary) might be helpful in taking an organization through a redesign.

Information systems used to monitor implementation were not adequate: use systems that are quick, simple and transparent to monitor implementation. A balanced scorecard approach works well. Getting all the information on one sheet weekly and paying attention to this week's progress compared with last week's is helpful (see Chapter 6). A complex information system is unnecessary. Metrics that give relevant, progressive and actionable information are essential.

People resist the change, try to shift the burden and/or become accidental adversaries: the people issues that reviews uncover are often significant. Traditional operational metrics do not monitor people's responses to change. However, these shadow-side responses act against the project. Emotional and behavioural barriers may be the cause when:

- the changes have been announced but implementation does not get under way;
- change is taking longer than reasonably expected;
- old ways are cropping up and people have gone back to doing what they used to do;
- the change does not run by itself it needs constant reinforcement;
- the same problem pattern repeats;
- people still have an investment (or are rewarded) for doing things the old way;
- there is an 'us and them mentality', or 'in-groups and out-groups'.

One organization reviewed aspects of their progress nine months after their 'go-live' to the new design. The HR director explains the background:

Nine months ago our new design went live. We'd restructured in order to become more responsive to stakeholder wishes and to be flexible enough to meet future changes in the external context. We'd arrived at the design through a significant amount of staff communication, involvement and participation and the design chosen was the one proposed by the staff representatives working group. No one could say this was a top-down mandated, surprising restructure.

So we were very surprised to experience a bumpy and difficult ride in the period from the go-live date to now. A staff survey (30% response rate) about the new design, conducted a couple of months ago, revealed a number of dissatisfactions and anxieties about the way the change has impacted employee life, work and business relationships. We're baffled about what to do now. We can't change the structure so we've got to make it work.

Once this situation had been identified the organization commissioned a third party to help with the task of making the new design work. He discussed the situation with the HR director and a couple of others and summarized this initial conversation, saying:

It seems as if much of the dissatisfaction stems from the point of moving from the theoretical practicality of the new structure and the benefits it was intended to achieve to the actual reality of what it is like living and working in it.

I'm guessing that people didn't know, or could not imagine, what it would be really like until they were in the new situation.

We've thought of many reasons for this 'shock of the new':

1   The matrix structure is complex to operate and people do not have the skills to manage in it (either as an employee or as a manager).
2   The shared resource pools cut into people's self-esteem and professionalism. They feel they are losing professional credit and skill by being part of a pool rather than in a specialist team.
3   There are questions around power and status in a matrix structure – who will be seen as experts? How will reward and recognition be apportioned?
4   There are some highly influential, vocal informal leaders who may be swaying general employee opinion about the new structure.
5   There was insufficient work done following the 'go-live' to address concerns, anxieties and questions.
6   There is now more of a focus and necessity for team working than the more individually focused working in the previous structure. Staff may not have the disposition or skills for team working.
7   People do not know what they are in control of, what they have responsibility and authority for and how much autonomy they can exert in a matrix structure. (This may be an emotion not a deficiency in a job description.)

And we're of the view that all, any, or perhaps even none of these but other factors, may be contributing to the overall feeling that things are not going as well as hoped. Just to add though we do have pockets of things going well in the new design.

This scenario illustrates the almost circular and iterative nature of organization design. This preliminary conversation, although post-implementation, is very similar to the preliminary conversations in the assessment phase (see Chapter 4), and in a sense the requirement to adjust the design is, itself, a mini-redesign.

In this particular case the organization set up a small-scale project to validate the list of possible reasons for disaffection and to take action on those confirmed. Their subsequent task was to scope the project and propose the way forward. They presented their conclusions and got support for their approach. A couple of weeks later the project manager reported:

We have set up three teams to work on three priority areas:

1   leadership and management of people;
2   internal organization, planning, programming and reporting;
3   information, communication and knowledge management.

All the groups have identified already the low-hanging fruit and first proposals have been formulated and first actions have taken place, primarily raising the awareness of how the issues identified will be tackled. This has produced some innovative ideas to put into practice on how to engage the staff in the process and keep them informed of progress.

Some of the identified low-hanging fruit have already been processed into concrete proposals and are now to be fed into our annual planning cycle.

This organization's review confirmed the assessment of the feelings of staff following the go-live of the new design. Although this was surprising to the project team given the amount of involvement staff had had in the design process, it is not unusual. Look back at the list of the common findings of transition reviews and it is evident that this response is almost to be expected. Theorists suggests that this reaction stems from 'cognitive dissonance' – a theory based on the notion that:

Individuals strive to achieve consistency in their beliefs and behaviors. Dissonance or tension is thought to result when individuals experience new events or are exposed to new information that results in cognitions that are incongruent or at odds with each other. The resulting tension, in turn, is thought to be uncomfortable and to motivate individuals to seek ways in which consonance between the cognitive elements can be re-established. Dissonance reduction can be achieved through changes in behavior (and the corresponding behavioral cognitive elements), changes in beliefs, or selective exposure to new information. However, resistance to dissonance reduction through behavioral change may occur when (1) the change is considered painful or involves loss, (2) the present behavior is satisfying, and (3) making the change is not possible. Finally, evidence suggests that forced compliance with dissonance-producing changes – through the use of rewards or threats – does not lead to meaningful cognitive change. (Zablah *et al.*, 2004)

Knowing in advance that this response is likely to occur almost regardless of the amount of participation and involvement up to the point of go-live can prepare OD consultants to work with it when it does.

In some instances, reviews come up with major problems that may call in question the whole rationale for doing the redesign. These types of findings include:

• making organizational changes that are unrelated to any desired business benefits;

- restructuring to fix yesterday's problems, not recognizing that the world has changed and moved on;
- implementing a redesign of generalized organizational concepts (or current management fad) rather than one tailored to the enterprise's specific needs and objectives;
- fiddling with the organization chart instead of redesigning;
- politics rather than business benefit and customer requirements have determined the shape of the organization.

Handling this is complex and requires admission of what has happened and facing up to what can be done going forward. Uniqlo provides a good example. CEO Tadashi Yanai writes:

> Learning from mistakes is something that Uniqlo has had to do – several times, unfortunately.
>
> We opened our first store outside Japan in 2001, in London. And we failed spectacularly. We quickly opened 21 outlets in Britain – and shut down 16 of them by 2003. In retrospect, that was probably good, because we learned so much. Our big mistake was to try to do things the British way. We never capitalized on our strengths.
>
> China, the second overseas market we entered, was a failure at first, too. We faltered in China because we went too far in adapting to China. Per capita income is low – about 5 percent of Japan's – so we figured we should sell at much lower prices. That was a mistake.
>
> Vegetables were a disaster too. We saw food distribution as a backward sector, so we went into partnership with a food group, Ryokuken, in 2002. But vegetables are not an industrial product; you don't know exactly when they will be ready or in what volume.... After two years, we shut operations down.
>
> The important thing is not so much that we failed in these instances, but that we learned and eventually succeeded. In Britain, we now (2011) have more than a dozen stores, including a flagship on London's Oxford Street, and are doing well. China is our fastest-growing market, with almost 100 stores.
>
> Failures are always unpleasant; from the right perspective, though, they can be useful. Our travails in Britain and China fostered resilience and led us to understand three important things. First, to create the best possible Uniqlo in other countries, we had to use the best aspects of our own organization. Second, while globalization is difficult, it is also essential. And third, to succeed outside Japan requires understanding other markets on their own terms. (Adapted from Yanai, 2011)

Adjusting the design means testing it again (as done at the end of the design phase) to confirm that adjustments are making intended improvements. The nine tests of a well-designed organization are frequently used.

1   The market advantage test. Does your design direct sufficient management attention to your sources of competitive advantage in each market?
2   The parenting advantage test. Does your design help the corporate parent add value to the organization?
3   The people test. Does your design reflect the strengths, weaknesses, and motivations of your people?
4   The feasibility test. Have you taken account of all the constraints that may impede the implementation of your design?
5   The specialist cultures test. Does your design protect units that need distinct cultures?
6   The difficult links test. Does your design provide co-ordination solutions for the unit-to-unit links that are likely to be problematic?
7   The redundant hierarchy test. Does your design have too many parent levels and units?
8   The accountability test. Does your design support effective controls?
9   The flexibility test. Does your design facilitate the development of new strategies and provide the flexibility required to adapt to change? (Goold and Cambell, 2002)

Whether Uniqlo actually applied the nine tests is not known, but take a quick glance back at their story and it is obvious that their various designs failed several of the nine tests. In each case they recognized their mistakes, took drastic action and moved on.

OD short

Adjusting the design post-implementation takes a certain amount of courage to recognize and address the deficiencies. Many of the deficiencies are attributable to the cognitive dissonance people feel when they are faced with the actual reality of the new situation – something they could not experience before the event. In other cases failures of strategies, systems, management and business processes must be addressed. Applying the nine tests of good design will support appropriate adjustment to the design. Where the design is a major mistake and cannot be adjusted the only thing to do is to recognize the failure, take the hit, learn from it and move on.

Project closeout

The project closeout differs from the PIR in that the closeout is specifically related to assessment of the project management operation, activity and governance. It is not really concerned with the way the transition to the new design is proceeding. The project closeout comes at a point when the project is deemed finished and when the project team has handed over responsibility for the effective operation of the design to line managers.

Table 8.3 Example project closeout template

General project information

[Enter high-level general project information. Expand this section to include more information if needed for the project.]

	Description		
Project name	[project name]		
Project description	[description of project]		
Project manager	[project manager name]		
Project sponsor	[project sponsor name]		
General comments	[any additional general comments]		

	Baseline	Actual	Variance	% Variance
Start date	[mm/dd/yyyy]	[mm/dd/yyyy]	[000 days]	[00.0%]
Finish date	[mm/dd/yyyy]	[mm/dd/yyyy]	[000 days]	[00.0%]
Hours	[000 hours]	[000 hours]	[000 hours]	[00.0%]
Days	[000 days]	[000 days]	[000 days]	[00.0%]
Budget	[$0,000.00s]	[$0,000.00s]	[$0,000.00s]	[00.0%]

Management effectiveness

[Summarize how effectively the management needs of the customer and project were met. Highlight the significance of approved changes to the baseline, their impact on the project and how they were managed. Compare baselines to actual and describe discrepancies. Identify and discuss specific issues that challenged the project/project team. Consider areas such as cost, schedule, scope, quality, risk, issue, change, communication, implementation and transition, regulatory compliance and overall project-team performance.]

Lessons learned

[Summarize project lessons learned including the cause of issues, reasoning behind the corrective action chosen and other types of lessons learned. Identify and discuss specific issues that challenged the project/project team. Make lessons learned available to others in a way that makes them want to read and apply them, Organize the critical information in an easy-to-understand way that makes its relevance apparent. Ensure that the different stakeholder groups are aware that the information is available.]

Administrative closure

[Summarize project administrative closure activities such as procedures to transfer the project products or services to production and/or operations; stakeholder approval for all deliverables; confirmation that the project has met all sponsors', clients' and other stakeholders' requirements; verification that all deliverables have been provided and accepted; validation that completion and exit criteria have been met; regulatory compliance items.]

Contract closure

[Summarize project contract closure activities such as formally closing all contracts associated with the completed project.]

Information distribution and archive

Table 8.3 (cont.)

[Summarize the data archived in the project repository. The type of information actually archived will differ depending on the scope and type of project. Consider items such as contracts and proposals, business case, charter, scope statement, schedule, budget estimate, project management documents, surveys, status reports, checklists and emails.]

[Archived items distributed to individuals upon project closeout. Note that this list may include individuals without access to the project's archive repository. This should be considered when deciding on an appropriate distribution medium.]

Item	Distribution list	Distribution medium
[archived item]	[name]	[email, fax, website, etc.]

Project management methodologies describe the closeout activity and tasks, often providing templates, checklists and descriptive processes on how to conduct it. Table 8.3 shows a standard reporting template for a closeout.

If it hasn't already happened, have a closeout celebration or ceremony that recognizes the work of the team members and marks the formal end of the project. If possible, arrange for the sponsor or a senior leader to participate in the celebration, demonstrating endorsement of the project work and the contribution of the various members. In some organizations celebrations sometimes feel forced or that they are tokens rather than authentic recognitions. If this is the case find other forms of appropriate recognition for project-team members.

OD short

A formal project closeout is an important marker in the life cycle of an organization design piece of work. It signals the handover to line managers of the responsibility for realizing the benefits that were intended at the start of the project and written into the business case and/or project charter. (See Chapter 4.) Project management methodologies describe the approach and good sources of information on this are the Association for Project Management and the Project Management Institute (http://www.apm.org.uk/DirectingChange).

Preparing for the next phase of the design

Rapid change in organizational landscapes (see Chapter 10) suggests that continuous design changes should be the norm, and intermittent design changes the exception. Google is an example of a company that regularly examines its design, as its blog writer explains:

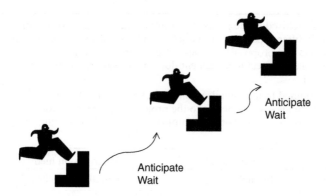

Figure 8.3 Step and wait approach to organization design

We're living in a new kind of computing environment. Everyone has a device, sometimes multiple devices. It's been a long time since we have had this rate of change – it probably hasn't happened since the birth of personal computing 40 years ago. To make the most of these opportunities, we need to focus – otherwise we spread ourselves too thin and lack impact. So today we're announcing some more closures, bringing the total to 70 features or services closed since our annual spring cleaning began in 2011… These changes are never easy. But by focusing our efforts, we can concentrate on building great products that really help in their lives. (Hölzle, 2013)

Organizations that are not engaged in continuous design changes still need to build the capability to meet the future, and various writers make suggestions on these. The extract presented in Chapter 3, and shown again here for revision, offers a set of four that are actionable by organization design and development consultants:

Anticipating. This means developing a view of possible or likely changes – not trying to predict actual changes. Anticipating includes a rigorous review of customer needs and industry forces, and an evaluation of likely scenarios of industry consolidation, product development, pricing and customer needs.

Sensing. This involves continual reviews of market conditions, looking for trends and especially anomalies in customer behavior, competitor moves, supply chain shifts, supply/demand changes, and macro- and microeconomic developments. It requires strong analytics capabilities.

Responding. The key is to respond to market shifts faster than competitors do. This includes rapid decision-making, testing responses on a pilot basis and then scaling for a broader response. It frequently includes preset 'plays,' where management teams have agreed ahead of time how they will respond to certain situations – for instance, to a price drop by a competitor or the merger of two rivals.

Adapting. Once initial market changes have been identified, organizations often find that they need to rework some of their business processes. Some may tailor their organizational structures to better handle ongoing changes in their markets. (Shill *et al.*, 2012)

Not shown in Chapter 3 is the related series of questions that organizations would do well to keep asking themselves:

1 Does your organization have at least three scenarios for how your enterprise is most likely to evolve over the next 36 months? Does it have good options for responding?
2 What three big opportunities would your organization be pursuing if it were more agile?
3 Imagine three possible sources of competition that you haven't thought would be likely until now. How will you respond to them?
4 Put yourself in your top competitors' shoes. What could they do to disrupt the market in the next year, and what are your plans for outsmarting them?
5 How is your company augmenting its ability to quickly sense new market anomalies? Are you taking full advantage of the new capabilities of today's analytics tools?
6 What are the three biggest factors preventing your organization from being more agile? How do you plan to overcome them?
7 Have you make such big cuts during downturns (particularly in terms of talent) that your agility and ability to grow have been damaged? If so, how are you compensating now for those cuts?
8 In what areas should you be *collaborating* with your competitors to drive changes in the market?
9 Who among your organization's potential formal and informal leaders will be most effective at taking advantage of volatility? What makes them different from your current leaders?
10 Which of your customers are the best leading indicators of future market opportunities?
11 Where would faster decision-making be of most benefit to your organization?
12 Have you been able to cut your organization's fixed costs in the past few years to improve its agility? (Shill *et al.*, 2012)

Another method of preparing for a new design is to do the 'Planned Abandonment' exercise recommended by management thinker Peter Drucker. This involves an organization's leadership team regularly reviewing its operations (essentially what Google's annual spring cleaning is about) and making design and other changes in response to this (Drucker, 2001). His view is that abandonment should be considered when:

1   The product, service, market, process or whatever still has a few good years of life.
2   Its greatest virtue is that it is fully written off. Ask instead 'what is it producing?'.
3   An old and declining product, service, market, process, etc. is being maintained at the expense of new and growing products, services, markets, processes, etc.

These two exercises reinforce the point that an organization design is better seen not as a static end state but rather as an ongoing process of adaptation and renewal.

Helping reinforce this is the ability, via collection, analysis and interpretation, of big data (see Glossary) to point to opportunities. The relevance of big data to organization design is 'significant because hidden among the daily terabytes that a single organization can generate are insights that can lead to better customer service, improved revenues, and deeper market understanding' (DailyTekk, 2013), i.e. an improved organization design.

Continuous redesign may be inappropriate, and another way of thinking about preparing for a new design is a 'step and wait'. This term comes from research in technology forecasting. Recent research suggests 'that advances in performance are often followed by a waiting period before the next step forward. The steps can be big or small, and the waiting periods long or short' (*The Economist*, 2013). This might well be applicable to organization designs. The step is the new design, the wait is the sustaining and embedding of it whilst doing the context anticipation and planned abandonment type of work mentioned above. The next step is taken at an appropriate point depending on what the anticipating and sensing during the wait uncovers. Then there is repeated period of waiting and so on (Figure 8.3).

OD short

No design is perfect in its conception and implementation and neither is it a static state. Following from the PIR comes adjustment of the current design and preparation for the new design. There are various ways of preparing for the new design, beginning with developing the capability to recognize when a design change is needed: regular reviews of one type or another and big data analysis and interpretation highlight areas of design/redesign opportunity. Design changes may be continuous or they may follow more of a 'step and wait' pattern.

Tools

1   Planned abandonment exercise

Adapted from Drucker, 2001.

Step 1

Complete this worksheet using your best estimates (doing it with a group or leadership team works well).

1   List your organization's top products or services.
2   For each product/service, ask yourself, 'If we didn't do this already, knowing what we now do, would we do it?'
3   Based on your answers to the preceding question, which products or services should be abandoned? Why? Pick dates to end those that will be abandoned.
4   What might replace them? List your ideas.

Step 2

Follow up by creating a worksheet related to each organizational element (one worksheet per element). Ask a range of people to complete, e.g. individuals or groups at each level of management and each function or business unit. You could also survey all employees.

Example elements to be examined (add others and delete those that aren't relevant to your organization):

Products, Services, Processes, Policies, Markets, Marketing Strategies, Distributors, Distribution Channels, Suppliers, Technologies, Partners.

1   In the area you have selected, which of your organization's products, services, processes, markets or whatever should be abandoned?
2   Why? Pick a date to end each.
3   What, if anything, might replace them?
4   List some other things that your organization is investing resources (time, money, energy) into that you think it should stop doing. Make a few notes about each and pick a date to end each.

2   Big data checklist

1   Are you getting insights from your producers of business analytics or are they just producing data?
2   Are your business analytics insights in sync with any business planning/decision-making cycles?

3 Do potential users of the analytics have a strategic planning process or decision-making process that builds in a step to use available analytics?

4 Are your business analytics systems sufficiently customized to the organization's business decisions?

5 Is there a strong relationship between your producers and users of business analytics? One that allows the analyst to understand or anticipate users' needs?

6 Do your users have sufficient training to understand business analytics? A crash course in regression and other simple analytic tools may be necessary.

7 Are you clear that business analytics are often viewed as a silver bullet and companies fail to collect deep, non-quantitative insights that provide the bigger picture into which analytics needs to be placed? How will you collect, analyse and interpret the corresponding qualitative data?

8 Are you building your big data use capability to figure out how to use the analytics to create new growth, innovation or to compete in wholly new ways?

9 Are you investing in tools that inspire confidence in the analytics? It is not enough to rely on the traditional three Vs of big data – Volume, Velocity and Variety. Add in another two – Veracity and Value – and invest in tools that give you this.

10 Are your managers modelling the use of business analytics? Asking for the data, asking questions about the data, pushing for insights and taking actions in response to those insights show the rest of the company what role business analytics plays in decision-making.

(Adapted from Moorman, 2013.)

Summary

The review and embed stage is often missed out of the original project charter and business case of a design project. However, it is a critical part of the process. Done at two points – almost immediately after 'go-live' and then six months to a year later – it yields valuable operational and behavioural information that highlights necessary design adjustments. Conducting a project closeout related to the project management and governance is also required. This yields a different set of information that, if the lessons learnt are passed on, can profitably inform the smooth running of future projects. A new organization design is not a static end state. Develop the skills to do continuous sensing and anticipation of when a new design is needed, using big data to help with this.

References

CDC. (2010). 'Project Management Guide'. Retrieved 22 March 2013, from Centers for Disease Control and Prevention: http://www2.cdc.gov/cdcup/library/pmg/default.htm.

DailyTekk. (2013). 'Big Data: What Is It and Why Does It Matter?', 7 January. Retrieved 23 March 2013, from DailyTekk: http://dailytekk.com/2013/01/07/big-data-what-is-it-and-why-does-it-matter.

Drucker, P. (2001). *'Leading in a Time of Change' Viewer's Workbook*. New York: Peter F. Drucker Foundation for Non-Profit Management.

The Economist. (2013). 'The Law and the Profits', *The Economist* (*Technology Quarterly*), 9 March.

Efficiency Unit. (2009). *Serving the Community through Successful Project Delivery*. Hong Kong: Government Logistics Department.

Goold, M. and Cambell, A. (2002). 'Do You Have a Well-Designed Organization?', *Harvard Business Review*, March, 117–24.

Hölzle, U. (2013). 'A Second Spring of Cleaning', 13 March. Retrieved 22 March 2013, from Google Official Blog: http://googleblog.blogspot.com/2013/03/a-second-spring-of-cleaning.html.

Mind Tools. (2013). 'Post-Implementation Reviews'. Retrieved 20 March 2013, from Mind Tools: http://www.mindtools.com/pages/article/newPPM_74.htm.

Moorman, C. (2013). 'The Utilization Gap: Big Data's Biggest Challenge', 19 March. Retrieved 23 March 2013, from The CMO: http://cmosurvey.org/blog/the-utilization-gap-big-datas-biggest-challenge.

Nadler, D. A. and Tushman, M. L. (1997). *Competing by Design*. Oxford: Oxford University Press.

Pyne, A. (2013). *Transition into Business as Usual*. London: The Stationery Office.

Shill, W., Engel, J., Mann, D. and Schatteman, O. (2012). 'Corporate Agility: Six Ways to Make Volatility Your Friend', October. Retrieved 23 December 2012, from Accenture: http://www.accenture.com/us-en/outlook/Pages/outlook-journal-2012-corporate-agility-six-ways-to-make-volatility-your-friend.aspx..

Yanai, T. (2011). 'Dare to Err', June. Retrieved 22 March 2013, from *McKinsey Quarterly*: https://www.mckinseyquarterly.com/Dare_to_err_2827.

Zablah, A., Bellenger, D. and Johnston, W. (2004). 'Customer Relationship Management Implementation Gaps', *Journal of Personal Selling and Sales Management*, **24**(4), 279–95.

9 Communication and engagement

Treat people as if they matter.

Peterson, 2013

What you will learn

This chapter discusses the importance of communication and engagement through the life cycle of the project – beginning at the point of first discussions. A range of communication channels are considered and methods of using these effectively with a range of different stakeholders are discussed. Encouraging engagement is key to communication.

Overview

Social media and all things 'neuro' are upending long-standing approaches to stakeholder communication, change management and engagement. Keeping up with what is going on in these fields is daunting but necessary because they will have a profound impact on the design of organizations and the way employees work and interact with one another.

Social media are 'transforming the way we connect, communicate, collaborate and relate to each other' (Social Media Club, 2010) and will continue to do so as they advance. At intervals, the Conversation Prism produces an updated visualization of communication channels (Figure 9.1). Looking at the number of channels gives pause for thought on which to choose, why those ones and how to best use them in organization design work.

Learning from other users' experiences and trying out the various media are both worthwhile. There are many ways of doing this. One avenue to explore is the Social Media Club, established in 2006. Its aim is to 'to host conversations around the globe that explore key issues facing our society as technologies transform the way we connect, communicate, collaborate and relate to each other' (Social Media Club, 2010). It has many chapters around the world and an extensive programme of support and activity. Another avenue is via LinkedIn, which has several social media groups.

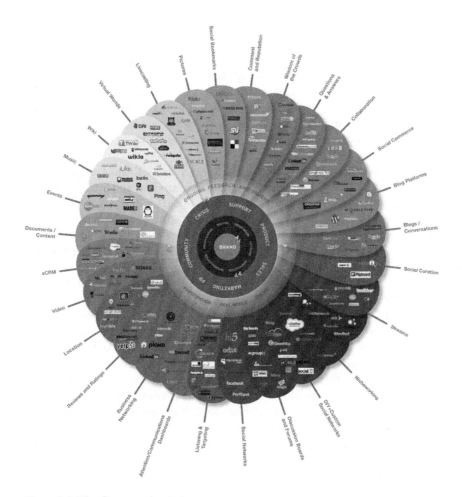

Figure 9.1 The Conversation Prism
Source: Solis and Thomas, 2010.

Increasingly, traditional change-management methods are giving way to those based in engagement approaches. This is happening as we learn more about neuroscience, behavioural economics and related fields. Engagement, defined as 'the intellectual and emotional attachment that an employee has for his or her work' (Heger, 2007), occurs when employees have:

> Connection – that is, they feel a strong sense of belonging with their organization both in terms of sharing the same beliefs or values and in their readiness to follow the direction the organization is heading.

Support – which comprises the practical help, guidance and other resources provided to help people do a great job. In particular how managers support employees in good times and bad.

Voice – this means the extent to which people are informed, involved and able to contribute to shaping their work context.

Scope – concerns the degree of opportunity employees have to meet their own needs, to have control over their work and to play to their strengths. At its best this reflects the two-way nature of an adult–adult employment relationship. (Holbeche and Matthews, 2012)

Where change is happening and it limits any one of the four aspects of engagement, people tend to switch off, resist, get anxious and finally disengage from the process. Unfortunately, many planned and/or desired changes, including organization design, often ignore or compromise the four aspects necessary to maintain employee engagement. Even if intellectually people can understand and appreciate the reasons for the change, this doesn't translate into emotional comfort and acceptance of it.

One of the reasons for this may be people's desire to avoid what they perceive as losses. In a useful discussion of loss averseness, psychologist and economist Daniel Kahneman says that his research finds that there is a 'loss aversion ratio' – that is, for every one thing that might be lost there has to be a gain of in the range of 1.5–2.5: a salutary point for organization designers and their communications teams.

In simple terms this means that if an individual feels he/she is going to lose something in a redesign – for example a familiar commute to work because there is an office relocation – he/she has to gain something worth, in her estimation, twice that. Note that the things that individuals value cannot be generalized across the employee population. Thus engaging each individual in agreeing to a loss and accepting something that they do not necessarily see as a gain is one of the challenges of organization design work and a contributor to the difficulties some projects experience in the transition and implementation phase.

A different issue, but coming from the same idea of loss versus gain, illustrates the power of small lobbying groups. In Kahneman's words:

The same simple rule explains much of what happens when institutions attempt to reform themselves, in 're-organizations' and 'restructuring' of companies.... As initially conceived, plans for reform almost always produce many winners and some losers while achieving an overall improvement. If the affected parties have any political influence, however, potential losers will be far more active and determined than potential winners; the outcome will be biased in their favour and inevitably more expensive and less effective than initially planned. (Kahneman, 2011)

This situation is one explained from a different perspective by Mancur Olson, economist and social scientist. He argued that 'the narrow "special interests" of the small group tend to triumph over the (often unorganized and inactive) interests of "the people"' (Olson, 2002). This observation has become known as the Olson Paradox.

Small, vocal groups who can mobilize easily and who can sway the intended outcome of a project abound in organizations. One such example is that of moving from people having offices to people working in an open-plan environment. Lawyers are a case in point:

> Many firms still use the promise of prime office space and million-dollar views as a recruitment tool for lawyers who measure their worth in square feet.
>
> Show open-office plans to law firms, and 'the hairs go up on the backs of their necks,' said Barbara Liberatore Black, a managing principal at Cresa, a real-estate advisory firm.
>
> 'Lawyers, their whole mind set is based on precedent,' said Barbara Dunn, a principal and co-chair of the law firm practice group at Gensler, a global architecture and design firm, which designed the Holland & Knight and Proskauer offices. 'None of them want to be first ... but they'll all get in line to be second,' she said. (Smith, 2012)

In-house lawyers are no different from firms of lawyers in defending their 'entitlement' to an office, and again Kahneman has an interesting discussion on the behavioural economics of entitlement, what individuals perceive as fair and the way they will 'fight harder to prevent losses than to achieve gains'.

Both Kahneman's and Olson's perspectives are material when it comes to stakeholder engagement in change projects. Communicating with stakeholders and engaging them effectively goes part of the way towards helping people understand and participate in change rather than feeling that something is being 'done to' them. It may help, too, with the emotions around loss aversion and defending the status quo.

As noted in the chapter opening, paralleling the research into brain and behaviour is the expanding domain of social media. Blending employee engagement strategies with these new media channels and what we are learning about behaviour through neuroscience offers communication specialists a different landscape in which to deploy their skills: they can now use insights derived from economics and the social sciences together with new social media channels.

These new communication approaches supplement tried and tested ones: stakeholder mapping, business and change readiness assessments, change networks/community building, policies updates, frequently asked questions and so on. This means using the best of the conventional communication strategy approaches in new and adaptive ways. This chapter discusses first communication strategies, then moves into social media with their impact on organizational interactions and finally links these to employee engagement, specifically in the aspects of voice and connection.

Communication strategies

Very few organization design consultants and managers afford communication the importance it deserves. They seem unaware that people rapidly pick up on what they intuit, see and hear going on, or what they guess might be going on. Take this example:

> We were thinking of moving offices and invited some architects in to give us their ideas. We had decided it was far too early in the process to tell our staff, but what we hadn't thought through was the fact that we held the meeting with the architects in a room opposite the staff coffee area. Although the door was closed it had a glass panel in it. People could look in. After the meeting I went to get some coffee and someone asked me straight out if we were moving offices.

This is not an isolated type of finding. The rumour mill runs far more rapidly than any form of formal communication and is aided in its widespread repercussions via use of Twitter, Facebook and so on. People respond to rumour in various ways – some will be wary, sceptical or anxious, others will be fearful and a minority will be energized and excited. All will have a point of view and start talking about it.

Mitigate the risk of having to counter rumours and/or misinformation. As soon as the first thought of a design project is mooted start thinking about communication: what, why, when, how, where and to whom. There are many books and resources available to help construct a robust organization design communications strategy and plan. For example, the Change Management Institute has chapters in many countries and can help on communication planning. Most plans follow a similar format:

- Determine the goal of the communications. These will change as the project proceeds but they follow the five-phase organization design methodology and can be summarized as follows:
  - Phase 1: aspects of awareness – capturing attention, developing understanding of the project and the case for change and stating what is negotiable and non-negotiable about the change.
  - Phase 2: issues of individual concern – assuaging anxieties, seeking views, looking at losses and gains and building engagement and commitment.
  - Phase 3: focus on aspects of mental try-out – reinforcing the case for change and linking the goals of the OD project to the well-being of individuals and the organization.

- Phase 4: centre on identifying and mitigating risks, applying new ways of doing things and demonstrating the accruing benefits.
- Phase 5: evaluate the effectiveness of the content and implementation of the communications plan, providing recommendations for future projects and lessons learned. Also, communicate successes and provide evidence that the change is sustainable (or not).

- Identify and profile the various stakeholder groups. There is more on this later in the chapter.
- Identify any constraints that might affect communication about the project.
- Agree who is responsible for drafting, developing and implementing each type of communication and whether specific forms or templates will be used. See Table 9.1 for an example of a template. Decide, too, who has overall accountability for the plan. Ensure that the accountable and responsible people understand, support and have the capability and motivation to communicate accurate and timely messages. For this they need:
  - knowledge of, and support for, the OD project;
  - knowledge of the audience and position and credibility within the organization;
  - interpersonal skills and ability to listen and gain confidence of the audience;
  - an acknowledged role in the OD project.
- Agree resources for the communication development and delivery.
- Develop messages and feedback mechanisms – including the level of detail and the format according to stakeholder audience. The message can be defined as 'what the recipient will be thinking or doing as a result of the communication'. For example, the purpose of the message may be to:
  - convey information (no action required);
  - stimulate action;
  - promote changing behaviour;
  - convey caring and reassurance;
  - motivate towards a goal;
  - promote feelings of unity;
  - provide the 'big picture';
  - show concerns are being captured and listened to;
  - provide feedback.
- Select communication channels. See Figure 9.1 for some options (including consideration of sensitive or confidential information and who will authorize this). The selection of the appropriate medium depends on the size of the audience, the likely reaction of the audience, the response sought from the audience and the type of channels they are likely to use.
- Determine timing, frequency and flow of communications. Getting this wrong can give rise to all sorts of issues. When communicating with

Table 9.1 Extracted example using a communications plan template

AUDIENCE 1: *General managers*

Audience	Objectives	Key messages	Channel	Timing	Accountable
GMs	Obtain their engagement and support Ensure GMs understand their personal role and undertake appropriate action	Rationale for change We need your support and action to make this happen Efficient delivery of business plan and budgets Focus on commercial awareness Efficient use of resources Branches able to focus on delivery Effectiveness in process, systems and infrastructure Issues/project for first year Organizational structure and rationale Timescales for roll-out	*Face-to-face* Strategy Away day Monthly update Project update presentations 1:1s *Social media* Jabber Yammer	March Each month TBC April	

stakeholder groups at different times, take great care to manage possible leaks, misrepresentations and chatter on the rumour mill.

- Develop a communications contingency plan for any unexpected events that might occur, including an escalation plan for resolving any communication-based conflicts or issues.
- Implement the plan.
- Evaluate and make ongoing adjustments and corrections. Aspects to evaluate include:
    - the timing of the communication;
    - whether it is perceived and accepted as accurate by the relevant stakeholders;
    - how far two-way communication is being achieved;
    - what type of feedback is being gathered;
    - whether co-ordination and consistency of messaging and materials is being achieved;
    - whether key influencers are showing their commitment to the project.

Remember that both the *channel* (the conduit for sending the message to the chosen target audience) and the *purpose* of communicating information influence the message design. A 140-character Tweet is a very different design from a blog piece or a short video. Whatever the channel and purpose, there are some key principles to follow:

Clarity: messages must clearly convey information to ensure target audience understanding and to limit the chances of misunderstanding or inappropriate action. Clear messages contain as few technical/scientific/ bureaucratic terms as possible, and eliminate information that the audience does not need. Readability tests help determine the reading level required to understand drafted material and help writers to be conscientious about the selection of words and phrases.

Consistency: in an ideal world all messages on a particular topic would be consistent. Unfortunately, consistency is sometimes elusive. Different leaders and managers put their own spin on things, words used can differ and different perspectives show through. Nevertheless, make the overarching points and direction consistent.

Main points: the main points should be stressed, repeated and never hidden within less strategically important information.

Tone and appeal: messages are reassuring, alarming, challenging or straightforward, depending upon the desired impact and the target audience. Messages should also be truthful, honest and as complete as possible.

Credibility: the spokesperson and/or sources of the information should be believable and trustworthy.

Target audience need: for a message to break through the 'information clutter' people receive every day, messages should be based on what the target audience perceives as most important to them, what they want to know and **not** what is most important or most interesting to the organization's communication team.

Effectiveness: effective two-way communication occurs in a culture of openness and trust where there is willingness to obtain and share information and to listen and act on feedback. If one of the OD project objectives is to develop or build on this type of culture then communication processes and messages must be consistent with this. People look for behaviour, signs and symbols which work together to reinforce the communication messages. Without this consistency people are likely to become disillusioned or sceptical. A survey checking on the effectiveness of communication might look like that shown in Table 9.2.

Prior to dissemination, messages should be pretested or at least checked with the target audiences and/or channel gatekeepers to mitigate risks of misinterpretation or unintended confusion. (Adapted from W. K. Kellogg Foundation, 2006)

Table 9.2 Extract from a survey on communications effectiveness

Statement	Level of agreement
Communications are clear, concise and consistent	1 2 3 4 5 6
Communicators are effective	1 2 3 4 5 6
I benefit from the communications I receive	1 2 3 4 5 6
I feel involved in the decisions that are made by my organization	1 2 3 4 5 6
Top management is committed to good communication	1 2 3 4 5 6
Communication is ongoing, not a series of special events	1 2 3 4 5 6
Communications mirror the vision/values/goals of my organization	1 2 3 4 5 6
Communication has a consistent image and brand which I can relate to	1 2 3 4 5 6

Bearing in mind the desire to maintain the status quo and avoid feelings of loss it is helpful to communicate what is not part of the new design and the transition plan: the things that will continue in relative stability. Reassure people that some of the familiar ways will continue and show that the legacy and heritage of the past and the part people played in the organization up to now is still valued. (Make sure that these statements are true.)

One new CEO who was redesigning his organization told the story of working with the board of the company to construct a visual timeline of its history. Several of the board were long-servers and others were new but all were able to contribute. He shared the timeline with staff, who added their contributions and were then able to use it to see what was enduring and what had changed in their organization. Facebook has a timeline feature that organizations are using to construct histories – a useful item for the communications and engagement toolkit (Facebook, 2013).

Remember, however, that is it almost impossible to avoid at least a few accusations of poor communication, no matter how much is put into it. It is a well-worn truism that there is never enough communication. This is sometimes because there is not enough and sometimes because there are various barriers to messages getting across. These include:

- poor communication skills of the senior communicators (this can be compounded if staff have a negative attitude towards senior management and do not forgive lack of skill);
- a structure which favours top-down communication rather than interactive (downwards, upwards and lateral) communication;
- the strength of internal politics working against the effective transmission and reception of the messages;
- wrongly chosen channels. For example, using Google+ or Pinterest, which may not be accessible/ available to all staff (some geographies and countries do not allow the use of certain social media channels);

- not seeking feedback on communication effectiveness;
- gaps or mistimings in communication;
- too few channels for feedback;
- lack of trust in the messages;
- information overload of recipients.

Many projects have foundered because of ineffective communication – avoid this possibility by regularly reviewing the effectiveness of communications. This will give insight into any improvements or deteriorations during the course of the project, which can be used to take appropriate action.

OD short

Interactive planned communication ideally begins when the first thought of an organization design is raised. A robust communications plan has several standard features, and its implementation success should be evaluated regularly. People will notice if the content, tone and approach of the communications do not square with the prevailing (or intended) culture, which can jeopardize project success. Disseminate regular and consistent messages carefully targeted through a variety of channels that encourage feedback.

Social media

'Social media' refers to the means of interactions among people in which they create, share and exchange information and ideas in virtual communities and networks. Expanding on this definition, Andreas Kaplan and Michael Haenlein define social media as:

> [A] group of Internet-based applications that build on the ideological and technological foundations of Web 2.0, and that allow the creation and exchange of user-generated content. Furthermore, social media depend on mobile and web-based technologies to create highly interactive platforms through which individuals and communities share, co-create, discuss, and modify user-generated content. It introduces substantial and pervasive changes to communication between organizations, communities and individuals. (Wikipedia, 2013)

Note the last sentence in the quotation above. The platforms for interaction (the social media) have changed the way people can and do interact, build relationships, generate content, develop ideas, form and influence opinions, share experiences and perspectives, and 'talk' one-to-one, one-to-many and many-to-many.

From an organization design perspective this evolving communication/ interaction capacity changes the design of the organization in many respects, including the way companies relate to customers, the way products and services are designed and modified/improved, the way user data can be mined for customer insights and so on. In the daily use of social media most of the organizational effort is directed at stakeholders outside the organization, with much less strategic use of its capabilities directed at employees.

Each year Burson Marsteller, a public relations and communications firm, conducts a Social Media Check-Up, examining the Fortune Global 100's use of popular social networking platforms, including Twitter, Facebook, YouTube and, for the first time in 2012, Google+ and Pinterest. What is interesting is that in 2010 the 100 companies were just beginning to engage in social networking, but by 2012 they were actively engaging with users, with the highest volume of activity being on Twitter. Statistics quoted show that during 2012 each of the Fortune Global 100 companies was mentioned an average of 55,970 times per month on Twitter, and 79 per cent of companies engaged with users via retweets and @mentions. Beyond Twitter, 75 per cent of the companies had a Facebook account and again were actively engaging with users. Seventy per cent of the companies had YouTube channels (Burson Marsteller, 2012).

The same Burson Marsteller survey found that companies have multiple accounts on the platforms to enable targeting by audience, geography, topic and service/product. Additionally, as new platforms emerge companies are adopting them as part of their ongoing strategy to interact with external stakeholders.

As the external interaction channels and opportunities change so should the internal interactions and channels. In this respect, using social media as part of an organization design project's engagement with employees should be a no-brainer. As mentioned, this is not yet the case. There are relatively few companies at this point (2013) that are using social media internally with the same facility and capability that they are using them externally – a missed opportunity for rapid collaboration, feedback and interaction that, used effectively, could raise levels of engagement and knowledge-sharing around a project and provide insights into what is working well and not working well and how to do things better.

Euan Semple, in a series of 15 one-minute videos, offers sound advice on social media for internal business use, suggesting various ways that business performance can be heightened via its use and arguing that it offers more to managers than traditional command-and-control ways of communicating. In a brief talk on the impact of social media on the culture of a business, he comments:

> I think the excitement for me is the significant impact social media does have on [a business's] culture, in that so much of the business world has been based on command and control presumptions that you have a Taylorist sort of machine that people get plugged into, and all your systems have to be maintained and managed and most managers set up with that in mind. The potential for these more connected conversational [social media] tools is that more people are more able to deal with issues, become innovative, find other people dealing with issues and connect

with each other to begin to practically do stuff using these tools, with the need for a lot less management.

That doesn't mean you don't need good managers – a lot of managers feel a loss of control with these tools ... I think they're of interest to the middle and the top of organisations ... so for example a middle manager having a place to express the challenges he's facing and express the priorities he's trying to work to, even express the limits in which people have to work, all make more people more likely to understand what he's trying to achieve and more likely to line up behind it. (Semple, n.d.)

If managers are dubious about social media then helping them see the value of it in engaging staff should be a key element in any organization design communications plan.

In a 2011 report, *Driving Collaboration Through Social Media*, the Corporate Leadership Council notes that only 11 per cent of companies felt they collaborated effectively or very effectively and offers a list of reasons why this might be the case. Note that the study was about social media and collaboration in general rather than collaboration related to the engagement of employees in an organization design project. Nevertheless, for those considering using social media as an involvement and participation tool in organization design, the list offers a number of the common barriers which limit its effective internal use:

- Employees don't know who to connect with.
- It is difficult to facilitate collaboration across information 'silos'.
- Legal, security and confidentiality constraints inhibit collaboration.
- Managers don't encourage collaboration and/or don't know how to use social media.
- Senior leaders don't support collaboration and/or don't know how to use social media.
- The organization does not communicate a purpose for collaboration or social media use.
- The organization is too focused on short-term results to invest time in social media support and development.
- The organization lacks the appropriate social media technology or platforms to effectively facilitate collaboration.
- The organizational environment is not supportive of collaboration or the use of social media.
- There are poor processes/policies for collaboration and social media participation.
- There is a lack of budget and other resource for social media capability development.
- There is a lack of clarity regarding who should participate in what social media – and how, why and when.
- There is a lack of incentives to encourage social media use, participation and collaboration among employees.

- There is insufficient time created for employees to collaborate, share information, comment, put a point of view or give feedback.
- There is no co-ordinated approach to social media use and skills development.
- There is no organizational accountability for driving collaboration or metrics to track its effectiveness.
- People don't see the point of using social media. (Adapted from Corporate Leadership Council, 2011)

To have so many aspects to address seems daunting, but the same Corporate Leadership Council report comes to the rescue, offering several ideas for developing a social media strategy for internal use (Table 9.3). All are useful in the context of an organization design communications plan.

OD short

As new platforms and designs for social media emerge, organizations are adopting them and adapting their designs to accommodate the business potential. At this point (2013) social media are used more effectively for interaction with external stakeholders than for interaction with employees. This is a missed opportunity for fostering engagement in an organization design project, and for adapting the organization design in line with these new ways of doing business. A number of barriers to internal social media take-up exist in many organizations, but these can be addressed via an internal social media strategy that specifies the organizational benefits and return on investment that would accrue from their use.

Stakeholder engagement

'How companies define their stakeholders can make an enormous difference in how they implement their business idea' (Schwarz and Gibb, 1999) and defining stakeholders is another of the challenges of organization design work. It becomes critical in relation to the communication and engagement aspects of the project, because, as implied in the earlier discussion (Chapter 7) on the shadow side of the organization:

> Much of the real work of companies happens despite the formal organization. Often what needs attention is the informal organization, the networks of relationships that employees form across functions and divisions to accomplish tasks fast. These informal networks can cut through formal reporting procedures to jump-start stalled initiatives and meet extraordinary deadlines. But informal networks can just as easily sabotage companies' best-laid plans by blocking communication and fomenting opposition to change unless managers know how to identify and direct them. (Prusak, 1997)

Table 9.3 Developing an internal use social media strategy

Focus	Filter	Facilitate
• Focus on identifying the underlying goals for collaboration – and the social media systems and processes that would be necessary to achieve these – agnostic of the specific social media technology. • Create a focus for the social media initiatives (whether that's on enterprise-wide goals or improving individual work needs, or an organization design project) to make participation more effective. • Identify the organization design challenges and then determine which social media management model or combination of models best addresses those challenges. • Continuously review the social media networks for business relevance and direction.	• For an organization design project use multiple accounts to filter and target participants as many companies do their external users. • Establish filters to find the right contributors and create quality content, and manage governance systems that facilitate effective collaboration. • Ensure the right participants are in a particular network or community. • Consider capping the size of each network to militate against the law of diminishing returns.	• Take a quasi-organic approach to social media: allow for open discussion among employees, but actively direct social media towards specific collaborative goals. • Use an evolving set of measures to engage in rapid-cycle reviews of social media use/effectiveness to identify and implement against key learnings. • Manage social media against three principles: 1 Manage to the behaviours that drive effective collaboration rather than to the technical skills used in social media interactions. 2 Extend the scope of social media management from creating to implementing the best ideas. 3 Continuously improve collaborative social media strategies and processes by focusing on the different needs of users and capturing goal-oriented measures.

Source: Adapted from Corporate Leadership Council, 2011.

Stakeholders are those internal and external individuals and groups who are affected by an organization design project, who can influence it for good or bad and who have an interest of some sort in it. The way an OD project is shaped and implemented is interwoven with stakeholder needs and responses. Working with stakeholders is more than communicating with them. It is involving them, listening to them and being responsive to what they are saying. That is, it is engaging with them. Working with stakeholders from the start is in the long-term best interests of an OD project even if it may seem a heavy investment of resource to begin with.

Stakeholder engagement starts in the assessment phase of an OD project. Ideally this is intentional activity aimed at:

- segmenting or mapping stakeholders into categories: Mind Tools has a useful template for this (Thompson, n.d.);
- understanding their positions and perspectives;
- developing an engagement plan that invites support for the new design.

Without this early-stage intentional activity the task of engagement will be harder further down the line.

Segmenting or mapping stakeholders into categories

This helps in effective engagement. But beware of typecasting and know that as things proceed stakeholders can and do change their views. Each stakeholder category (and/or individuals within the category) will have specific needs or concerns that the OD consultant should be aware of. Different stakeholders perceive the same changes in quite different ways depending on various factors, including their:

- expectations of the organization;
- vested interests;
- previous experience of OD and change;
- existing pressures of work;
- interests and affiliations;
- particular characteristics and priorities.

Recognize these differences and segment appropriately. There are various ways of doing this depending on the type of OD project and the organization culture and business.

One method is to think of stakeholders as falling into one of seven categories as shown in Figure 9.2. This classifies them more or less into the roles they have vis-à-vis the new design. Notice that people can fall into more than one category. For example, an employee might be a target of the new design, and knowing that he/she may be asked to take a new job in it could be a blocker or an advocate (and his/her roles may switch during the life cycle of the project).

A second method of classification is to identify stakeholders as falling broadly into three main categories, which are then sub-categorized. Table 9.4 explains.

Understanding stakeholder positions and perspectives

Once stakeholders are categorized, gather information about them in order to do an informed analysis of their opinions, wants and interests. As mentioned, this information-gathering on stakeholders ideally forms part of the assessment phase activity which includes desk research, workshops, interviews and surveys (see Chapter 4).

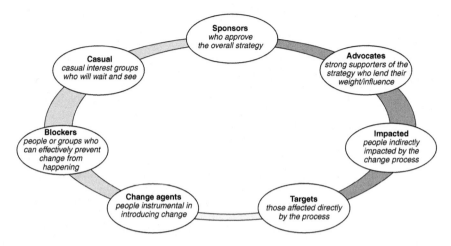

Figure 9.2 Stakeholder segmentation

Different levels of data detail may be necessary for different kinds of stake-holder, depending on the characteristics of the organization, the information readily available and the nature of the proposed changes. For example, an organization with few suppliers may require only a high-level review of them as a group, whereas one with a strong dependency on many key suppliers may need to treat each differently.

If a 'quick and dirty' analysis is all there is time/resource available for, think about each stakeholder in relation to their power, the impact the project has on their interests (their stake in it), their assumed commitment to the project and the level of importance they attach to project success. Then note whether they are low, medium or high on the dial (Figure 9.3).

A likely and common finding of this analysis is that in most OD pro-grammes, the concerns, preoccupations and objectives of different stake-holder groups are found to be in conflict with one another. This is useful, if difficult, information as it points to the requirement to work out systemati-cally a plan to engage critical mass in favour of the new design. Before start-ing the planning, map the stakeholders – there are various templates for doing this, and as well as Mind Tools, Google Images is a good source of them. An example is shown in Figure 9.4.

Note that this example mentions 'sacred cows'. These represent the organi-zational dominant logic and/or non-negotiables that create difficulties. Often they are not explicitly acknowledged or are so much a part of the fabric of the organization that they are unquestioned. The original thinking on domi-nant logic comes from management theorists C. K. Prahalad and R. A. Bettis (Prahalad and Bettis, 1986). Blog writer Sean Silverthorne offers a three-question test for sacred cows:

Table 9.4 Categorizing stakeholders

Main category	Sub-category
Key individuals	**OD sponsor:** the director, senior manager or person who initiates and drives the new design and who takes overall accountability for it
	Promoter: the person(s) promoting a particular kind of solution to address given problems
	OD programme manager: the person responsible for the performance outcomes of the OD process
	Project managers: those responsible for particular projects within the overall OD programme
	Change agents: staff assigned to specific roles to facilitate change and support line management in the process, based on their enthusiasm for the changes the OD project brings and their available skills
	Targets: users of the changed design, including those who expected to benefit from it in other business areas – normally the employee and contractor groups
	Champions: those supporters or enthusiasts in the business who shape opinions, and lead and influence in generating support for the proposed changes coming out of the OD project
	Anti-champions: those nay-sayers or opponents in the business who shape opinions, and lead and influence in generating opposition to the proposed changes coming out of the OD project
	Support players: those whose functional support is required for effective implementation of the project but who do not have direct accountability for it or a strong stake in it
Key groups	These comprise mainstream employees whom the proposed change will directly impact and whose jobs and performance standards will be changed as a direct result of the change process, including:
	Senior management: this group is usually the board or an executive body, which is responsible for organizational performance. Members make key decisions. Their sustained and mutual commitment will be required to endorse the changes required and to maintain energy within the OD process
	Change owners: these are the management groups who will implement the new design. It will have day-to-day operational impact on their business area
	Line management: this is the intermediate management/supervisory group between top management, change owners and employees. Without their positive engagement project success is dubious
	Employee representatives: this group represents the interests of the non-managers in the organization. It may be through works councils, trades unions or similar. Whichever representative bodies are present in organization their involvement is critical
	Specialists: this includes those groups who may be responsible for policy, design, planning, technical specification or functional control of various aspects of the change, e.g. IT, Finance, Recruitment, Training and Development

Table 9.4 (cont.)

Main category	Sub-category
	Support: this category of staff includes those who support the key operational groups, e.g. secretarial staff or facilities management. They often wield power in their role of gatekeepers for other stakeholder groups **Employees**: this is the largest group, comprising the rank and file of the organization **Contract staff**: where there are significant numbers of contractors, decide whether they are a key group to engage. Make this a conscious decision. Often their work is critical to organization success but they are excluded from communication and engagement activity **NOTE**: Other methods of identifying key internal groups are according to their business division, level of management, skill areas, location or roles in the OD process, etc. Again, note that a single individual could appear in more than one category or group
Key external stakeholders	What constitutes an external stakeholder will vary according to the size and scope of the OD programme. For some organizations, planning major OD change without involving suppliers as stakeholders is inconceivable. For others, a broader view of the likely impact on third-party groups is sufficient. If there are outsourcing agencies or partnerships/alliances with other organizations consider what role they play as project stakeholders. A typical list of key external stakeholders includes: • customers • shareholders • suppliers • strategic partners • consultants and advisers • competitors • government agencies • local community • advisory bodies • NGOs and lobby groups

1   What do we consider good performance?
2   Whom do we promote: executives who can extract profits from the current business model or those who can lead the company into new businesses?
3   Do middle managers focus on change or the status quo?

By looking at these questions through the Kodak lens (pun intended), we can see how effective these questions can be in identifying the sacred cows that anchor us to the past.

At Kodak, I'm sure the three questions were answered thus: Increasing film sales is a key measure of good performance; we promote people who

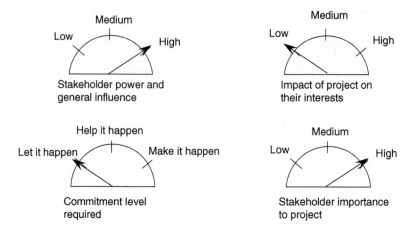

Figure 9.3 'Quick and dirty' stakeholder analysis

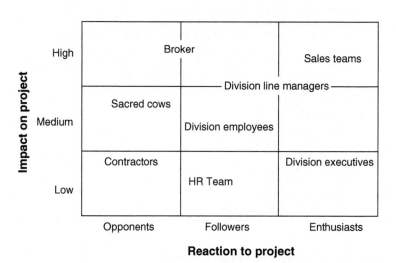

Reaction to project

Figure 9.4 Example stakeholder map

can extract profit from the current business model; middle managers focus on the status quo.

How would your senior managers answer these questions? How do you think managers at Apple or P&G or Google would answer? (Silverthorne, 2010)

Assessing and mapping stakeholders has to be done regularly through the project life cycle. As the organizational environment changes the stakeholder group and their response to what is going on are likely to change also. If, for example, a key individual leaves the organization their successor may take quite a different view of the project and work may have to start from square one to gain the new person's support. In other circumstances a competing project might suddenly jockey for stakeholder attention. Get a running picture so that engagement activity can be adjusted to meet the changing situation.

Once the initial stakeholder analysis and mapping is completed develop a clear plan for engaging stakeholders appropriately. The plan should include, for each stakeholder group, techniques and approaches to use to increase level of commitment to the OD project and its outcomes. A combination of tactical activity, nudge activity based in behavioural economics (see Glossary), carrot/stick incentives and infrastructure reinforcement works best.

Developing an engagement plan that invites employee support for the new design

People directly affected by the changes the OD work brings, and for the most part this is the rank and file employees, benefit from the planning and delivery of empathetic and ordered activities to support them through the transition from current to new design. This engagement plan is different from a communication plan but interactive with it.

Broadly the employee engagement plan is based in the notion that:

> For the most part people voluntarily join an organization because they are attracted to the 'deal' it offers them in exchange for their work. Different organizations offer different deals but this 'employee value proposition', as it is known, includes benefits, career development opportunities, rewards, culture and management style, work location and workplace design: if the 'deal' changes, then the level of engagement changes.
>
> Any planned radical change, for example a new organization design, impacts, for better or worse, the deal the employee has with the organization. An employee who has joined an organization because, among other reasons, they liked the easy commute from their home to the office is not going to appreciate the plan to relocate to offices that require changes to the length of their commute, their child-care pick-up arrangements, the lack of the route-home supermarket, etc.
>
> In this sort of situation employees are not just considering what the organization is offering and/or changing. They are positioning the new deal in the context of their work/life balance and juggling other changes they are affected by – society, the economy and in their personal lives, for example life-stage or 'generational' change. Changing the deal changes the level of engagement the employee has with the organization. (NBBJ, 2013)

Developing employee engagement with the 'new deal' is another challenge faced by organization design consultants. The challenge is that it has to overcome the loss aversion mentioned earlier and be accepted as a gain. Briefly it requires four types of activity:

1   **clarifying** the impact of the change on the employee deal;
2   **consulting** with employees and stakeholders on change and what it means for individuals, the teams they work in and the organization as a whole;
3   **confirming** the new situation at the individual, team and organizational level;
4   **communicating** and actively soliciting communication throughout the organization using multiple channels and consistent messaging.

These four 'C's are not a sequence of activities but rather an iterative, emerging and interrelated approach involving careful and sensitive methods of attraction, co-option and engagement of people in the organization design, ideally using social media. The activities encourage employees to help influence and shape the design from the moment it is first being considered within a framework of what is negotiable and what is not – not in the sense of a formal union-style negotiation but rather as a discussion on what they can change and what is a given. This last point is important because, as one consultant remarked on reviewing this approach:

> My only question is with the four Cs. In item two, we talk about consulting with employees and stakeholders about the change and what it means to them and the organization. We have run into conflicts in the past with employees being consulted but not being in a position to act on their ideas. Or leadership on the project doesn't want to. Is there a way we can address that at least in the methodologies and processes?

The clarifying part of the methodology involves leadership statements on what is and is not negotiable. So, for example, a leader might say:

•   We are moving to a new location and I and my leadership team will decide where, based on criteria that we will share with you.
•   The current teleworking/remote-working policies will not change in the new design.
•   There will be a desk-sharing policy in the new location and no one will have his/her own office.

> All of these are non-negotiable. The things I am expecting input and ideas on are currently the following:
> What departments and teams it makes sense to co-locate.
> The methods of developing teleworking/remote-working capability so that it works better than currently.

The logistics and protocols around desk-sharing.
We will take your views and preferences into account and meet as many as
we can, communicating with you on the why and why not as we go.

Clarifying also involves reminding people of the part the redesign plays in
the strategic direction of the organization in both the short term and the long
term. It means providing and discussing, with conviction, a sound case to let
people know that things are changing not for the sake of it but with the intention of achieving agreed business results.

This form of clarification helps to answer the questions 'why redesign, why
now, why us?' which pop up in every phase of the project and means that clarifying activity is both time- and event-driven – that is, it continues through the
life cycle of the project as new things to clarify emerge.

Consulting with stakeholders involves making it clear that not everyone
will get what they want and that consultation involves compromise and balancing competing interests. Consulting involves enabling people to feel positive and optimistic in the face of change – willing to take accountability and
risks in order to benefit from the redesign. Even if job loss is a possibility,
there is every reason to help people prepare for this and help them believe that
they have a good future ahead of them. Again, the consulting is an ongoing
process through the project life cycle.

As things are decided there is confirmation of the new state of play. For
example, the plans for co-location are fixed following the consultation. As
with clarifying and consulting this confirming activity is ongoing.

Integral to each of these three activities there is communication using
multi-channels and targeted at the appropriate audiences.

This four-part iterative approach enables employees to understand why an
organization redesign is happening and then make a choice around whether
they still feel connected with the organization, its mission, purpose and values. Part of this choice relates to the losses and gains they feel they are incur-
ring. Additionally it encourages voice – being asked for their opinion, being
involved and being kept in the know sustains engagement.

The four-pronged approach to engagement is not all plain sailing. It involves
dealing swiftly and constructively with negative behaviours and disengagement.
Leaders have to face the fact that their actions and decisions may be called
into question if the proposed redesign cannot avoid taking actions unpleas-
ant to individual stakeholders, and an organization redesign is very likely to
have unfortunate consequences for some. It is important that leaders and OD
consultants maintain a strong sense of perspective and have the personal confidence to manage complex, perhaps distressing, dilemmas and situations.

OD short

Stakeholder engagement is more than communication. It is planned activity
to develop or maintain support for the new design. Segmenting stakeholders

enables appropriate engagement activity to be planned. Employees are a critical group and engagement activity designed to give them a voice in an organization design project, and a sense of continued connection with the mission and values of the organization, helps mitigate feelings of loss commonly associated with changes to the status quo. Behavioural economics and emerging work in neuroscience offer new ways of developing engagement.

Tools

Tool 1 The brains, behaviour and design toolkit

This features five tools to help designers apply findings from the field of behavioural economics to their practice in order to provide a head start on framing research as well as developing new strategies for solving user problems. The toolkit is downloadable (Brains Behavior and Design Group, 2012).

The toolkit includes:

- Reference cards: behavioural economics research findings organized and described.
- Concept ecosystem poster: the relationships between concepts.
- Irrational situations guides: when people act irrationally, what to look for and how to design for these situations.
- Strategy cards: ways to design for the irrational mind.
- Loss/gain worksheet: understanding and designing for tradeoffs.

Tool 2 Communication and engagement checklist

Summary

Social media and advances in behavioural economics and neuroscience are transforming organizational communication stakeholder engagement. Taken together they offer a powerful way of working with stakeholders to develop and maintain their support for a new organization design. Successful communication and stakeholder engagement require systematic and carefully planning, implementation and continuous evaluation. Because the context in which the design is happening is changing irrespective of the design activity, it is essential to be alert to course corrections and changes, to maintain engagement and to keep communication timely, transparent and trustworthy. Inevitably some stakeholders will be disaffected by the changes and swift action is needed to prevent powerful groups derailing the project.

References

Brains Behavior and Design Group. (2012). 'Toolkit'. Retrieved 18 May 2013, from http://www.brainsbehavioranddesign.com/index.html.

Table 9.5 Communication and engagement checklist

Communication	N/A	Yes	No
Open and effective engagement involves both listening and talking			
Two-way communication (Who do we need to talk and listen to?)			
1 Foster co-ownership of the communication process.			
2 Clearly define lines of communication.			
3 Maximize community and stakeholder opportunities to say what they want and to provide information and feedback.			
4 Ensure appropriate representatives take part in consultation and are accessible to communities and stakeholders.			
5 Demonstrate active listening by responding to the issues of each community and stakeholder group and being sensitive to their concerns.			
6 Determine and use the right channels of communication to ensure the method of communication is appropriate to the relevant communities and stakeholders.			
7 Identify appropriate individuals and contacts to ensure the right people are engaged. Ensure the contacts are representative of their group.			
8 Build and maintain honest working relationships through the provision of accurate and timely information.			
9 Understand individual and group capacities to participate and incorporate this into planning.			
10 Recognize the importance of engaging at the most direct level and ensure the level is appropriate for the purpose.			
Clear, accurate and relevant information (What is communicated? What do key stakeholders want to know?)			
1 Identify and assess all relevant social, environmental and economic effects of activities.			
2 Provide information and analysis (where appropriate) that is technically or scientifically sound and relevant.			
3 Provide information in a form that is understandable by the target audience and in a way that genuinely helps people to understand and make informed decisions.			
4 Use independent expert advice when appropriate.			
5 Ensure access to information.			
6 Ensure the information provided is delivered in a culturally appropriate manner.			

Table 9.5 (cont.)

Communication	N/A	Yes	No

7 Provide opportunities for communities and stakeholders to ask questions, to seek clarification of information provided and to contribute their own experiences and information.

Timeliness (When do we communicate?)

1 Seek community and stakeholder views as early in the proposal development stage as possible.

2 Understand and recognize the need to build relationships, capacity and knowledge before making decisions.

3 Allow enough time for community and stakeholder issues to be raised and addressed and for stakeholders to review and respond to information.

4 Establish clear and realistic time frames for community and stakeholder input.

5 Maintain engagement throughout the life of the project, from the planning stage through to construction/implementation, operation/review and finally through to closure.

7 Respect time frames that will allow for community and stakeholder participation.

8 Provide information within appropriate time frames and contexts and identify the reporting period. Make any critical deadlines and time frames clear to communities and stakeholders.

9 Ensure timing is convenient to allow adequate community and stakeholder representation.

10 Recognize, respect and accommodate changes to time frames where necessary.

Transparency (How is information about the engagement process communicated?)

1 Clearly identify objectives for the project. Clearly articulate the preferred outcomes of the engagement process.

2 Identify the objectives of the community and stakeholders.

3 Clearly explain or negotiate (where required) the decision-making processes and ensure that communities and stakeholders understand objectives.

4 Clearly outline and negotiate (where required) the boundaries of the engagement process, commitment of resources and level of influence of the various parties involved in the process.

5 Clearly articulate the preferred outcomes of the project (for example operating conditions, environmental objectives, effective implementation of changes to minimize impact on clients).

6 Clearly set out the process and provisions for two-way feedback.

7 Reinforce the expected outcomes throughout the process. Provide information immediately on any changes to the expected outcomes.

8 Report openly the input from all communities and stakeholders and include feedback on their input.

Reporting (What is documented?)

1 Document decisions and outcomes of meetings with communities and stakeholders.

2 Report appropriate performance information on the consultation through an agreed process.

3 When appropriate and practicable, support performance information with verification.

Collaboration (How to work co-operatively to seek mutually beneficial outcomes)

1 Recognize that adequate time and resources are needed to effectively engage stakeholders.

2 Share expertise.

3 Work in co-operation.

4 Establish joint ownership of outcomes, seeking mutually beneficial outcomes where feasible.

5 Comprehensively deal with the issues and seek stakeholder input into responses.

6 If appropriate, take an active role in local community affairs.

7 Consider independent mediation processes to deal with disagreements and disputes.

Inclusiveness (What are the cultural characteristics of communities and stakeholders? Do they have the ability, experience and/or access to support or deal with this process?)

1 Identify the relevant communities and stakeholders, recognizing they may change over time.

2 Identify and, where possible, understand community and stakeholder issues, interests, aspirations and concerns to better define what matters most to the community.

3 Facilitate (where appropriate) community and stakeholder engagement.

4 Acknowledge and respect the diversity of communities and stakeholders.

5 Respect the culture and heritage of local communities and stakeholders.

6 Accept the different agendas of different communities and stakeholders and ensure that dominant groups are not the only voices heard.

7 Ensure there are appropriate systems, with minorities and other marginalized groups having equitable and culturally appropriate ways to engage, so groups that may be under-represented or hard to reach take part.

Table 9.5 (cont.)

Communication	N/A	Yes	No
8 Acknowledge that in few circumstances is it feasible to involve the entire community.			
9 Prepare a consultation plan and tailor engagement strategies to meet the needs of community and/or stakeholder groups, their accessibility and information needs.			
Integrity (What is the ability to build credibility and confidence?)			
1 Agree on the ground rules for the process and obey them – explain what the process is trying to achieve.			
2 Be open about the nature of the engagement process and make it clear from the beginning what decisions are outside the scope of the process.			
3 Clearly articulate what is negotiable and what is not negotiable in the engagement process. Give reasons for decisions.			
4 Ensure realistic expectations are set and agreed early in the process.			
5 Take responsibility for project actions and decisions and live up to promises.			
6 Report often on progress – accurately and promptly.			
7 Ensure the proclaimed values of project policies and codes of conduct at the corporate level are consistent with practice on the ground.			
8 Ensure that all stakeholder opinions and rights to object or support a project/policy are respected. Acknowledge and respond to stakeholder concerns.			
9 Treat people fairly and without discrimination.			
10 Respect legal, ethical and human rights.			
11 Be honest, even when the news is not good or favours others.			

Source: Adapted from Department of Immigration and Citizenship, 2008.

Burson Marsteller. (2012). 'Global Social Media Check-Up 2012', July. Retrieved 30 March 2013, from Burson Marsteller: http://www.burson-marsteller.com/social/ Presentation.aspx.

Corporate Leadership Council. (2011). *Driving Collaboration Through Social Media.* Washington, DC: The Executive Board.

Department of Immigration and Citizenship. (2008). *Stakeholder Engagement: Practitioner Handbook.* Retrieved 7 August 2013, from Australian Government: National Communications Branch of the Department of Immigration and Citizenship: http://www.immi.gov.au/about/stakeholder-engagement/_pdf/stakeholder-engagement-practitioner-handbook.pdf.

Facebook. (2013). 'Introducing Timeline', 13 March. Retrieved 29 March 2013, from Facebook: https://www.facebook.com/about/timeline.

Heger, B. K. (2007). 'Linking the Employment Value Proposition (EVP) to Employee Engagement and Business Outcomes: Preliminary Findings from a Linkage Research Pilot Study', *Organization Development Journal*, **25**(2), 121–32.

Holbeche, L. and Matthews, G. (2012). *Engaged: Unleashing Your Organization's Potential through Employee Engagement.* San Francisco: Jossey-Bass.

Kahneman, D. (2011). *Thinking Fast and Slow.* New York: Farrar, Straus and Giroux.

McGregor, J. (2007). 'The Business Brain in Close-Up', July 22. Retrieved 24 March 2013, from Bloomberg Business Week: http://www.businessweek.com/ stories/2007–07–22/the-business-brain-in-close-up.

NBBJ. (2013). 'Engaging Change', April. Seattle: NBBJ.

Olson, M. (2002). *The Logic of Collective Action: Public Goods and the Theory of Groups.* Cambridge, MA: Harvard University Press.

Peterson, C. (2013). *Pursuing the Good Life.* New York: Oxford University Press.

Prahalad, C. K. and Bettis, R. A. (1986). 'The Dominant Logic: A New Linkage between Diversity and Performance', *Strategic Management Journal*, 7(6), 485–501.

Prusak, L. (1997). *Knowledge in Organizations.* Newton, MA: Butterworth-Heinemann.

Schwarz, P. and Gibb, B. (1999). *When Good Companies Do Bad Things: Responsibility and Risk in an Age of Globalization.* New York: John Wiley & Sons Inc.

Semple, E. (n.d.). 'Social Media Advice for Business'. Retrieved 30 March 2013, from Guru Online: http://www.guruonline.tv/euansemple/business-social-media/3817/ social-media-affect-business-culture.

Silverthorne, S. (2010). 'The Sacred Cow Test', 30 June. Retrieved 31 March 2013, from CBS Moneywatch: http://www.cbsnews.com/8301–505125_162–31547234/ the-sacred-cow-test.

Smith, J. (2012). 'Law Firms Say Good-Bye Office, Hello Cubicle', 15 July. Retrieved 29 March 2013, from *Wall Street Journal*: http://online.wsj.com/article/SB10001424 05270230361280457752894029167010 0.html.

Social Media Club. (2010). 'About Us'. Retrieved 24 March 2013, from Social Media Club: http://socialmediaclub.org/about-us.

Solis, B. and Thomas, J. (2010). 'The Conversation Prism'. Retrieved 24 March 2013, from http://www.theconversationprism.com.

Thompson, R. (n.d.). 'Stakeholder Analysis'. Retrieved 15 May 2013, from Mind Tools: http://www.mindtools.com/pages/article/newPPM_07.htm.

W. K. Kellogg Foundation. (2006). 'Template for Strategic Communications Plan', 1 January. Retrieved 29 March 2013, from W. K. Kellogg Foundation: http:// www.wkkf.org/knowledge-center/resources/2006/01/template-for-strategic-communications-plan.aspx.

Wikipedia. (2013). 'Social Media', 30 March. Retrieved 30 March 2013, from Wikipedia: http://en.wikipedia.org/wiki/Social_media.

10 Trends and organization design

The spread of computers and the Internet will put jobs in two categories: people who tell computers what to do, and people who are told by computers what to do.

Brynjolfsson and McAfee, 2012

What you will learn

In this chapter you will learn about the future of work and its impact on the design of organizations; specifically, you are asked to consider four types of work and how these are changing in response to various context factors. You will find out how to identify and follow the trends that may have an organizational impact and then assess whether to respond to these. Three trends that you will discover more about are digital transformation, neuroscience and demographics.

Overview

Throughout the book the emphasis has been on designing the structure of an organization around the work of the organization. This implies that as the nature of work changes so will the design and structure. So it is worth first considering what work is and second looking at aspects of the environment that are changing the nature of work. Writing in 1992, Robert Reich, a US political economist, defined 'the work of the future' in three categories (he was talking about paid employment):

Routine production services: these are repetitive tasks done over and over. Reich explains that 'Routine producers typically work in the company of many other people who do the same thing, usually within large enclosed spaces. They are guided on the job by standard procedures and codified rules, and even their overseers are overseen, in turn, by people who monitor – often with the aid of computers – how much they do and how accurately they do it.' Examples of this type of worker are assembly-line workers and data inputters. This type of work can be done anywhere in the world.

In-person services: are those that are supplied person to person. In-person workers work alone or in small teams and 'are in direct contact with the immediate beneficiaries of their work; their immediate objects are specific customers'. In-person workers include waiters, flight attendants, taxi drivers and physical therapists.

Symbolic-analytic services: are those that involve problem identifying, problem solving and strategic brokering, using data and analytic tools. Reich includes in this category people who call themselves research scientists, software engineers, lawyers, real estate developers, management consultants, advertising executives and film makers. He makes the point that symbolic analysts manipulate symbols. 'They simplify reality into abstract images that can be rearranged, juggled, experimented with, communicated to other specialists, and then, eventually transformed back into reality. The manipulations are done by analytic tools sharpened by experience.' Analytic tools include algorithms, principles, psychological insights, 'or any other set of techniques for doing conceptual puzzles' (Reich, 1992).

These three categories of work still hold good. But think about how the work done in each of the categories has changed in the past couple of decades and is continuing to change. Also consider that an activity that is paid employment for one person may not be for another. For example, someone may iron their own shirt, in which case the activity is unpaid 'work'. But the same person may opt to pay someone to iron the shirt, in which case the activity becomes that person's paid employment. This example leads to a consideration of the characteristics of paid work. In her 1982 book *Employment and Unemployment: A Social-Psychological Analysis*, social psychologist Marie Jahoda identified five important features of the employed life and thus of work:

1   It imposes a time structure on the day and thereby on our experience.
2   It enlarges the scope of relationships beyond those of the immediate family or neighborhood where one lives.
3   It provides meaning through the shared purposes and activities of a social group.
4   It assigns social status and clarifies personal identity. Work (or employment) need not be 'high status' to meet this need.
5   It requires regular activity. (Peterson, 2009)

Each of these is changing expression as digital transformation takes hold. ('Digital transformation refers to a broad strategic initiative in which multiple parts of an organization use new digital technologies, such as social media, mobile, analytics or "smart" devices, to enable critical business improvements, such as enhancing the customer experience, streamlining operations, or creating new business models' (MIT Sloan, 2013).)

Work, in the clichéd phrase, can now be 24/7, the scope of relationships can be global and virtual; shared purposes can be transient as people move from one work project or team to another; visible manifestations of social status are eroded as private offices give way to open-plan; regular activity can give way to spasmodic activity as people multi-task, respond to the urgent and neglect the important or move in and out of the workforce.

Responding to these changes a fourth category of work is re-emerging: that of artisan. This form of work is defined as trade or handicraft work produced in limited quantities, often using traditional methods such as in rug-making or glass-blowing. The digital angle on this artisan category of work is the emerging maker movement, described as:

> [A] trend in which individuals or groups of individuals create and market products that are recreated and assembled using unused, discarded or broken electronic, plastic, silicon or virtually any raw material and/or product from a computer-related device. The maker movement has led to the creation of a number of technology products and solutions by typical individuals working without supportive infrastructure. This is facilitated by the increasing amount of information available to individuals and the decreasing cost of electronic components. (Janssen, n.d.)

This changing nature of work, what people consider work and how they do the work has a profound impact on the design of organizations. Designing organizations capable of responding to the changing meaning and expression of work requires identifying and tracking trends and planning how to best respond to them. So this chapter continues with a discussion of trends in general and then considers three major ones – digital transformation, neuroscience and demographics. The chapter closes with a brief discussion of some emerging organization designs.

OD short

Four categories of work – routine, in-person, symbolic analytic and artisan useful – cover most types of paid employment. Work in all four categories changes as the context changes, and as organizations are designed around work it is important to keep abreast of the trends that offer insight into how work may change.

Trends

A trend is a month-by-month or year-by-year movement of a metric. Trends in organizations are collected on performance-based data, obviously the financials, but also include customer satisfaction, company reputation,

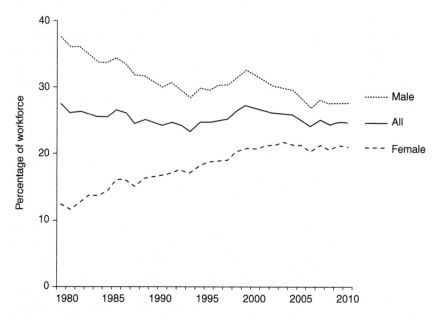

Figure 10.1 Share of workers with good jobs, by gender, 1979–2010
Source: Schmidtt and Jones, 2012.

productivity and employee engagement among others. Trends are often shown graphically as 'trend lines' drawn from quantifiable metrics collected over time (Figure 10.1).

Organization design consultants need to be aware not only of internal trends but also those in the external environment. Whatever is going on outside the organization may well have an impact on its design and redesign. They need to be able to answer three questions.

1   What are the emerging macro trends – economic, political, societal and business – that are rising to the top of the agenda?
2   Are our senior executives across the board aware of the significance of these and the potential impact on the organization?
3   Do we have the right individual and organizational capability to succeed in the future business landscape indicated by the trends?

As an example, take social media. Since 2010, use of social media has been increasing significantly, and at the beginning of 2013 Edelman Digital, a brand and media firm, reported that:

> 300 million photos are posted to Facebook every day. 5 billion photos have been shared on Instagram. Visual sites such as Tumblr and

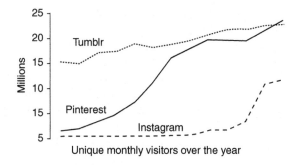

Figure 10.2 Visual sites surging in traffic and attention
Source: Lutz, 2013.

Pinterest have surged in interest, with 23 million unique visitors per month [during 2012]. Consumers aren't just visiting visual sites, they are interacting more with visual content. According to Simply Measured, visual content generates 5× more engagement than non-visual content on Facebook.

Having presented the trend lines (Figure 10.2), the author continued:

Brands are taking note. Johnnie Walker made the shift in 2012, launching on Instagram by partnering with established Instagram influencers and evolving its Facebook presence to highlight fan-generated photos in cover photos. Visual storytelling is evolving on mobile as well. Twitter's purchase of Vine is driving a surge in campaigns using bite-sized videos. McDonald's, Skylanders and Toyota have each jumped in with games, fans and a stop motion ad to start.

Think what this trend means for organization designers. It requires thinking about an appropriate organization response – one that will maintain competitiveness, planning how to take action and then taking the action. The response from some organizations has been to establish a social business 'command centre', defined as:

A physical space where companies coordinate to listen and engage their market in social channels to achieve business use cases in marketing engagement, customer care, risk management, or operational efficiency of coordination and contact center deflection. (Owyang, 2012)

Now go back to the systems model (Figure 1.3) and think how establishing a command centre of this type requires aligning all elements of the organization's system. Michael Brito, a commentator on the topic, explains, in a video presentation, the elements that need addressing:

> [In the video] I get into the Command Center Framework and discuss the importance of having a set strategy taking into consideration the goals and objectives and dashboard and technology requirements. I used the Social Business Framework to illustrate the need to consider People, Process and Platforms for command center deployment. This included building the right team, creating a social business center of excellence, create processes for crisis management and customer support workflows. (Brito, 2013)

From this example it is clear that external forces – in this instance social media – heavily influence organization design, and organizations have to know when to respond quickly to a trend and when to wait and see. Very often the response is laggardly and organizations then struggle to regain lost ground. The Kodak story is one frequently held up as a warning in this regard: Fujifilm of Japan undercut Kodak's prices, and people switched from traditional film (which in 2003 it stopped investing in) to digital photography.

> For the best part of two decades, Eastman Kodak [founded in 1880 and one of America's most notable companies] has been a case study in whether a global pioneer in an earlier, analogue technology can success-fully make the transition to the digital era.
>
> The answer finally came shortly after midnight on Thursday morning [19 January 2012] in its home town of Rochester, in upstate New York: the company that local entrepreneur George Eastman founded 131 years ago after he was bitten by the photography bug filed for bankruptcy. (Waters and Nuttall, 2012)

Kodak was not alone in losing ground to companies swifter on the uptake of new technologies and new competitors. The Borders Group liquidated in 2011 after failing to gain a toehold in e-books, while Blockbuster sold itself to Dish Network, also in 2011, as its retail outlets lost ground to online competitors like Netflix (de la Merced, 2012).

Tracking trends is a skill all organization designers need to have (also see Chapter 2), but it is not always easy to know what trends to track and then whether something is a trend to act on or a short-term 'fad' that requires no action.

> A fad is the 'newest thing'. In the business world brainstorming, corpo-rate social responsibility, customer relationship management, delayering, double-loop learning, empowerment, lean, learning organization, matrix management, outsourcing, process improvement, project management, quality circles, six sigma, succession planning, sustainability, total quality management, vertical integration and/or zero-based budgeting are some

things which have all at one time or another been the 'newest thing'. Many of them have disappeared within a few years, others have remained part of business life and proved valuable and others not. (Stanford, 2013)

Because it is hard to know whether something is a fad or a trend, few organizations successfully adapt to changes in the environment, or positively and attentively engage with change and stay competitive and successful over the long term, but many aspire to. A systematic process for scanning and choosing whether to take action on a trend or to dismiss something as a fad are actions that make adaptation more likely, and it is worth the investment of resources in doing so. However, as one writer points out, in approaching this:

> Trust yourself. Trust your own experience and apply it to the current market place. You won't do any worse than the consultants to whom you'd otherwise pay good money. To truly understand what any given business is doing right or doing wrong, you have to fully understand what it is doing. Most businesses don't have the machinery and/or can't afford the time to do that, so we stagger on as best we can with the best-available data. (Mason, 2010)

The enduring areas in which to look for trends are more or less covered by the STEEPLE acronym (described in Chapter 3) and the tool at the end of this chapter shows how it can be used. As mentioned, digital transformation, neuroscience, demographics, sustainability and social value are all topics for trend watchers and likely to remain so.

OD short

Keeping an eye on trends likely to have an impact on a particular organization is a crucial activity for organization designers. To maintain competitiveness in a constantly changing environment, knowing what trends to act on and what not to be too concerned about requires knowing the business and also knowing the competitor landscape. It is less risky to act on trends tracked over time than to respond to fads.

Digital transformation

As the definition in the first section of this chapter indicates, 'digital transformation' is a catch-all phrase for many technologies, and earlier in this chapter social media were discussed. One of the fields of digital transformation that is having, and will continue to have, a significant impact on organization design generally is that of robotics. Interestingly, robotics touches all four types of work.

In many types of routine, assembly-line/manufacturing work robots are replacing human workers (in 2011 the sale of robotics for manufacturing grew 44 per cent: Brooks, 2013). This example illustrates:

At the Philips Electronics factory on the coast of China, hundreds of workers use their hands and specialized tools to assemble electric shavers. That is the old way.

At a sister factory here in the Dutch countryside, 128 robot arms do the same work with yoga-like flexibility. Video cameras guide them through feats well beyond the capability of the most dexterous human.

All told, the factory here has several dozen workers per shift, about a tenth as many as the plant in the Chinese city of Zhuhai. This is the future. (Markoff, 2012)

In-person work is not immune from robotics. In the field of healthcare, for example, the Huggable™ is a new type of robotic companion,

designed to function as a team member that is an essential member of a triadic interaction … the fully autonomous Huggable™ interacts with the patient to provide therapeutic benefit of a companion animal, and can also communicate behavioral data about this interaction to the nursing staff to assist them in promoting improved well-being of the patient. (Huggables, 2008)

And there is significant work in the field of robotics on using them as care and/or service assistants.

Service robots are already used in a wide variety of areas today, including for household chores, surveillance work and cleaning, and in hospitals and care homes. Our aging population is making it necessary to keep older people as autonomous as possible for as long as possible, which means caring for aged people is likely to be an important area for the deployment of service robots. (Kurzweil Accelerating Intelligence, 2012)

However, this is not without barriers. A 2012 European Union Report, *Public Attitudes towards Robots*, reported that:

EU citizens also have well-defined views about the areas where robots should be banned. Views are most emphatic when it comes to the care of children, elderly people and people with disabilities, 60% of EU citizens saying that this is an area where robots should be banned. There is also considerable opposition to the use of robots in the other more 'human' areas included in the survey: 34% of respondents believe robots should be banned in education, 27% are against the use of robots in healthcare and 20% oppose their use for leisure purposes. Less than ten percent oppose the use of robots in any of the other areas. Overall, ten percent of respondents spontaneously said that robots should not be banned in any of the areas listed. (European Union, 2012)

In work classed as symbolic analytic, IBM's supercomputer, Watson, for example, is being asked to

> soak up all the information it can about oncology and case histories at Sloan-Kettering. It then learns about specific patients, and comes up with a ranked list of treatment options. It offers a kind of second-opinion for the consulting doctor based on its ability to sift through a colossal amount of data and make new associations that doctors might not see … Watson doesn't really give you an answer. It gives you a list of answers and then it ranks based on its certainly and probabilities which ones it thinks are the most likely. (McMillan, 2012)

Meanwhile in the world of artisan work, individuals are building robots from a variety of recycled materials and, for example, using them to engage children in making their own robots and explore the world of creative engineering (Bal, 2013).

Although there is a fear that robots are taking jobs away from people, a moment's pause to reflect may prompt the thought that in order to develop, manufacture and service robots, people are needed. Jobs may move to a different sector, requiring different skillsets, but there may not be an overall loss of jobs. However, quickly skilling up people to do jobs requiring new capability is not easy. These two aspects of the spreading use of robots in the workforce introduce two organization design challenges: designing for new forms of work, and designing for different skillsets – if the skillsets are not readily available in the market place it may be useful to consider more innovative forms of organization design – for example, sharing skilled people with another organization, or delayering to free up staff and paying for those with the capability to do a rapid retraining.

An organization development challenge is that of teaching managers and employees the skills to work with a workforce comprising humanoid robots and human beings. Anybots, for example, produces a robot avatar.

> Anybots QB Telepresence robot lets you be at the office without being there But don't worry. It doesn't want your job. QB is a robotic stand-in for workers. You control it remotely as a videoconference system on wheels. Embodied as a QB, you can attend meetings, drop by a coworker's office, even confab at the water cooler.
>
> You can control your robotic self from anywhere using a computer connected to the Net. It's a bit like the recent Bruce Willis movie *Surrogates*. Except QB is less, uh, muscular. (Guizzo, 2010)

OD short

There are many aspects to 'digital transformation'. Beyond social media one that is likely to become increasingly prevalent in the workplace is the spread of robots. Their use is already evident in all four types of work. The increasing use of robots brings several organization design challenges including designing for different forms and mixes of work. An additional challenge is that of learning the skills of managing a diversity of in-person, avatar and robot workers.

Neuroscience

There is a rising swell of information on the impact of neuroscience on organizations and some new fields of investigative research are emerging. One example is that of 'organizational cognitive neuroscience (OCN)', defined as 'the cognitive neuroscientific study of organizational behavior. OCN lets us start to understand the relationship between our organizational behavior and our brains and allows us to dissect specific social processes at the neurobiological level and apply a wider range of analysis to specific organizational research questions' (Senior *et al.*, 2011).

This field appears to offer huge potential for understanding more about management, although this is the start of the journey, and there are significant

> technological limitations of functional magnetic resonance imaging (fMRI), which appears to be the method of choice for cognitive neuroscience research at present. A fundamental limitation in neuroimaging is an inability to infer complex social behavior from observations of specific activated brain regions ... Organizational researchers who wish to investigate the potential of neuroscience to inform their work need to engage with these inference problems in order to avoid the nonsensical claims that seem to appear with such frequency in the popular press. (Lee *et al.*, 2012)

Based in neuroscience is 'behavioural economics', the study of the effects of psychology on economic decision making. In other words, how people's emotions and thoughts can affect how they make decisions about things. Research into behavioural economics is fast being applied in business and in government, often in relation to the routine work of decision making. Google, for example, applies some of the behavioural economics techniques – also called 'nudge techniques' – in managing and developing the workforce.

> Google is one organization that believes that when employees are healthy, they're happy. When they're happy, they're innovative and in pursuit of that healthiness, happiness, and innovation, Google has turned to nudges: simple, subtle cues that prompt people to make better decisions. Behavioral economists have shown the idea works, but Google has taken it out of the lab and into their cafeteria. For example, when people walk into the cafeteria the first thing they see is the salad bar. The less healthy eating options are further away and more hidden. (Kuang, 2012)

A useful book on the topic is *Nudge: Improving Decisions about Health, Wealth, and Happiness,* by Richard Thaler and Cass Sunstein (Yale University Press, 2008). The UK and US governments have both engaged the authors to work with them.

As understanding of neuroscience grows so it will change the nature of work and the design of organizations. Some researchers believe it is likely to have as great an impact as the human genome project has had on medicine and medical treatments, similarly creating the jobs and industries of the future while improving lives (Collins, 2013).

Exactly how this will happen is more difficult to predict, but there are plenty of people in the field of management, leadership and marketing who are right now leaping on the bandwagon of neuroscience: neuro-leadership, brain-based coaching and neuro marketing are three that are worth taking a critical view of: are they perhaps making the 'nonsensical claims' mentioned above?

For example, neuroscience is being used in the film industry to help develop box office success:

> Some big Hollywood studios such as Fox and Paramount have been experimenting with neuroscientific research in order to gain a reliable, direct, real-time read of moviegoers' (non-conscious) brain and emotional responses to movie stimuli such as trailers … The study's real value to the film industry is in putting this new method to work. Biometrics can be used to evaluate the trailer up to eight weeks prior to movie launch – enough time to rework the trailer based on high and low points in the target audience's emotional experience, put the promotion back into market, and improve the ultimate performance on opening weekend. (Randall, 2013)

Knowing whether the reworking of a trailer is related to the findings of neuroscience research or something else requires not only the trust in experience mentioned above but also casting a critical eye on such claims. This involves four processes:

Getting some context and deciding what to observe and consider
This includes an awareness of what's happening in the context. In this instance, questions to ask include: Is the evidence for the claims reliable, valid and current? Who is endorsing the claims?

Surfacing assumptions
This involves analysing assumptions about the claim as well as examining the beliefs that underlie them. Sample questions include: What has been taken for granted in this claim? Which beliefs/values shaped any assumptions? What assumptions are being made that might be influencing decisions?

Exploring and imagining alternatives

This involves thinking about and imagining other ways of looking at the claims. It involves exploring many alternatives for other choices or approaches. Sample questions include: What is one possible explanation for [insert what is happening] in the claims? What are other explanations for what is happening? What are two more possibilities/other alternatives? Are there others who might be able to help develop alternative thinking?

Reflecting with scepticism. Deciding what to do

This involves questioning, analysing and reflecting on the rational for decisions about the claim. Sample questions include: Are the interpretations believable? What rationale is there for the decisions made? What aspects of this claim require the most careful attention? What else might work in this situation? (Brookfield, 2001)

This critical eye is an important one for organization designers to develop, and it is in action in former director for international theatrical research at Fox Entertainment Group, Melissa Mullen's, view of neuroscience-based methods as an 'exciting new frontier for cinema marketing research' – but then comes the voice of strong caution.

> A movie studio may be able to use bio- or neuromarketing research to get the best possible trailer out there for consumer eyeballs, but one cannot ignore the extremely weighty aspects of marketing spend, publicity and promotions upon levels of awareness, interest and buzz. It makes sense that high engagement (high attention along with high emotional connection) by a wide fan base would indeed lend itself to high box office receipts. But high engagement without high marketing spend can cause a box office flop, regardless of how well the trailer plays to audiences. If consumers don't know about the film, it won't succeed at the box office. All the variables must be brought to bear in a prediction of this nature. (Randall, 2013)

Molly Crockett, a neuroscientist, in her TEDX talk 'Beware Neuro-Bunk', offers three more comments indicating caution:

- If someone tries to sell you something with a brain on it ... ask to see the evidence. Ask for the part of the story that's not being told.
- [Neuroscientists] haven't found a 'buy' button inside the brain, we can't tell whether someone is lying or in love just by looking at their brain scans, and we can't turn sinners into saints with hormones.
- When you see activation in [a brain region], you can't just pick and choose your favorite explanation. (Crockett, 2012)

But as advances are made in neuroscience research the nature of work and thus the design of organizations will feel the impact. The body of evidence so far suggests that neuroscience has the potential to influence how work is done and how individuals can learn to be effective, happy and productive in organizational roles.

Additionally, the field is creating new and different jobs. One exciting area is the design and manufacture of neurally controlled prosthetic limbs. In December 2012, for example:

> [R]esearch participant Zac Vawter utilized the world's first neurally controlled, powered prosthetic limb to climb 103 floors (2,109 steps) of Chicago's Willis Tower at the SkyRise Chicago fundraiser. In this most grueling test of the technology to date, Vawter demonstrated that this advanced research is quickly on its way to becoming available to lower-limb amputees worldwide. (PRNewswire, 2012)

In this small example we see the confluence of changes in routine work (production of a new type of prosthetic limb, requiring new employee skills), in-person work (teaching the person to use the limb effectively), symbolic-analytic work (researching and developing a neurally controlled prosthetic limb) and artisan work (fitting the limb to the specific individual).

OD short

Neuroscience research is a burgeoning field that has started to have, and will continue to have, a significant impact on the way work is done and organizations are designed. Some of the current claims made about neuroscience are suspect and it is wise for organization designers to keep informed on the topic and to view findings with a critical mindset, making careful judgments on whether to apply them in their organizations.

Demographics

In 2013 the largest survey of the British class system ever carried out revealed a new structure of seven social divisions, ranging from an 'advantaged and privileged' elite to a large 'precariat' of poor and deprived people. This new model of class offers a powerful way of comprehending contemporary Britain, and provides some insights into how the four types of work are represented in the seven social divisions. The seven classes are:

1   The Elite, comprising 6% of the population
    Demographics: average age of 57; 4% ethnic minorities; 50% female
    Average household income, after tax: £89,000
    Typical professions include: company directors, barristers and dentists.
2   The Established Middle Class, comprising 25% of the population
    Demographics: average age of 46; 13% ethnic minorities; 54% female
    Average household income, after tax: £47,000

Typical professions include: town planners, midwives, occupational therapists.

3   Technical Middle Class, comprising 6% of the population
     Demographics: average age of 52; 9% ethnic minorities; 59% female
     Average household income, after tax: £37,000
     Typical professions include: radiographers, pharmacists, scientists and social scientists.

4   New Affluent Workers, comprising 15% of the population
     Demographics: average age of 44; 11% ethnic minorities; 43% female
     Average household income, after tax: £29,000
     Typical professions include: plumbers, sales assistants, electricians, housing officers.

5   Traditional Working Class, comprising 14% of the population
     Demographics: average age of 66; 9% ethnic minorities; 62% female
     Average household income, after tax: £13,000
     Mainly retired workers.

6   Emergent Service Workers, comprising 19% of the population
     Demographics: average age of 34; 21% ethnic minorities; 55% female
     Average household income, after tax: £21,000
     Typical professions include: bar staff, chefs, customer services operatives, call centre workers.

7   Precariat, comprising 15% of the population
     Demographics: average age of 50; 13% ethnic minorities; 57% female
     Average household income, after tax: £8,000
     Typical professions include: cleaners, caretakers, shopkeepers, cashiers or unemployed.

The study as a whole comments that:

> It is striking that we have been able to discern a distinctive elite, whose sheer economic advantage sets it apart from other classes. Although this is not necessarily surprising, our analysis is the first time that this group has been elaborated within a wider analysis of the class structure in which they are normally placed alongside a larger group of professionals and managers. The fact that this elite group is shown to have the most privileged backgrounds also is an important demonstration of the accentuation of social advantage at the top of British society.
>
> At the opposite extreme, we have discerned the existence of a sizeable group – 15% of the population – which is marked by the lack of any significant amount of economic, cultural, or social capital. We have identified these as the 'precariat'. The recognition of the existence of this group, along with the elite, is a powerful reminder that our conventional approaches to class have hindered our recognition of these two extremes, which occupy a very distinctive place in British society.

The 'new affluent workers' and the 'emergent service workers' are an interesting focus. They seem, in many respects, to be the children of the 'traditional working class', and they might thus be said to exemplify the stark break in working class culture which has been evident as a result of de-industrialisation, mass unemployment, immigration and the restructuring of urban space. To this extent, new social formations appear to be emerging out of the tendrils of the traditional working class. (Trueman, 2013)

This portrait of a society where there is increasing polarization between the tiny elite and the increasing number in the precariat is not limited to Britain. There is a similar picture emerging globally, as the Organisation for Economic Co-operation and Development (OECD) finds. According to its 2011 report on income inequality:

Over the two decades prior to the onset of the global economic crisis, real disposable household incomes increased by an average 1.7% a year in OECD countries. In a large majority of them, however, the household incomes of the richest 10% grew faster than those of the poorest 10%, so widening income inequality ... Earners in the top 10% have been leaving the middle earners behind more rapidly than the lowest earners have been drifting away from the middle. (OECD, 2011)

The OECD discusses three possible causes of this widening gap in income inequality: globalization, technology and policy and regulation choices. In this discussion the authors note that '[t]he empirical evidence as to the key drivers of inequality remains largely inconclusive', but conclude the report on a positive note:

The new OECD work presented in this report shows that there is nothing inevitable about growing inequalities. Globalization and technological changes offer opportunities but also raise challenges that can be tackled with effective and well-targeted policies.

Regulatory reforms can be designed in such a way that they make markets more efficient and encourage employment while reducing inequalities at the same time. Labour market and social policies also need to be adapted to changing household structures. Policies for inclusive growth are required in the current situation. Any policy strategy to reduce the growing divide between the rich and poor should rest on three main pillars: more intensive human capital investment; inclusive employment promotion; and well-designed tax/ transfer redistribution policies. (OECD, 2011)

Note that all three of the pillars are also in the power and remit of organizations to address in their designs. The emergence of new social classes and the related growing disparity in income equality is only one part of a complex demographic picture including factors such as diversity, educational attainment, health profile and longevity that organization designers have to consider as they design flexible, scalable, adaptive and socially conscious organizations.

OD short

The rise of new social divisions, growing income disparity, youth unemployment, work–life balance choices and increasing numbers of people eligible for retirement staying in the workforce are a few of the many demographic dimensions that pose organization design challenges into the future. Included in these challenges are social and moral issues around healthcare, longevity, employer–employee relationships and so on. Responsible organization designers keep abreast of demographic trends and factor them into their work.

Emerging organization designs

John Lewis, a UK retailer, is an example of an organization that although established in 1864 and taking its present form as an employee-owned business in 1928 demonstrates the hallmarks of one type of design that has flourished, and continues to be adaptive to a changing operating context. In a radio broadcast given in 1957 John Spedan Lewis made the point that:

> Rightly or wrongly I feel quite certain that the general idea of substituting partnership for exploiting employment is now-a-days in the air and will spread through industry of all kinds. It is already dear to many hearts besides my own, for it makes work something to live for as well as something to live by. Here may be the new source of working energy of which our country is in such grave need. (Lewis, 1957)

The notion that organizations need to be sustainable and offer social value, as John Lewis does, are two characteristics of several types organization designs that are capitalizing on the three trends discussed earlier. Table 10.1 summarizes a range of other types of organization design that are challenging traditional command-and-control hierarchies.

Tools

1   Trend mapping

Look again at the STEEPLE analysis (Table 3.1). This can be used as a trend map building on the information you gained in the design phase.

Table 10.1 Newer organizational forms

Organizational design	Characteristics	Example
Sharing	Rather than an individual buying an item for single use, companies are offering shared use of a variety of goods that people use intermittently. Technology advances mean that sharing is more than hiring or renting for a fixed period of time or from a fixed location. It 'has reduced transaction costs, making sharing assets cheaper and easier than ever – and therefore possible on a much larger scale. The big change [from traditional hiring models] is the availability of more data about people and things, which allows physical assets to be disaggregated and consumed as services. Before the internet, renting a surfboard, a power tool or a parking space from someone else was feasible, but was usually more trouble than it was worth' (*The Economist*, 2013).	**Car2Go** is a car-sharing scheme operating in several cities across the globe. 'By using one of the third-party Car2go smartphone apps, you can locate an available vehicle and walk on over. No reservations are required, but they are possible, up to 24 hours in advance. Taking control of a Car2go is easy as can be' (Blanco, 2011).
Social entrepreneurship	A social entrepreneur identifies and solves social problems on a large scale. Just as business entrepreneurs create and transform whole industries, social entrepreneurs act as the change agents for society, seizing opportunities others miss in order to improve systems, invent and disseminate new approaches and advance sustainable solutions that create social value. Unlike traditional business entrepreneurs, social entrepreneurs primarily seek to generate 'social value' rather than profits. And unlike the majority of non-profit organizations, their work is targeted not only towards immediate, small-scale effects, but sweeping, long-term change (PBS, 2005).	**Acumen Fund** Acumen is a non-profit that raises charitable donations to invest in companies, leaders and ideas that are changing the way the world tackles poverty. The organization invests in entrepreneurs who have the capability to bring sustainable solutions to big problems of poverty. It is a venture capital fund for the poor, supported by a global community of philanthropists willing to take a bet on a new approach.

Table 10.1 (cont.)

Organizational design	Characteristics	Example
Ecosystems	A business ecosystem is a dynamic structure which consists of an interconnected population of organizations. These organizations can be small firms, large corporations, universities, research centres, public-sector organizations and other parties which influence the system. Business ecosystems are self-sustaining. This means that no government interventions are needed in order to survive in local or global markets. Business ecosystems develop through self-organization, emergence and co-evolution, which help them to acquire adaptability. In a business ecosystem there is both competition and co-operation present simultaneously (Peltoniemi and Vuori, 2004).	**European Institute for Innovation and Technology (EIT)** The creation of the EIT represented a radical change, often described as a reinvention, of EU innovation policy. It aims to take a holistic approach to innovation by assuming an integrated perspective among the three sides of the 'knowledge triangle', which are education, research and innovation. In this respect, the EIT is a unique institution, not only with regard to European policy, but at a worldwide level. The EIT's route for facilitating innovation is to encourage the creation of KICs. The activity of a KIC 'must involve at least three independent partner organizations. The partners must be established in at least three different EU Member States and must include at least one higher education partner and one private company' (Ernst & Young, 2013).
State capitalism	State capitalism organizations are a new kind of hybrid corporation, backed by the state but behaving like a private-sector multinational. The best national champions are outward-looking, acquiring skills by listing on foreign exchanges and taking over foreign companies (*The Economist*, 2012a).	**Petrobras** 'The state controlled Brazilian oil company is aiming to pump 5m barrels a day by 2020, up from around 2m ... This can only be achieved, according to Graça Foster, CEO, if the government understands that the firm needs to concentrate on pumping oil if it is to generate the revenues to invest in job-creating refineries and terminals. She rejects the idea that Petrobras is run for Brazil's good, rather than its own. "Petrobras does not see developing the country as its core business," she says. "Not every project that would be great for the country will be undertaken, because not all are economically justified"' (*The Economist*, 2012b).

People power	Internet companies are increasingly tapping into the collective knowledge of their online communities to improve services. Among the best examples of such collaboration efforts are wikis, which are websites that can be quickly edited by visitors with simple formatting rules (*Information Week*, 2007).	**Google Maps** has several features that call on people power to improve the map quality: one that lets people correct the location marker for street addresses, businesses and other places. Another is map-creation tools that let people make maps, and then share the information with other users. In addition, map-makers can publish profile pages highlighting their creations.
Co-ordinators	Co-ordinating organizations are those that enable peer-to-peer rental of 'beds, cars, boats, and other assets directly from each other, co-ordinated via the internet'. They may pay a fee to the co-organization but essentially the payment for the service is to the owner of the item (PBS, 2005).	**AirBnB** co-ordinates peer-to-peer accommodation rental: 'Airbnb collects payment from your guest electronically and transfers it to you via direct deposit, Paypal, check, or wire transfer. The money appears in your account 24 hours after your guest checks in. In addition, we collect an optional security deposit on your behalf in case you need additional peace of mind. It's free to list your space on Airbnb, and we make money when you make money. Based on your reservation total, the 3% host fee covers transaction fees. The guest contributes a 6% to 12% guest fee' (AirBnB, n.d.).
Boundary organizations	Boundary organizations are those that form strategic alliances between multiple organizations and then interact on the partners' behalf with the users or purchasers of their products/services.	**U2** is an online education 'company that partners with graduate schools to build, administer, and market online degree programs … the first real example of a collective of top higher ed institutions offering the same courses and teachers that a student would find in the physical classroom, yet in an online-only setting that actually offers credited courses to students who aren't enrolled at the universities offering them' (Empson, 2012).
Open source	Open source organizations are non-profit enterprises that generate products and services via the involvement and contribution of anyone.	**Mozilla** is a 'proudly non-profit organization dedicated to keeping the power of the Web in people's hands. We're a global community of users, contributors and developers working to innovate on your behalf. When you use Firefox, or any Mozilla product, you become a part of that community, helping us build a brighter future for the Web' (Mozilla, 2013).

Table 10.2 Emerging trend

Emerging trend	Potential impact on customers	Potential impact on competitor markets	Potential impact on …
Social/demographic			
Technological			
Environmental			
Economic			
Political			
Legal			
Ethical			
Other stuff			

Use the vertical axis with the STEEPLE elements. Use the horizontal axis to name aspects of the trends that are of organizational interest, for example, customers or competitor markets.

Do some work on identifying the trends. See whether they are tracking up, or down or are static. Compare the trends. Look for patterns and interactions. Consider how things might develop and what the organization response could or should be. How might the design of the organization need to develop or be adapted?

2   Is your organization design with-it or past-it?

Gary Hamel, a management theorist, has compiled a list of 12 work-relevant characteristics of online life. These are the post-bureaucratic realities that tomorrow's employees will use as yardsticks in determining whether a company is 'with-it' or 'past-it'. Use it to check the relevance of your organization's design.

1   **All ideas compete on an equal footing.** On the web, every idea has the chance to gain a following – or not, and no one has the power to kill off a subversive idea or squelch an embarrassing debate. Ideas gain traction based on their perceived merits, rather than on the political power of their sponsors.

2   **Contribution counts for more than credentials.** When you post a video to YouTube, no one asks you if you went to film school. When you write a blog, no one cares whether you have a journalism degree. Position, title and academic degrees – none of the usual status differentiators carry much weight online. On the web, what counts is not your resumé, but what you can contribute.

3   **Hierarchies are natural, not prescribed.** In any web forum there are some individuals who command more respect and attention than

others – and have more influence as a consequence. Critically, though, these individuals haven't been appointed by some superior authority. Instead, their clout reflects the freely given approbation of their peers. On the web, authority trickles up, not down.

4 **Leaders serve rather than preside.** On the web, every leader is a servant leader; no one has the power to command or sanction. Credible arguments, demonstrated expertise and selfless behavior are the only levers for getting things done through other people. Forget this online, and your followers will soon abandon you.

5 **Tasks are chosen, not assigned.** The web is an opt-in economy. Whether contributing to a blog, working on an open source project or sharing advice in a forum, people choose to work on the things that interest them. Everyone is an independent contractor, and everyone scratches their own itch.

6 **Groups are self-defining and self-organizing.** On the web, you get to choose your compatriots. In any online community, you have the freedom to link up with some individuals and ignore the rest, to share deeply with some folks and not at all with others. Just as no one can assign you a boring task, no one can force you to work with dim-witted colleagues.

7 **Resources get attracted, not allocated.** In large organizations, resources get allocated top-down, in a politicized, Soviet-style budget wrangle. On the web, human effort flows towards ideas and projects that are attractive (and fun), and away from those that aren't. In this sense, the web is a market economy where millions of individuals get to decide, moment by moment, how to spend the precious currency of their time and attention.

8 **Power comes from sharing information, not hoarding it.** The web is also a gift economy. To gain influence and status, you have to give away your expertise and content. And you must do it quickly; if you don't, someone else will beat you to the punch – and garner the credit that might have been yours. Online, there are a lot of incentives to share, and few incentives to hoard.

9 **Opinions compound and decisions are peer-reviewed.** On the Internet, truly smart ideas rapidly gain a following no matter how disruptive they may be. The web is a near-perfect medium for aggregating the wisdom of the crowd – whether in formally organized opinion markets or in casual discussion groups. And once aggregated, the voice of the masses can be used as a battering ram to challenge the entrenched interests of institutions in the offline world.

10 **Users can veto most policy decisions.** As many Internet moguls have learned to their sorrow, online users are opinionated and vociferous – and will quickly attack any decision or policy change that seems contrary to the community's interests. The only way to keep users loyal is to give them a substantial say in key decisions. You may have built the community, but the users really own it.

11 **Intrinsic rewards matter most.** The web is a testament to the power of intrinsic rewards. Think of all the articles contributed to Wikipedia, all the open source software created, all the advice freely given – add up the hours of volunteer time and it's obvious that human beings will give generously of themselves when they're given the chance to contribute to something they actually care about. Money's great, but so is recognition and the joy of accomplishment.

12 **Hackers are heroes.** Large organizations tend to make life uncomfortable for activists and rabble-rousers – however constructive they may be. In contrast, online communities frequently embrace those with strong anti-authoritarian views. On the web, muckraking malcontents are frequently celebrated as champions of the Internet's democratic values – particularly if they've managed to hack a piece of code that has been interfering with what others regard as their inalienable digital rights. (Hamel, 2010)

Summary

This chapter discusses the organization of the future, not through a predictive lens, but through three trends that are already having an impact on the design of organizations: digital transformation, neuroscience and demographics. In looking at trends it is important to remember that they may or may not be heralds of something to act on. Treat them with judicious caution, as the discussion suggests. Nevertheless, looking at the newer forms of organization listed illustrates the fact that organization designs are continuously evolving.

References

AirBnB. (n.d.). 'How Do I Get Paid?'. Retrieved 27 April 2013, from AirBnB: https://www.airbnb.co.uk/life.

Bal, H. (2013). 'Meet the Makers: Steve Battle, the Man behind Battle Bot', 21 March. Retrieved 14 April 2013, from Bristol Mini-Maker Faire: http://makerfairebristol.com/archives/990#.

Blanco, S. (2011). 'In Depth: Daimler's Car2Go Program Is Simple, Amazing, but not Perfect', 24 March. Retrieved 26 April 2013, from Autobloggreen: http://green.autoblog.com/2011/03/24/daimler-car2go-program-carsharing-smart-fortwo.

Brito, M. (2013). 'The Emergence of the Social Business Command Center', 18 January. Retrieved 9 April 2013, from Britopian: http://www.britopian.com/2013/01/18/the-emergence-of-the-social-business-command-center.

Brookfield, S. (2001). 'Four Critical Thinking Processes', in *Using Your Head to Land on Your Feet*. A. Hafner and B. Raingruber (eds). Philadelphia: F.A. Davis Company.

Brooks, R. (2013). 'Robots at Work: Towards a Smarter Factory', *The Futurist*, **47**(3), May–June. Retrieved 15 April 2013, from *The Futurist*: http://www.wfs.org/futurist/2013-issues-futurist/may-june-2013-vol-47-no-3/robots-work-toward-smarter-factory.

Brynjolfsson, E. and McAfee, A. (2012). 'Jobs, Productivity and the Great Decoupling', 11 December. Retrieved 1 August 2013, from *The New York Times*: http://www.nytimes.com/2012/12/12/opinion/global/jobs-productivity-and-the-great-decoupling.html?_r=0.

Collins, F. P. (2013). 'BRAIN Initiative Challenges Researchers to Unlock Mysteries of Human Mind', 2 April. Retrieved 14 April 2013, from The White House Blog: http://www.whitehouse.gov/blog/2013/04/02/brain-initiative-challenges-researchers-unlock-mysteries-human-mind.

Crockett, M. (2012). 'Beware of Neuro Bunk', December. Retrieved 26 April 2013, from TED Ideas Worth Spreading: http://www.ted.com/talks/molly_crockett_beware_neuro_bunk.html.

De la Merced, M. (2012). 'Eastman Kodak Files for Bankruptcy', 13 January. Retrieved 9 April 2013, from *The New York Times*: Dealbook: http://dealbook.nytimes.com/2012/01/19/eastman-kodak-files-for-bankruptcy.

The Economist. (2012a). 'The Rise of State Capitalism', 1 January. Retrieved 27 April 2013, from *The Economist*: http://www.economist.com/node/21543160.

The Economist. (2012b). 'The Perils of Petrobras', 17 November. Retrieved 27 April 2013, from *The Economist*: http://www.economist.com/news/americas/21566645-how-gra%C3%A7a-foster-plans-get-brazils-oil-giant-back-track-perils-petrobras.

The Economist. (2013). 'The Rise of the Sharing Economy', 9 March. Retrieved 27 April 2013, from *The Economist*: http://www.economist.com/news/leaders/21573104-internet-everything-hire-rise-sharing-economy.

Empson, R. (2012). '2U One-Ups MOOCs, Coursera, Now Offers Online Undergrad Courses from Top Schools for Credit', 15 November. Retrieved 27 April 2013, from Techcrunch: http://techcrunch.com/2012/11/15/2u-one-ups-moocs-coursera-now-offers-online-undergrad-courses-from-top-schools-for-credit.

Ernst & Young. (2013). *Moving Europe Forward: Innovating for a Prosperous Future*. Ernst & Young.

European Union. (2012). *Public Attitudes Towards Robots*. Special Eurobarometer 382. Retrieved 7 August 2013, from http://ec.europa.eu/public_opinion/archives/ebs/ebs_382_en.pdf.

Guizzo, E. (2010). 'Anybots QB Telepresence Robot Lets You Be at the Office ... without Being There', 18 May. Retrieved 26 April 2013, from ieee Spectrum: http://spectrum.ieee.org/automaton/robotics/industrial-robots/051810-anybots-qb-new-telepresence-robot.

Hamel, G. (2010). 'The Facebook Generation vs. the Fortune 500', 22 September. Retrieved 27 April 2013, from Open Source: http://opensource.com/business/10/9/facebook-generation-vs-fortune-500.

Huggables. (2008). Retrieved 14 April 2013, from MIT Media Lab Personal Robots Group: http://robotic.media.mit.edu/?url=Projects.Robots.Huggable.Overview.

Information Week. (2007). 'Google Maps Taps People Power to Improve Results', 20 November. Retrieved 27 April 2013, from: http://www.informationweek.co.uk/google-maps-taps-people-power-to-improve/204200368.

Institute for Government. (2013). 'Cass Sunstein on Simplification and Nudging', 22 March. Retrieved 26 April 2013, from Institute for Government: http://www.instituteforgovernment.org.uk/events/cass-sunstein-simplification-and-nudging.

Janssen, C. (n.d.). 'Maker Movement'. Retrieved 13 April 2013, from Techopedia: http://www.techopedia.com/definition/28408/maker-movement.

Kuang, C. (2012). 'In The Cafeteria, Google Gets Healthy', 19 March. Retrieved 26 April 2013, from Fast Company: http://www.fastcompany.com/1822516/cafeteria-google-gets-healthy.

Kurzweil Accelerating Intelligence. (2012). 'Advanced Humanoid Roboy to Be "Born" in Nine Months', 26 December. Retrieved 14 April 2013, from Kurzweil Accelerating Intelligence: http://www.kurzweilai.net/advanced-humanoid-roboy-to-be-born-in-nine-months.

Lee, N., Senior, C. and Butler, M. (2012). 'The Domain of Organizational Cognitive Neuroscience: Theoretical and Empirical Challenges', *Journal of Management*, **38**(4), 921–31.

Lewis, J. (1957). 'Dear to My Heart', 15 April. Retrieved 27 April 2013, from John Lewis Partnership: http://www.johnlewispartnership.co.uk/about/our-founder. html.

Lutz, M. (2013). '10 Essentials for Social Media in 2013, part 1', 20 February. Retrieved 9 April 2013, from Edelman Digital: http://www.edelmandigital.com/2013/02/20/10-social-media-essentials-2013-part-1.

McMillan, R. (2012). 'IBM's Watson Machine Dons Lab Coat at World's Largest Cancer Center', 23 March. Retrieved 14 April 2013, from Wired: http://www.wired.co.uk/news/archive/2012–03/23/ibm-jeopardy-machine.

Markoff, J. (2012). 'Skilled Work, without the Worker', 18 August. Retrieved 14 April 2013, from *The New York Times*: http://www.nytimes.com/2012/08/19/business/new-wave-of-adept-robots-is-changing-global-industry.html?_r=2&nl=todaysheadlines&adxnnl=1&emc=edit_th_20120819&adxnnlx=1345370579-sxvBiwfg4ctjJPZAtTaGFg&pagewanted=print.

Mason, L. (2010). 'Review of *The Management Myth: Debunking Modern Business Philosophy* by Matthew Stewart'. Retrieved 25 March 2012, from http://www.thebookbag.co.uk/reviews/index.php?title=The_Management_Myth:_Debunking_Modern_Business_Philosophy_by_Matthew_Stewart.

MIT Sloan. (2013). 'Digital Transformation Survey', 6 April. Retrieved 14 April 2013, from MIT Sloan Qualtrics: https://mitsloan.qualtrics.com/SE/?SID=SV_0kSLIxI4 4rIMp7v&source=1.

Mozilla. (2013). 'Mission'. Retrieved 27 April 2013, from Mozilla: http://www.mozilla.org/en-US/mission.

My Shelter Foundation. (2011). 'About Liter of Light'. Retrieved 27 April 2013, from http://aliteroflight.org/about-us.

OECD. (2011). 'An Overview of Growing Income Inequalities in OECD Countries: Main Findings'. Retrieved 27 April 2013, from http://www.oecd.org/social/soc/49499779.pdf.

Owyang, J. (2012). 'Breakdown of a Dedicated Social Media Engagement or Command Center', 24 August. Retrieved 9 April 2013, from Jeremiah Owyang: http://www.web-strategist.com/blog/2012/08/24/breakdown-of-a-dedicated-social-media-engagement-or-command-center.

PBS. (2005). 'What Is Social Entrepreneurship?'. Retrieved 27 April 2013, from The New Heroes: http://www.pbs.org/opb/thenewheroes/whatis.

Peltoniemi, M. and Vuori, E. (2004). 'Business Ecosystem as the New Approach to Complex Adaptive Business Environments', February. *Proceedings of e-Business Research Forum* (pp. 267–81).

Peterson, C. (2009). 'Positive Psychology and Unemployment', 25 May. Retrieved 13 April 2013, from Psychology Today: http://www.psychologytoday.com/blog/the-good-life/200905/positive-psychology-and-unemployment.

PRNewswire. (2012). 'First Neurally Controlled, Powered Prosthetic Limb Is 2,109 Steps Closer to Realization', 7 November. Retrieved 13 April 2013, from PRNewswire: http://www.prnewswire.com/news-releases-test/first-neurally-controlled-powered-prosthetic-limb-is-2109-steps-closer-to-realization-177780951.html.

Randall, K. (2013). 'How Your Brain Can Predict Blockbusters', 22 February. Retrieved 14 May 2013, from Fast Company: http://www.fastcompany.com/3006186/how-your-brain-can-predict-blockbusters.

Reich, R. (1992). *The Work of Nations: Preparing Ourselves for 21st Century Capitalism.* New York: Vintage Books.

Schmidtt, J. and Jones, J. (2012). 'Where Have All the Good Jobs Gone?', July. Retrieved 14 April 2013, from Center for Economic Policy and Research: http://www.cepr.net/index.php/publications/reports/where-have-all-the-good-jobs-gone.

Senior, C., Lee, N. and Butler, M. (2011). 'Perspective – Organizational Cognitive Neuroscience', *Organization Science*, **22**(3), May/June, 804–15.

Stanford, N. (2013). *Organizational Health: An Integrated Approach to Building Optimum Performance.* London: Kogan Page.

Trueman, T. (2013). 'Largest Class Survey Reveals Polarized UK Society and the Rise of New Groups', 3 April. Retrieved 27 April 2013, from Eureka Alert: http://www.eurekalert.org/pub_releases/2013–04/sp-lcs040313.php.

Waters, R. and Nuttall, C. (2012). 'One Negative Too Many for Kodak', 19 January. Retrieved 9 April 2013, from *Financial Times*: Tech Hub: http://www.ft.com/cms/s/2/2a591538–42af-11e1–97b1–00144feab49a.html#axzz2PyacCy6U.

The White House, Office of the Press Secretary. (2013). 'Remarks by the President on the BRAIN Initiative and American Innovation', 2 April. Retrieved 14 April 2013, from The White House: http://www.whitehouse.gov/blog/2013/04/02/brain-initiative-challenges-researchers-unlock-mysteries-human-mind.

Appendix: Transitioning people from old to new design

1 Framework

Organization	Matching	Individual
Develop business plan Purpose/ objectives Long term – based, strategic Short term – operational, detailed	**Integrated matching process** • **Employment strategy** – what kind of employer do we want to be? • **Resourcing strategy** – acquire, shed, transform staff? What contracts are needed (e.g. annual, hours/homeworking)? Do we need to outsource/integrate our partners? • **Capabilities** – what future capability need to be? • **Training and development** – what development and training will build required capabilities?	
People plan Organization and culture Volume of activity Processes Impact of IT Manpower plan (roles, capabilities and numbers)	• **Career management** – how will people move through the organization? What are the career paths? How do processes need to be improved? What are the individual's aspirations? • **Performance management** – how can we achieve effective performance management processes? • **Management style** – what should managers spend more/less time doing? How can consistency be achieved?	**Individual needs** Occupational choice Employer choice Lifestyle requirements Career plans Self-assessment Expectations
Organizational action plans Develop, acquire, shed or transform skills Address an organizational weakness Revise people processes	• **Reward and recognition** – what do you want to reward? How are people recognized? • **Participation** – to what extent do you want employee involvement? • **Culture** – what is your desired culture and how will you achieve it? How can you achieve it? How can you reinforce L2000 principles? • **Collective relations** – how effective are your collective relations?	**Individual outcomes** Individual feedback on realism of aspirations Revision of individual plans

Organization	*Matching*		*Individual*
Organizational outcomes	**Assess resources and philosophy against business requirements**		**Individual outcomes**
Productivity			Job satisfaction
Flexibility			Motivation
Level of service	**Action plan**		Personal development
Unit cost improvement			Sustained/enhanced performance
			Optional integration of work and family

2 Considerations

Culture	Employee morale	Equal opportunities	Involvement
• What is the desired culture to support the business? • What is the current culture? • What is reinforcing it? • How can you reinforce the organizational principles?	• What systems do you have in place to maintain a work environment that supports the well-being and development of all employees?	• How effective are you in implementing and monitoring equal opportunity policy and practice?	• To what extent do you want employee involvement? • What is the type and level of involvement now? • What processes are in place to support this?

Job design	Job evaluation	Leadership style	Organizational structure
• How will tasks be organized? • What are the intrinsic reward factors in job design (skill, variety, autonomy, task, identity, feedback)?	• What structures would suit your business? • What are your job families and bargaining units? • How does this link to your pay system?	• What should leaders spend more/less time doing? • Do managers have the traits necessary for effective leadership? • Do managers display the behaviours required for effective leadership?	• What is the structure of the organization? • Is it the most effective for the business? • What are the decision-making processes? • How effective are they? • What are the barriers?

Performance management	Policy	Quality strategy	Recognition
• What criteria will be used to manage performance? • How effective is the current process? • What would make it really effective? • Which employees should the process cover?	• What policies are currently in place? • How effective are they?	• What continuous improvement mechanisms do you have in place?	• How are people recognized in your organization? • How satisfied are you with the levels of recognition?

3   Planning process

Deliverable	*Activities*	*Linkages*	*Action*
STEP 1 – MANPOWER PLAN TO BE INCLUDED IN BUSINESS CASE (to ascertain whether the organization has the capability to realize the benefits of the project)	FUTURE SKILLS • Identify future critical skill by level/family against different scenarios • Assess the population against the requirement (skills audit) • Define the skills gap • Define what is trainable • Define transition skill requirements NUMBERS • Identify headcount targets for yr 1, yr 2 and yr 3 against different scenarios, e.g. Scenario A re-engineer/automate; Scenario B relocate; Scenario C outsource • Identify future flexible resourcing requirements, e.g. part-time, annual hours • Identify manpower flows: (a) Natural flows (historical) Natural wastage Internal organization flows (b) Identify induced flows required against each scenario and skill requirement.	SEPARATION PLAN – STEP 4 RECRUITMENT PLAN – STEP 5 TRAINING PLAN – STEP 6 MANPOWER PLAN – STEP 1 RELOCATION PLAN – STEP 8	

Deliverable	Activities	Linkages	Action
	Number and skills to shed e.g. induced exit, redeployment, termination of temporary contracts. Number and skills to acquire, e.g. based on volume, performance. Numbers to reskill/ train (c) Identify manpower transition requirements including change programme resourcing • Develop resourcing plans for new locations (if appropriate)		
STEP 2 – CHANGE MANAGEMENT PLAN (to be included in the business case to ensure that organization has a change plan to transit from current state to be ready to receive project deliverables and realize the benefits)	• Develop a vision for the future • Define organization structure and resources to deliver change in the short and medium term • Define accountabilities and decision-making processes • Assess capability to deliver change and develop mechanisms to enhance ability • Identify post-change management skills required, e.g. contract management skills • Define the desired current and future culture including how to become the best-managed company and develop measurements, e.g. Employee Satisfaction Index	TRAINING PLAN	
STEP 3 – CONSULTATION PLAN	Involvement • Decide level of involvement required and involvement principles • Develop mechanisms to deliver involvement	ORGANIZATION CONSULTATION APPROACH LEGAL FRAMEWORK	

Deliverable	Activities	Linkages	Action
	Communication • Define all stakeholders • Identify a communications strategy for each group • Develop communications plan and processes Industrial relations • Develop consultative mechandisms • Develop dispute processes • Identify agreements that need to be changed • Review future bargining arrangements Legal • Identify how Transfer of Undertakings will occur if required • Identify posible changes to contracts and implications		
STEP 4 – REWARD AND PERFORMANCE PLAN	• Identify numbers of people available for possible redeployment and potential target areas • Assess the probability of redeployment with the potential receiving area • Identify and design options to meet requirements and associated costs to build into budget and reflect in business case • Identify who to retain and who to let go • Identify and develop support mechanisms for staff leaving or moving on a redeployment basis or on a localized basis, counselling • Identify approaches to Transfer of Undertakings scenario • Identify legal implications of terminating staff	DEPENDENCIES WITH OTHER PARTS OF ORGANIZATION	

Deliverable	Activities	Linkages	Action
STEP 5 – RECRUITMENT PLAN	• Identify external recruitment by skill and level against casual factor, e.g. volume, replacement, and build into HR budget • Assess future skill markets and how to target them • Identify internal movement through career development processes/ selection and what mechanisms need to be in place • Identify possible redeployment flows into project delivery area • Review contract types required for now and for the future depending on the nature of future work • Identify resources required to deliver the change programme • Develop a clear, detailed resourcing plan with built in recruitment lead times, e.g. 12 weeks to offer • Ensure that critical roles have sufficient succession cover		
STEP 6 – TRAINING PLAN	• Conduct a skills audit as part of the manpower plan • Identify opportunities to retrain staff to meet future needs • Assess and design management and other training and development to support change • Develop appropriate training budget to meet requirements		
STEP 7 – REWARD AND PERFORMANCE PLAN	• Identify performance measures to deliver and track the change • Develop performance targets in line with business objectives • Develop recognition mechanisms		

Deliverable	Activities	Linkages	Action
	• Develop incentive mechanisms for retention • Identify requirements for future reward processes, e.g. what will align with future business objectives?		
STEP 8 – RELOCATION PLAN	• Identify appropriate locations and assess availability of skills in the locality • Determine contract and terms and conditions • Develop and resource a local recruitment plan • Develop an induction and training plan		

4   Selection options

Essentially, there are five selection options available.

Make appointments through an involving bidding process

How you do this:

- Create the new organization and develop the new structure.
- Publish full job descriptions, criteria and person specifications together with the vision, the new organization chart, the mission and goals.
- Invite employees to consider the published jobs in relation to their career development plans, their match to the criteria, their skills and abilities.
- Hold 1:1 manager–employee discussions on options and possibilities.
- Ensure each staff member completes a bidding form for the jobs they are interested in.
- Recommend that they attach supporting documentation to the form, indicate the preference order of the jobs and nominate one or two referees to be contacted when the bids are considered.
- Collate bids.
- Convene a series of management meetings by grade. Each level of management selects the lower level of staff, making a team decision on appointees.

Use information collated from the bid, current manager, performance data, career development data and referees to inform the decision.

- Give everyone feedback on their applications and the reason for the decision (the current manager holds these discussions).
- Have an appeals process available.

Comprehensive selection process

How you do this:

- Publish the new organization and the jobs.
- Make available full job descriptions and person specifications and essential criteria.
- Communicate a summary of the selection process that you will use to assess suitability and potential for each role.
- Invite staff to apply for the jobs using a standard application form.
- Screen the applications to identify staff who meet the essential criteria.
- Call those who do meet the criteria for interview with the new owning manager and an independent representative.
- Give everyone feedback on their application and the reason for the decision (the current manager does this).

Management appointments

How you do this:

- Create the new jobs as you create the new organization.
- Lead the management team through a process of matching jobs to people in the organization.
- Offer jobs to individuals as you make the decisions.
- Publish the new organization chart with jobs allocated and names attached.
- Have feedback available to support the appointment decisions you make.

Career development appointments

How you do this:

- Create the new organization.
- Write the job descriptions and person specifications.
- Use succession plans and career development data to match staff to jobs (staff may not know the range of jobs available; management judgment drives the appointments).

Move with the job

How you do this:

- Move people who are currently in jobs that figure in the redesign with the job.

In practice, there is a combination of these five approaches, some jobs being bid for, others being allocated and yet other jobs moving with incumbents. Decide what will work best for you. Then design a robust and fair selection process.

Glossary

5 Whys a simple problem-solving technique that helps get to the root of a problem quickly. Made popular in the 1970s by the Toyota Production System, the 5 Whys strategy involves looking at any problem and asking: 'Why?' and 'What caused this problem?'

Very often, the answer to the first 'why' will prompt another 'why' and the answer to the second 'why' will prompt another and so on; hence the name the 5 Whys strategy. (Mind Tools, n.d.)

Behavioural economics a theory stating that there are important psychological and behavioural variables involved in the economic decisions of consumers or countries. (Business Dictionary, n.d.)

Big Data describes datasets that are too large or too difficult to store, manage and analyse using traditional database software and analytical tools, and therefore require a new approach using distributed models and parallel processes. 'Big data' is a relative term describing a situation where the volume, velocity and variety of data exceed an organization's storage or compute capacity for accurate and timely decision-making. The true value of big data lies not just in having it, but in harvesting it for fast, fact-based decisions. (SAS Institute Inc, 2012)

Bring your own device (BYOD) employees are able to bring their own tablets, smartphones and other devices to use in place of employer-provided equipment.

Community of practice a loose association of people who share a common interest and meet virtually or face-to-face to extend their knowledge, solve problems, ask for insights and so on.

Decent Work Agenda an International Labour Organization support programme based on the understanding that work is a source of personal dignity, family stability, peace in the community, democracies that deliver for people and economic growth that expands opportunities for productive jobs and enterprise development. (International Labour Organization, n.d.)

Design (verb) the process of designing. In this book the design process comprises five major steps, each with associated tasks and activities.

The outcome of the design process is the organizational structure or architecture or design.

Design (noun)   the outcome of the designing process. It may be a structure chart (organization chart) or it may be a more complex design involving other organizational elements.

Employee value proposition (EVP)   all the tangible and non-tangible benefits an organization provides in return for the employee's time, effort and productivity. While compensation plays a part in any company's full EVP, an EVP is far more than salary and benefits. EVP statements commonly include areas such as corporate culture, rewards, management style, training and development, advancement opportunities, and unique corporate policies. (Employee Value Proposition, n.d.)

Future Search   a form of conference – typically three days – that brings together large groups of people (60 to 80) in one room or hundreds in parallel rooms to collectively work on an action or issue and develop solutions or approaches that can be implemented following the meeting.

Hoteling (or hotelling)   a method of supporting unassigned seating in an office environment. It is similar to hot-desking, and is sometimes confused with it, since both methods support unassigned seating. Hotelling is *reservation-based* unassigned seating, whereas hot-desking is *reservation-less* unassigned seating. (Wikipedia)

Humanistic values   there are many views on what constitute 'humanistic values' but the British Humanist Association suggests the following 12, which, regardless of a consultant's religious beliefs, seem to be exactly what organization design and development consultants should role model.

1   The encouragement of free-thinking and the spirit of enquiry that seeks to describe the nature of the universe and of the diversity of life on earth.
2   An openness to new knowledge and the acceptance of uncertainty.
3   Self-reliance and independence of thought within the recognition of the ultimate interdependence of humanity.
4   Concern for the well-being of the whole of humankind. Compassion and concern for all humans who, in varying degrees, are deprived of the opportunity for self-fulfilment.
5   Respect for all humans, for other species, and for the environment. The promotion and preservation of an ecological balance.
6   An approach which seeks to understand the beliefs and values of others.
7   A co-operative and problem-solving approach to conflicts of interest. Reasoned argument as opposed to dogmatic assertion.
8   An approach to morals and ethics which takes account of the complexities of modern living and has as its starting point that moral

and ethical behaviour is that which, except in self-defence, does no harm to the well-being of others. In situations of moral dilemma, the choosing of solutions which do least harm to the participants.

9 The concept of the democratic ideal. Impartiality towards, and equal treatment of, individuals and groups whatever their … beliefs.

10 Social attitudes which militate against the exploitation, or physical or psychological abuse, of humans by humans. A society which educates its members in tolerant, co-operative living.

11 A humane approach to all actions affecting members of the non-human living world.

12 The creative and artistic potential of human nature. The capacity of the arts, literature, and recreational activities for expanding perceptions, for increasing the awareness of self, and for illuminating the human condition. All those circumstances that enable humans to be free to experience the physical and mental joys of living. (North East Humanists, 2005)

Neuro-leadership an emerging field of study connecting neuroscientific knowledge with the fields of leadership development, management training, change management, consulting and coaching.

Organizational network analysis (ONA) using a range of technology ONA can reveal the acknowledged or perceived relationships among individuals, teams, departments, divisions and organizations, as compared to the expected relationships prescribed or predicted by strategic intent, organization charts, job roles, workflow interdependencies, clients, demographics, time, place, process or functional boundaries. Capturing this information and interpreting it during the assess and design phases adds richness and subtlety to the design work.

Process consultant one who operates from a facilitative, coaching style, believing that the client has the answers to organizational concerns and in working with the consultant will come up with them. Contrast this with two other consulting styles: providing expert information and 'playing doctor', i.e. examining organizational issues and symptoms, diagnosing what is going on and proposing a remedy.

Seven flows of healthcare following lean principles (based in the Toyota method) and value-stream mapping, seven flows of healthcare have been defined: patients, clinicians, medications, supplies, equipment, process engineering and information.

Social network analysis using the same principles as organizational network analysis, social network analysis examines the relationships and dynamics between individuals and communities in a social (rather than work) environment.

Structure (noun) organization structure is commonly taken to mean the organization chart and what it represents in terms of levels of power and authority and reporting relationships.

Vision versus mission   there are fine (but fiercely defended) distinctions between an organizational vision and mission. Some organizations have both, some have one or the other and some have neither. In broad terms they are an aspirational and directional statement that guide an organization's strategy.

Walk-throughs   practical tests of an organization design based in real-work process-flow scenarios to check whether a proposed design meets the design criteria and delivers the intended outcomes.

References

Business Dictionary. (n.d.). 'Behavioural Economics'. Retrieved 7 August 2013, from http://www.businessdictionary.com/definition/behavioral-economics.html.

Employee Value Proposition. (n.d.). Retrieved 7 August 2013, from Head2Head: http://head2head.ca/index.php?o=library&id=76.

International Labour Organization. (n.d.). 'Decent Work Agenda'. Retrieved 7 August 2013, from International Labour Organization: http://www.ilo.org/global/about-the-ilo/decent-work-agenda/lang--de/index.htm.

Mind Tools. (n.d.). '5 Whys'. Retrieved 7 August 2013, from Mind Tools: http://www.mindtools.com/pages/article/newTMC_5W.htm.

North East Humanists. (2005). 'An Introduction to Humanist Beliefs, Values, and Actions', September. Retrieved 19 May 2013, from Humanist Values: http://www.humanistvalues.org.uk.

SAS Institute Inc. (2012). *Big Data Meets Big Data Analytics*. Cary, NC: SAS.

Index